THE INNOCENTS AT HOME

Lord Kinross

THE INNOCENTS
AT HOME

Readers Union · John Murray
LONDON 1961

To
Harry Martin

*This RU edition was produced in 1961 for sale to
its members only by Readers Union Ltd at Aldine
House, 10–13 Bedford Street, London W.C.2, and
at Letchworth Garden City, Herts. Full details of
membership may be obtained from our London
address. This book has been reset in 10-point Plantin
type and printed and bound by Cox & Wyman
Ltd at Reading, Berks. It was first published by
John Murray Ltd.*

Contents

๑

Map on pages 12 and 13

๑

Drawings by Harry Martin

Some of the material used in these pages appeared, in a different form, in Punch, *and is reprinted with the permission of its proprietors.*

NEW YORK

I AWOKE, and became aware, with a sense of unease, that the engines of the *Queen Mary* had stopped. We had docked in New York. My four-day respite, lulled on the limbo of the ocean, was over. I must now face, rather as a child does on his first day at school, a remote and unfamiliar world. Reluctant to do so, I turned over again with my face to the wall. But sleep refused to return. In a mood still of misgiving, I braced myself for the ordeal and went up on deck.

Reaching landfall before dawn, we had missed seeing the skyline. There was no sign of it now beneath the cold March sky: only nondescript buildings of normal height and, on a cliff across a grey stretch of water which I took to be the Hudson, gabled villas such as overlook innumerable seasides.

A cameraman, with a passenger-list in his hand, advanced to take my photograph, conventionally posing me by the rails and instructing me to look out as though towards the skyline. He asked me a few perfunctory questions. Then he asked for my opinion on the situation in Cyprus. I had no opinion, I said. He turned away in silence, with a deadpan look which said 'no story,' and approached more hopefully a television starlet, one of my cabin-class companions. She wore glass slippers, and had, or so she had told me, a Spanish grandmother, and Irish eyes, and she was taking back five hundred dollars' worth of English Victorian silver to her home in Pasadena.

'No cheese-cake,' the cameraman reassured her. 'But maybe sitting on that piano. Just a leg. No? Okay then. Let's see you strike something sort of nice, . . . break out into a nice expression . . .'

I breakfasted, and went ashore, treading for the first time American soil, American concrete. It was cold in the Customs hall. I stood by my baggage, trying to attract the attention of an officer. He turned, looked at me in silence, then turned away again, continuing a leisurely conversation with a sleek American passenger, admiring, as he valued them, his purchases of porcelain, and listening with evident interest to the detailed story of his European trip. Beside me a parson was being greeted effusively

9

by three squat ladies, with sprays of orchids on their shoulders. For nearly an hour I looked hopefully around me, my feet growing colder. Finally an officer, responding to my look, sauntered towards me, and in a few moments silently cleared my baggage. An inside porter, whom notices instructed me not to tip, carried it out to the pavement, and grumbled that I had not tipped him. An outside porter carried it across the pavement to a taxi and grumbled that I had not tipped him enough.

The taxi-driver drove me in silence through streets and across avenues of a crumbling plum-coloured brick, as shabbily Georgian and ungenteel—moreover as littered with refuse—as the slums of Dublin or Liverpool. Here a Victorian church-spire struck my eye, there an Irish pub, the Shamrock Bar, with frosted windows. A pot plant wilted before a lace-curtained window; the rail of a balcony fluttered with laundry. Then the buildings grew higher, and after a surprisingly short drive we drew up at the Algonquin Hotel. Here I rejected a front room with a television set, and took refuge in a back room without one. It was not yet ten o'clock in the morning, and having unpacked and bathed I lay back on my bed, seeking a last spell of respite before confronting the world outside.

Why, I wondered to myself, had I come? Not in any spirit of high expectation, for the American legend had never greatly attracted me. Not to see friends, for I had few in America, only some friends of friends to whom I had letters of introduction. Not for a 'good time': such a prospect, in middle age, intimidated me. Not to make money: to give lectures had seemed to me presumptuous. I had come, I suppose, to fill a gap—quite a big gap—in experience: for America is a country which all must see, sooner or later, who aspire to know anything of the world. I was an ordinary traveller, with no fixed programme, a V.U.P. with, I hoped, enough dollars to last me for three or four months or perhaps longer. I had come as I had gone to many countries before. But, for the first time in my experience, the prospect that lay ahead of me seemed forbidding. America was unpredictable, whereas Europe and Asia and Africa had always been half-known in advance. It might give me nothing. Yet it might give me everything. I roused myself to call up some strangers on the telephone. Then, curiosity awakening, I went out into the street.

I walked tentatively westwards, dawdling and gazing into the shops as I had dawdled and gazed in countless foreign cities.

Their windows boasted, surprisingly, of imported European merchandise, of trifles 'just arrived' from Germany and Italy and France, of 'English-style' fashions and 'London character' shoes. I paused before a shop selling nothing but ties, Old School ones for the most part, with a distinct touch of Harrow in the Etonian blue; before another selling nothing but driftwood, ingeniously fashioned into penholders, fruit dishes, lamps, candelabra; before a third selling indecent Easter cards, for this was Easter week. As I gazed I became half aware of the sound of a bell, ringing through the throb of the traffic, then of shouts behind me on the pavement, and the grating on which I stood began to rise into the air, dividing, and bearing me up with it. A firm arm dragged me back to the pavement, and an expressionless voice rebuked me for disregarding the warning call.

Intimidated, I stopped obediently on the pavement of an avenue, joining an orderly crowd, before lights which instructed me in red, DON'T WALK. The cars pouring past us were all vividly parti-coloured—yellow and violet and crimson and turquoise—like the Dodgem cars in a fairground. Permitted by the green light to WALK once more, I crossed the avenue, following the file of pedestrians, and proceeded westwards again. Then I turned into a square and, for the first time, the skyscrapers hit me. They reared up, astonishing but frightening, to heights unforeseen, an anarchy of towers, dominating the high, grey sky, bearing down upon the earth and, it seemed, down upon me, so that I backed involuntarily away.

I walked away across the square—Times Square it was—and up Broadway, passing a black nun with a begging bowl seated by the kerb, startled by a slot-machine shouting to passers-by, hypnotized by a hoarding where monstrous lips puffed out cigarette smoke and a glittering cascade of light spelled out Pepsi-Cola. Unable yet to comprehend the whole, I had eyes only for details: orchids on sale for half a crown on a street corner; a Salvation Army officer on another, changing hymn-tunes on a long-playing gramophone. A vehicle like a bus drove past, full of motor-cars. Wandering on through streets still indistinguishable except for a series of numbers, I passed, unexpectedly, by the Dorset, the Warwick, the Devon hotels. All around me the air was thick with the dust of falling masonry and loud with the roar of the bulldozer and the drill and the blow-lamp, as regiments of demons, wearing yellow asbestos skull-caps and overalls like space-suits, tore buildings down or built them up. Hypnotized

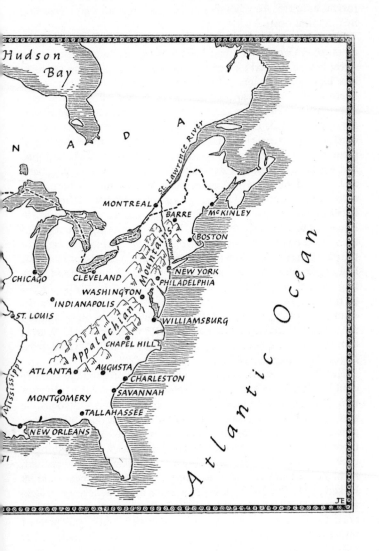

Hudson Bay

CANADA

St. Lawrence River

MONTREAL
BARRE McKINLEY
BOSTON

Mountains

CHICAGO
CLEVELAND
NEW YORK
WASHINGTON PHILADELPHIA
INDIANAPOLIS
ST. LOUIS
WILLIAMSBURG

Appalachian

CHAPEL HILL

ATLANTA AUGUSTA
CHARLESTON
SAVANNAH
MONTGOMERY
TALLAHASSEE

NEW ORLEANS
MISSISSIPPI
TI

Atlantic Ocean

JE

into silence, groups of people stood watching them, from observation platforms, beneath notices, HOUSE WRECKERS, BORING INC., JOSEPH P. BLITZ. An adjoining notice read, reassuringly, 'Building NOT coming down.'

Thus I came to the door of the Twenty-One Restaurant, the most expensive, or so I had been assured, in New York. In the street before it stood a racehorse, held by a negro groom, its forelegs bandaged, its loins clothed in a blanket bearing the words 'Kentucky Club.' Guarded outside by wooden effigies of jockeys in bright racing colours, the lush, panelled interior of the restaurant was adorned, in a cheerful style, with shelves of encrusted bottles, pewter pots and German beer mugs; ship models and plane models hung from the ceiling; sporting prints, photographs and caricatures crowded the walls. The waiters wore pink coats, and a band of them had gathered around a table where, as I entered, they were lustily singing, 'Happy Birthday To You.' The babel of voices, the buzz of vitality around me was such as, in Europe, I had seldom met far north of Naples. I singled out one of the several brothers who run this restaurant—and indeed ran it in the past as a speakeasy—a man upon whom a mutual acquaintance had urged me to call. He greeted me like a big brother and, putting an arm around my shoulder, steered me through the crowd to the bar, where he ordered me a double Martini. Beside us, drinking another, was a sleek-faced Colonel—the man, he assured me, who had invented the Sidecar in Paris after World War I; a man, too, he added aside, of immense wealth, derived from large cotton estates in Carolina.

He left us together, and the Colonel, as he ordered me another double Martini, talked of these estates, from which he flew nectarines and peaches to the Twenty-One daily. In his kitchens, he said, he had just installed a new stove which worked by radar—also a Chinese smoke-oven. The stove could cook anything in three minutes, by a process of remote control. But nothing it cooked tasted of anything. Thus, when the Colonel entertained, he had dishes flown over from Maxim's in Paris. Indeed—and he looked at his watch—he must now leave me to collect a consignment of *Sole Dieppoise* and *Canard à la Presse*, due at Idlewild Airport. He invited me to stay with him in the South, and pressed into my hand a book of matches, bearing a photograph of his villa ('on and often in the Ocean') at Myrtle Beach. It offered a number of amenities, including a Porte Couchère, a Psychiatric Lounge, a Snack Bar, a Smack Bar and a Bar Sinister. 'Guests with reservations,' I read, 'should keep them to themselves. No community singing in the showers. No Bouncing: Checks, Guests or Bottoms. No Throwing: Games, Fits, Parties, Wet Blankets, Dice, your Weight, or up.' This was my first millionaire.

I now lunched on the house, sitting on a banquette, accepting the restaurant tie emblazoned with '21's,' chewing at oysters too large to be swallowed at a single mouthful. Around me the chatter, as in an aviary, went on unabated. A smart lady on my right was saying to another: 'Your great talent is memory. I can't remember a thing.' A smart lady on my left was telephoning from her table to a series of friends. Farther off, big brother was giving lunch to his son, a fresh-looking college boy, and exuberantly assuring him, 'John, I love you dearly.' Leaving the restaurant, I mislaid my cloakroom ticket. The cloakroom attendant gave me that silent, deadpan look to which I was already accustomed. There was nothing to be done, said the look, but find it; and this I shame-facedly did.

That evening I dined with two friends of a friend, Kay and Andrew Jackson. He was a lawyer, she an editress for a publishing firm; they were not rich; they were relaxed and affectionate; their flat reflected themselves, and they had lived in it, unlike most New Yorkers, for more than twenty years. They cooked me a steak, which we ate at a candlelit table. They became my friends.

Thus ended my first day in New York.

○ **2** ○

City of Dreamless Spires · Marvels of Present and Past · From Hi School to Stork Time · 1001 Sleeping Problems · Old England in Clubland · Not 'With It'

A DAY or so later I wrote to Constance, in London:

'I am not quite acclimatized. I'm still an obstinate European. It's so unlike Europe in the sense that there's so little to look at. Little pleasure for the eye, as you pace the streets. No graceful buildings, no trees, no people—at least they haven't yet become people to me. And are they people to each other, this hurrying heedless mass? The traffic moves in a series of convulsive jerks, worrying to the nerves, from one set of lights to the next. The streets go on and on unendingly, with never a curve or an oblique angle, never a surprise, never a deviation from the standardized grid plan. But they're chaotic in height and in proportions, each building for itself, regardless of its neighbour and of the street below. It's all out of scale with man; that's what makes it so different from the cities of Europe. But the sky is miraculously high, and the light is radiant, and there's always a tang of the sea in the air. You never forget you're on an island. And this I like.'

Congested on Manhattan Island, New York is a city handy for a pedestrian to master. Stringing itself far out to the north and the south, it is narrow and compact at the centre, so that its distances seem shorter than those of London or Paris. At first, as I walked, the illusion of Englishness, born in that drive from the docks, returned. Here, coming up in the world from the Dublinesque slums, were streets like those of Kensington or Mayfair or Marylebone, neo-Georgian, Victorian or Edwardian in style; here was an architectural character belonging neither to America, as I had expected, nor to the European continent, but to Britain. The élite Sutton Place, facing the East River across lawns, reproduced Cheyne Walk. Away from the opposite bank there sprawled a Brooklyn as dingily Victorian as Wandsworth or Battersea. Downtown the Bowery was Whitechapel; uptown Harlem was Highbury. Only back towards the centre, striding down and across Madison, Park and Fifth Avenues, did the true America of the skyscrapers emerge. But even here, above the functional level, Europe had provided the finishing touches, so that the famous skyline became, in detail, a procession of swags and pediments and castellated ramparts, of towers capped with Gothic chapels, Roman temples, Renaissance palaces and Jacobean mansions. Only the more modern and functional among them, pillars of light fashioned from glass and aluminium and bronze, had shaken themselves free of such vestigial appendages, leaping skywards in confident and unrelieved mastery of their element.

Collectively, they oppressed me with a sense of claustrophobia. My walks became a series of escapes from the skyscrapers, seeking to come to terms with them from a more comfortable distance. The easiest line of escape was to Central Park—no park, it is true, in the London sense, since traffic encircles and invades it, crisscrossing and burrowing beneath its pastures, while its trees are stunted in growth by a substratum of rock for ever forging to the surface and sprawling over it in elephantine grey outcrops. It was, however, strangely empty of humanity, since few New Yorkers think to relax in the Park in the daytime; and from here, in comparative seclusion, I could contemplate, with equanimity and dawning enjoyment, the rectangular cliffs of masonry which soared up around me, each defiantly independent of its neighbour.

At night these cliffs become, as a friend vividly described them, 'celestial honeycombs,' and as such, on my second night in New York, I saw and was half-conquered by them. This time an acquaintance had taken me half-way up to meet the skyscrapers, to the roof of a twenty-storey building. No longer a pigmy on the pavement, I now saw them on a less intimidating scale, as a large mountain is seen from the top of a small one. Looking now downwards into the black canyons of the streets, where myriads of pinpoints and beams of light moved incessantly to and fro, now upwards towards the summits of the honeycombed colour-lit façades, I contemplated, as never before, a truly vertical landscape receding in perspective and rising to a diversity of levels bewildering to one familiar only with the horizontal world. Beneath the night sky it had all the fantasy and glittering allurement of a giant Luna Park. And indeed around it, by the edge of the encircling water, there revolved, in kaleidoscopic rings of light, an unending swift merry-go-round of cars, painted always in those bright fairground colours.

But the classic view of the New York skyline—this time the downtown skyline of Wall Street—is from the Brooklyn waterfront. Here, on my third evening in New York, I looked across the river from the bow-windowed Victorian apartment of Paul and Gabrielle Geier, to see range upon range of towers, racing upwards to a chaotic variety of heights, yet so compressed as to make an orderly form out of the chaos. I was reminded of the serried church-towers of San Gimignano, multiplied and blown up to a colossal scale—and indeed I have since noticed that San Gimignano provides a favourite subject for American painters in Italy. But these were not church-towers. They were towers filled with men. And to what purpose? Was New York, perhaps, the City of Dreamless Spires?

*   *   *

Filled with men they were indeed, as I was soon to observe, whisked up on a sightseeing tour, at a pace of fourteen hundred feet per minute, to the seventieth storey of the Rockefeller Center. Never was I able to find a staircase in this gargantuan hive of vertical living. Visiting it fairly regularly to call on my agent, often forgetting the number of his floor and of his office before I entered the elevator, I would guess at it and find myself wandering, on the wrong floor, with no means of checking the number and no apparent means of walking upstairs or down in search of his name on a door. I would thus be obliged to start all over again, taking the elevator right back to the ground, verifying the number from the reception desk and this time writing it down. In this world of numbers rather than names, I would get badly lost. I was for ever passing my floor in an elevator or my street on the subway or my house on a street, through inability to remember more than a single group of figures at once.

A whole mythology of numbers was now intoned to me by the guide, in a singsong chant like the liturgy of a priestess. She recited to us of the hundred million dollars which the skyscraper had cost, the three hundred and sixty four million tons which it weighed, its thirteen thousand telephones spanning the 'known world,' the fifteen million people who visited it annually. Here was an edifice Roman in its mammoth conception, and it seemed suitable enough that its approach should be guarded by an immense bronze figure of Prometheus, spouting water. For all its external starkness, its foyers and halls were in the sumptuous tradition of decadent Rome, with mosaics and sculptures and golden ceilings and marble galore, some of it Travertine, some from the island of Tinos. One of the mosaics consisted of a million pieces of glass in two hundred and fifty shades of colour; it represented 'Thought Enlightening the World.' Commanding the entrance, a huge painted effigy of Atlas followed the visitor around with its eyes.

The priestess called my attention to the fact that the lighting here was derived from that of Pompeii, that the stone there resembled that of the Colosseum. She indicated also two great white columns facing towards the east, towards the rising sun and towards Fifth Avenue, and through them the great flower-beds where, shortly, six thousand Easter lilies and three thousand daffodils would be planted for the Easter parade. Up above, at a height of some three hundred feet, were hanging gardens, four times the size of those of Babylon, but this time of Spain, Italy, Japan, Holland, America and England—the latter with a sundial and yews. Beneath the ground life became horizontal once more, lived in a warren of catacombs, cooled or heated according to season, and so furnished with shops and cafés and restaurants and places of entertainment that it was possible, so the priestess assured us, to spend whole days in them without coming to the surface. But there were churches too. She pointed out to us St. Patrick's Cathedral, seeming to revere it as much as the Rocke-feller Center, though it weighed less and took thirty-six years to build. Later I was to see the Riverside Church, twenty-two storeys high (and no men in them) and the site of the largest cathedral in the world, which was still being built.

Meanwhile my sightseeing tour led me to the Empire State Building, at the summit of which I was later entertained to luncheon in a lush apartment with views all round, like some luxurious belvedere at the top of an alp. Here, I learnt, strange natural phenomena occur: sometimes the snow falls upwards, sometimes the rain is red. The guide, a man this time, showed off to us other marvels: the Woolworth Building, with a Gothic tower reminiscent of Westminster; the Municipal Building, with a classical rotunda on top of it and a triumphal Corinthian arch going through it; the Flatiron Building, a skyscraper of great antiquity, indeed the father of them all, built in 1902. In these parts, the guide assured us, if all the people in all the buildings came out at once, they would be unable to walk on the sidewalk. He showed us the street of the nineteen night-clubs, the street of the hundred and fifty thousand garment-workers, the street of the Forgotten Men, the street known as Bridal Row and selling the most beautiful wedding-gowns in the world, the street with Sloppy Louie's in it ('If the place's sloppy you ought to see Louie'), and street after street after street, but only an occasional square.

He was a guide with a streak of nostalgia for the past, showing us not only Macy's (Motto: 'It's smart to be thrifty'), where eleven thousand assistants sold a million dollars' worth of goods each day, but also the first house in the city to have electric light, on a street once only two-and-a-half metres wide; not only the Statue of Liberty, the Colossus of the New World, with its index finger eight feet long and its eyes one-and-a-half feet wide, but the oldest Presbyterian church and the smallest motion picture house, with a seating capacity of less than one hundred. Had I chosen to dig deeper into the past, I could have joined a hike planned by the Municipal Art Society in co-operation with the Society of Architectural Historians, whose members rejoiced in ancient Victorian statues, marvelled at the ornamental doorway of a building erected in 1878, and talked about it all afterwards, or so I read in the *New York Times*, over drinks at Pete's Tavern, a favourite resort of O. Henry. 'The flamboyant architectural adornments of the last century had impressed them, but they bemoaned the encroachment of bleak and sterile streamlined apartment buildings.'

New York, however, seemed to me a landscape not of buildings alone but of words. From all sides, insistent on hoardings and shopfronts and the façades of the buildings, words jumped out at me—signs, commands, warnings, names, slogans, jingles, the catchwords of advertisers—and here again there was a Roman flavour. Here was the Lubritorium, for the service of motor-cars, the Giftorium, for the purchase of gifts, the Bowlatorium, the arena where the popular game of bowls (otherwise skittles) was played. Cinerama, of course, was already familiar; not so Burgerama, for the purchase of Hamburgers; Icearama, for skating; Frigerama, for the purchase of frigidaires; Motorama, for that of motor-cars, a doll-like lady—or was it a ladylike doll?—stepping nonchalantly into one, behind the plateglass window, before the wondering pavement crowds. There were the Bustorama and the Sexorama and the Thrillarama, the Bargainorama and the Birthdayrama and the Juniorama. Affecting a different but similarly classical suffix were the Beauteria, the Gasateria, the Steakateria and the Donuteria.

But New York's Roman temples, lining its triumphal avenues, are its shops—its emporia. For this is a nation of shoppers. Jerking down Fifth Avenue on a bus, a lady behind me chanted the names of these stately houses, as we passed them one after the other, in hushed and reverent tones: 'Bergdorf Goodman, Tiffany, Bonwit Teller, de Pinna, American Express, Saks Fifth Avenue, St. Patrick's Cathedral, Lord and Taylor . . .' Their windows, I thought, were dressed with less imagination than some in Paris or London. But within their swing-doors the devotee is enveloped in a rich scentless warmth, where 'suddenly it's spring, and every costume is gay with accessories in bloom'; where, amid the clothes ranged in ranks, tropical greenery may flourish and canaries sing from golden cages.

Magical escalators transport her skywards from marble hall to marble hall, where the wondrous treasures of a modern civilization, fashioned from Miracle Fabrics, are spread out for her temptation and delight. Here all is order, through the hierarchy of income-groups from Budget Dresses and Budget Hats to Better Dresses and Better Hats, through that of age-groups, for 'young worldlings from tots to teens,' from the Junior Hi and the Hi School Shop through the Camp Fire Girl Shop to the Junior Deb Center, and thence in the fullness of time to the Graduation Shop, the Bridal Shop, and the Maternity Shop ('Stork Time'). Here is provision for all shapes, up to the Stylish Stout; provision too for all occasions, from Brunch Coats and Fashion Dusters to Date Dresses and Boulevard Dresses, Country Club Dresses and Gracious Lady Gowns, with pickings of all kinds from the Commuter Bar, the Thrift Table, the Clutch Bar, the Panty Bar, the Bra Bar, the Needle Clinic or the Remnant Riot. Even here, however, an English influence penetrates, with Lady Manhattan shirts, Lady Baltimore luggage, Lady Berkleigh pajamas, or, as a present for a gentleman, a Lord West dinner-jacket, in raw silk of red, white or blue ('It's fun to go formal'). A more select emporium displayed tweeds in its windows, around a photograph of the Queen Mother, twice life size.

For the male, meanwhile, there are more robust establishments, like the Bar Mart. Here he may buy brassières to put round his bottles, jock-straps, attachable to glasses, to give his highballs a lift, flannel diapers for their wet bottoms, an eyeball or a fly to float in them ('adds a laugh to all iced drinks'), or a Manneken Pis to pour water into them. If he likes his cocktails really dry, there is a Vermouth Spray for them, while for subsequent use there is a tube of toothpaste or a mouth-wash flavoured with Bourbon, and a pillow or a bath-mat composed of the softest foam-rubber bosoms. For 'the man who has everything' there is a toothbrush of mink. For relief from a hangover, it is now possible—or so I was assured—to have an oxygen mask plugged into the bathroom wall, beside the electric razor.

Joke shops abound, where the male may buy toys for himself or his friends; an insomnia bib for an expectant father, a 'crying towel' for a disappointed sportsman; a set of false teeth which talks, or serves as an ashtray; a pair of 'refuge specs,' with eyes behind them, Shy, Demure, Eager Beaver or Cool Intellectual, for use At Dinner Parties, In Conference, At the Opera, On the Bench—'Nap Politely, yet look Alert and Intriguing.' On Broadway there is a shop where he may have his portrait painted or his handwriting analysed; buy himself a tie and have his or her name painted on it, or a pair of bosoms, or a wise saying; join a society called the Exalted Order of Stupid Imbeciles, or one called Idiots Anonymous ('for having accomplished and negotiated at least three preposterous blunders'); have a newspaper printed with his name in large headlines; photograph himself, record his own voice, or shoot himself (failing an alternative bull's-eye) with a tommy-gun. Such versatility extends to the tobacconist, who will sell him a clipper for either his cigars or his fingernails, and also plan his tax returns. Next door he may hire a detective to follow his wife; ('We give you peace of mind. Let us help you.') or, if he prefers, he may buy a toy for her, at a neighbouring establishment—a musical tea-pot playing 'Tea for Two,' a silver feather ('saves fingernails') for dialling on the telephone, a plastic handbag disguised as a telephone, or the lady's new electrical razor (no larger than a compact, designed to shave both legs and underarms and so 'always safeguard your personal charm').

Hungry, with the world on his Roman doorstep, the New Yorker may be tempted by the Caviar-teria or Delicacy Supermarket, 'a place where you can browse freely among two thousand exciting packaged foods from twenty-nine countries.' Here are Fresh Romanoff Caviar ('the Aristocrat of the Table of All Ages'), imported fried grasshoppers, fried Mexican agave worms, Japanese quail eggs, Brazilian palm-hearts, liquorice buttons from Holland, oatcakes ('ideal for health') from Scotland, or a Do-it-yourself gingerbread house.

Tiring, he may finally ascend to the Sleep Shop. 'Study our uninhibited Sleep Shop,' he reads, 'for progressive beducation.' Here Americans are put to sleep, as no Romans ever were, by magic beds and learned diagrams. The Sleep Shop outdoes all the sages of psychiatry. Beneath the life-size close-up of a sleeper, Freud is quoted: 'His aggressive sleeping position signifies a subconscious desire to reject or eject his mate. His pre-natal position indicates his desire to return to his mother.' But the Sleep Shop knows better: 'The man is not aggressive. He is thin-blooded and his feet are difficult to warm. All he needs is our electrical footwarmer.'

A rich variety of beds solves '1001 sleeping problems.' There is the Jack Spratt Bed, soft on one side for Sybarite She, hard on the other for Spartan He; the Electromatic Bed for the misogynist (or misandrist) who prefers his (or her) own company; the Compatibility Bed, for consoling proximity without restraint; the Veto Bed, for ambivalent mates ('Sometimes I love you, Sometimes I hate you') for reassuring proximity or cooling aloofness; the Modern Bundling Bed ('How to sleep on the level together'), discouraging involuntary rolling too close.

A Mattress Clinic discusses the relative merits of sleeping

positions: the right supine sprawl or the left kitten coil. A poll decides the graver question 'Should twin beds be abolished, Yes or NO?' The double-beds have it; but the Sleep Shop proposes a Delphic compromise—Tête-à-Tête Twins, to promote cultural exchange. Thinking is encouraged in addition to sleeping. Here Rodin is put in his place, like Freud. The position of his *Penseur*, compared with Our Thinking Chair, begets cramped thinking, discourages intuitive activity, inhibits fruitful thought. 'The wise boss ... insists that hard-pressed executives restore their flagging expensive energies with rejuvenating catnaps.' 'Sitting is Believing'—and sure enough the Saleslady, reclining in the chair before all the shoppers, has thought herself to sleep.

The minor 'shrines' of New York are its drug-stores, which cater without discrimination for the needs of the human body. DRUGS, LUNCH, reads the notice above it. Vaccines, Hot Dogs, Biological Milk Shakes, Perfumes are indiscriminately purveyed. Choose between a Hot Butterscotch Fudge Sundae and a Glycerine Suppository. Have your Corns and Calluses removed while drinking a Chocolate Coke. Squeamishly, I avoided eating in these drug-stores, disliking the conflict of smells between antiseptics and sausage-meat. To the logical American mind, there appeared to be no such conflict, each contributing its share to the same task of maintaining the body. On the highways the notice above the gasoline station, FUEL, FOOD, suggests equally no incongruity. Is not food simply the process of refuelling the body? Such and little more, in the down-to-the-pavement American fashion, I found it to be. But the fuel was fortifying enough, more in a Germanic than in an English style.

I preferred to eat in cafeterias or snack-bars or 'hash-houses'—even in automats, where a dish, hot or cold, was released from a pigeon-hole by a coin in the slot. Together with the Hamburger, varied to Beefburger, Steakburger or Cheeseburger, promoted to Twinburger, Kingburger or 'Hamburger with a College Education,' the basic element in American food is the sandwich—but a sandwich which has grown, as the house has grown into the skyscraper, to be a hi-decker or at least a structure on a substantial scale. 'THE BEST HAND-CARVED SANDWICH IN TOWN' might mean a full portion of Roast Sirloin of Beef, bursting out from between two slices of hot-buttered toast; a triple-decker tuna fish and tomato sandwich with Potato Frills and Pickle Chips, glorified with relishes; or, at the Bunnery, a meal of 'Butterfly Shrimps (4), Jumbo, Tender, Meaty, with French Fried and Cole Slaw,' all on a soft-toasted bun. Lacking adequate jaw muscles, I would scrape all this food off its bun or from between its slabs of bread and, to the deadpan scorn of the waitress, demand a knife and fork. The alternative was to eat most of it with the fingers—as most Americans in practice do.

In the hash-houses the bread was dispensed with, and there were mammoth helpings, described on the menu with an uninhibited licking of chops, of 'Tender Milk-Fed Veal, Pan-Fried in Pure Creamery Butter and served with Tasty Tomato Sauce, Golden Fried Idahos and Tossed Green Salad,' of a 'Jumbo Chopped Steak Sizzling Platter. Choice Angus Steer Beef, thick cut, tender; pink center; charcoal-boiled and served with Curley-cue Potatoes, French Fried Onions and Fresh Mushroom Sauce.' All was dished on to a spacious platter, with a separate compartment for each delicacy.

The food advertisements in the newspapers read as lusciously, even introducing an element of sex into food. In the *New York Times* my eye was caught by a headline 'SEXY SHRIMPS STUN SOPHISTICATES. Curvaceous shrimps, embracing the saucy marriages of spices and wine, tantalizing taste-buds, luring and tempting you to more.' After this the Chock Full o'Nuts, offering a Hot Fudge Fantasy, a Nut 'n Fudge Fancifree, or an Ice-cream selected from twenty-eight varieties, seemed an anti-climax—even washed down by drinks served with the latest straws, with built-in chocolate, vanilla or strawberry flavourings.

* * *

The days went by and I was lonely. I made a few new acquaintances who invited me to lunch, or drinks, or sometimes dinner. The restaurants in which we lunched had often an English character, being decorated with sporting prints, or heraldic escutcheons, or coach-wheels. But Guys and Dolls, for Gents and Ladies (and in one Italian restaurant Romeos and Juliets), struck a less familiar note. The clubs were more English still, whether furnished in the Jacobean manner, with lattice windows and wheel-back chairs, or decorated in a style which might be defined as Knickerbocker Adam, with Georgian plasterwork and Chippendale furniture. Here American gentlemen, in Old English School ties, reclined in leather armchairs and were served with 'House of Lords' gin by deferential Scots servants. But they were sober establishments. Only water was served with the meals.

The apartments in which I drank were well-warmed, well-carpeted, well-upholstered; they were furnished, as they might not have been in London, in invariable good taste, whether that of the owner himself or that of an interior decorator. Always they had a new look; there was never an object out of place or a stain to be seen on the well-polished furniture. Their kitchens were immaculate, with a white-enamelled armoury of sleek machines for freezing and washing and heating and cooking. But there was never a whiff of food, as though they were seldom cooked in. This was indeed often the case, since these New Yorkers, opulent as some of them were, had little or no domestic help. 'We are lucky,' one of them said to me. 'We have a woman who comes in once a week.' Often they preferred a meal in a restaurant or a light snack at home to the chores of more serious cooking. Most of them, since restaurants were expensive, thus entertained little. They were busy people, for New York is a hard-working city, or at least a city which works long hours. Often I was the only guest. Seldom did one new acquaintance lead to another. No gregarious whirl of hospitality bore me off. And for this at least I was grateful.

Generally, in the evenings, I would wander down the avenues in search of some café or modest-priced restaurant, then drop into a few bars, before retiring to bed. These bars as a rule were tenebrous places, relics of the days of the speakeasy, with shaded lights and dark divans. They were usually silent places too. I am not good at talking to strangers; but I had been assured that in America strangers would all talk to me—in the street, in buses, in the subway, in these bars. They did not do so. Perhaps they thought me a stuffed-shirt. But I noticed that they talked hardly more to each other.

One evening, feeling perhaps that I wasn't seeing or hearing the Real America, I decided to take the initiative and, downing a good gulp of Scotch, turned to my neighbour and remarked, unimaginatively, 'Not many people in here this evening.' He slowly focused on me the expressionless, deadpan gaze, and, looking me up and down, replied, 'Not with that accent.' Determined not to accept defeat, I downed another gulp of Scotch and made another, equally insignificant remark. At this his expression relaxed, and he exclaimed, to my surprise, 'Why, you're British.' He went on to explain that he had taken me for an American trying to be taken for an Englishman—a type he did not care to encourage. Then he talked for quite a time, about his job, and his recent promotion, and the three successive houses into which they

26

had enabled him, during the past five years, to move his wife and family.

But New York was proving slow in its impact. For me, it still lacked an identity—and I myself lacked an identity in relation to it. The city still was a mass of unrelated detail: the wood could not be seen for the trees. The unending streets and towering buildings and gleaming apartments and hurrying cars and staring signs and bewildering numbers would not cohere into a whole. It was an impersonal city, an assortment of things rather than people. The Americans have an expressive vernacular phrase, 'Get with it!' I was not yet 'with it.'

∽ 3 ∽

*A Chance Encounter · The Hundred Great Books · Nine
Different Lives · Beginning to Belong*

THE New Yorker taxi-driver is proverbial; as much so—and perhaps as much of a myth—as the London policeman. My friends had promised me frequent and enlightening conversations with taxi-drivers. Rather to my relief, since I like to relax in a taxi, these did not materialize. The taxi-drivers seemed taciturn— perhaps because I was—and when they talked their conversation was not always rewarding. There was one who asked me, charm-ingly, 'Are you a lover of nature?' If so, he added, he would drive me through Central Park. There was another, late one night, who assured me that he needed only three or four hours' sleep each night. 'I'm healthy,' he added. He had once worked as a rigger, stripped to the waist all day—and that was why. Mostly the taxi-drivers unloaded their grievances—about the traffic, its regulations, lady drivers, pedestrians, their fares and the disputes they had with them.

Then, one Sunday evening, I was returning home from a dinner with some rich, kind acquaintances. Their apartment was spick and span and Victorian, in the style of the smart Madison Avenue decorators. Their conversation was affable, their steaks were rare, and moreover served, to my agreeable surprise, with little glasses of wine. But somehow, for all their friendliness, I knew we should never become friends, and I needed friends: I needed personal intimacy in this city which, in its own person, seemed so aloof.

I left around eleven, the hour at which my New York acquaintances, faced with an early journey to business next morning, liked as a rule to retire: late nights they seemed to regard as a little provincial. Not yet ready for bed, I turned into a bar and spent a profitless hour in its dim-lit mirrored recesses, observing again how few of its patrons talked. Finally I left and took a taxi back to my hotel.

From a sense rather of duty I said a word to the back of the head of the driver. He was a fair-headed, well-built young man in a scarlet sweater whose face glared at me, like that of a wanted criminal, from his photograph pasted on his licence inside the cab. His name, Harry Martin, was inscribed beneath it. He answered and talked amiably, in an educated way. Soon he revealed that he was not a taxi-driver at all, but a painter, who drove a cab at weekends to augment his living. He added, 'I don't do so much painting, though. I guess it's just an excuse to lead a Bohemian sort of life.' We talked about Abstract Expressionism in American painting. I asked him if he often had conversations with his fares, and he said 'Yes. They treat the cab as a sort of confessional. They sit there as though they were on the couch at the psychiatrist's, pouring it all out in the dark.'

When I paid him off I said I would like, sometime, to see his pictures. He seemed pleased, and promised to call me. He did so a day or two later, inviting me over to his studio the next after-noon. This was a 'cold-water flat'—that is to say, a flat without central heating—on the fourth floor of a slummy tenement on York Avenue, uptown on the East Side of New York. The stairs were shabby, with dilapidated treads and flaking walls and a musty, damp-ridden smell. But the flat itself was airy, with an atmosphere of its own. There were three small rooms, one of them a kitchen containing a frigidaire and a bath with a lid on it. The windows looked out on to rooftops with an anarchic array of skylights and chimney-pots and television aerials. Abstract paintings lined the walls, unframed; mobiles hung from the ceil-ing; a row of painted masks formed a cornice above a small model theatre; a few neglected plants in pots straggled over an opening between the kitchen and the living-room. Books were stacked everywhere—books on philosophy and painting, modern poetry, fiction, the classics, biographies, the lives of the Saints, ranged along the mantelpiece and by the bedside, and overflowing from the bookcases on to piles on the floor, among stacks of old numbers of *The New Yorker* and *Time*.

There was a long untidy writing-table, and another table

holding a gramophone—but no television set. His canvases were stacked behind an easel in the kitchen, and over the disused fire-place one of them hung, a painting in oils of a stark bedroom in a Paris hotel, where he had once lived for a while. This helped to give to the room a nostalgic flavour, as of some garret in Mont-parnasse in the nineteen-twenties. It was a casual room, and essentially a personal one, where each object reflected the taste and activities of its owner. It contrasted warmly with the impersonal good-taste interiors of the New York apartments I had known. I at once felt at home in it.

Harry—for Christian names come easily in America—made some instant coffee, and as we drank it we looked through a port-folio of his drawings. As a painter he was emerging from an abstract phase, but no new style had yet taken its place, and these were haphazard sketches of people in the parks and of animals in the zoo, showing sensibility of line and expression. We talked about pictures and books and places and people, and to my sur-prise, since he had only once spent a few days in London, dis-covered two friends in common. One of them was Peter Watson, an English friend and patron of artists. The other was Alice Bouverie, an American by birth and wealth but a European in spirit, who had lived much in London but was now living here in New York.

Harry himself, direct in manner and quick in response, showed a blend of disillusion and zest, of sensitivity and toughness, which I found sympathetic. Here, I judged, was a capacity to embrace life without being too far deceived by it. Part German and part Irish in extraction, the son of a New York railway employee, he had been born, as strangely few New Yorkers are, in the heart of Manhattan, and had grown up in the narrow, conventional world of a small suburb. He had found an escape from it through the war, in which he had served as a medical orderly in the Navy. Afterwards he had gone to college on a G.I. Grant. The college he chose was an unorthodox one—St. John's, Annapolis—which, forsaking the conventional university curriculum, concentrated entirely on the study of the Hundred Great Books. Harry, tall and athletic in build, had excelled at basketball, and had supervised the sports at St. John's. But such sports were not encouraged; it was the books that counted, and he had thus absorbed an unusual degree of culture and a humanist outlook wider than that of the average college boy. This had born in him, however, a spirit of revolt against his environment, making him reluctant to conform to the material values of the life around him. Rather than strive to come to terms with the world of success, rather than join in the struggle for lucrative contacts in the various branches of commercial art and advertising, he preferred to keep his independence, as he saw it, and a degree of integrity, by driving his taxi-cab.

This gave him—since he only did it at weekends—more leisure than most, which he spent, if not in painting, then in reading voraciously or simply in absorbing life, drifting idly through it or seeking its cosmic significance in terms of a youthful contemplation of the navel. Harry, as I was to find, was a rebel, but a passive one. In his way of life, aspiring rather to be than to do, counting poverty and leisure and reflection to be virtues in a society wedded to wealth and work and action, I was to see America, as it were, through a looking-glass. In his own nature, warm and impulsive, enthusiastic and curious, I was to see it directly.

*   *   *

New York is a city, perhaps above all others, where life thus depends on the chance encounter. This applies not to foreigners only but to New Yorkers themselves. It is the city of the 'Lonely Crowd', to which millions come from all parts of America and from Europe, forsaking family backgrounds and seeking a new personal framework for living. They do not easily find it. They find, covering the City's immense expanse, a society which is not cohesive, as European and provincial societies tend to be, but broken up into an infinite number of social fragments, of atomic units, as it were, isolated one from the other. It may well be that a stranger in London finds the same. But here the composition of the units is different. In London they stem, as a rule, from the family, from the domestic interior. In New York they stem rather from the professional category, from the fraternity of the job.

Russell Lynes writes of American society in *A Surfeit of Honey*:

'Instead of being divided horizontally into levels and strata, as we are used to thinking of it, our society has increasingly become divided vertically. Instead of broad, upper, middle and lower classes that cut across the society of the native like the clear but uneven slices on a geological model, we now have a series of almost free-standing pyramids, each with its several levels and each one topped by an aristocracy of its own. It is a far cry from the top of one of the pyramids to the next, and communication between the members of the aristocracies is, to say the least, difficult; they not only speak different languages, but their minds are on quite different things. They have different notions of what constitutes success (though they all like money, of course) and their 'status symbols,' to use a sociologist's term, are as unlike as, say, a swimming pool and an academic hood.'

The divisions of this society are between the various categories of big business, small business, publicity, entertainment, politics, the intelligentsia and sport. By its standards, it is more important to be Something than Somebody. It is desirable to be categorized as 'in' something—in steel, in insurance, in public relations. Specialization, I found, extends in its sub-divisions even to charitable works, where ladies describe themselves as being in cancer, in polio, in cerebral palsy.

Moreover, each vertical pyramid has its own horizontal divisions, between the various levels of income and status and age. Thus there is in New York little sign of a 'society' in the European sense, based on a diversity of human elements and interests. It is a city without salons or cafés, lacking that eclectic urban culture such as is stimulated in Europe by the differing ideas of differing individuals in differing walks of life. Here personality tends to be overridden by category, as in the more rigid European societies it is overridden by class. Who your parents were is indeed of no consequence; but what you do counts more than what you are.

In London there exists a fluid society, in which one world quickly overlaps into another. In New York, outside the limited international world of Café Society, I had not found this to be so. Few of my new acquaintances knew any of the others. It was no place for name-dropping, for personal gossip: conversation was less about people than about things or ideas, and hence had a more serious trend. But here was a society, or a series of societies, with certain positive benefits. One of these was privacy. In E. B. White's *Here is New York*, I read: 'On any person who desires such queer prizes, New York will bestow the gift of loneliness and the gift of privacy.' 'I like living here,' an English friend remarked to me, 'because I can lead nine different lives, none of which ever meet.' New York is essentially a city of small intimate groups, in which no one enquires what his neighbour is up to; and to one of these groups, through the good fortune of a chance encounter, I now belonged. They were Harry's friends, and very soon they were mine. I was no longer one of the Lonely Crowd.

There were perhaps a dozen of them, all relatively poor and outwardly unconcerned about money, living for the most part in cold-water flats; perplexed by personal problems, psychological and otherwise, but creating around them an atmosphere in which I at once felt at home. They were people with a respect for civilized values, in the arts and in personal relations; with an approach to life which was zestful and essentially human, but with an honesty of mind which made them uneasily critical of much of the life going on around them.

There was Ellsworth Kelly, an abstract painter, sallow and withdrawn and misanthropic, who had begun to achieve some success but was for ever in a mood of perverse, perhaps romantic protest against it, and against the people to whom he was indebted for it. He would deliberately shun or discourage prospective patrons. 'I've never heard,' remarked one of them, anxious to buy one of his pictures, 'such negative salesmanship.'

There was Gerrit Lansing, mercurial and versatile, with an alert pug-face and a quick, paradoxical mind, who counterbalanced a safe University Press job with a pursuit of the esoteric and a private life of exuberant and restless disorder. There was Howard Griffin, spectacled and dome-headed as an owl, a poet of talent, a modest Boswell to the literary lights he revered, a loyal counsellor to many friends and an indefatigable correspondent, exchanging letters on all subjects with intellectuals, many of them strangers, in all parts of a Europe which he himself had yet to know.

There was Ruth Yorck, a writer and a 'refugee' from that Europe, who had shone as a bright light in the Berlin of the nineteen-twenties, and now challenged drabber surroundings with the flame of angry loyalties and warm enthusiasms, a sharp sense of perception and an imaginative talent for writing. There was Lo-Maria Schonburg, fresh and wayward with a dash of royal blood and a glow of Central Europe about her, earning a haphazard income by peddling manure to the owners of roof-gardens and window-boxes. There was Harry's sister Teresa, cool and relaxed and oddly untouched by the turbulence of American life.

This was a Bohemian world, perhaps over-romantic and, in European terms, 'dated' in its spirit of protest against things established. It was a spirit which in London had flourished in the nineteen-twenties, but had since won many of its battles. It was perhaps a passive spirit. But in terms of the America of today, of the conventional family backgrounds, rich or poor, against which these young people reacted; in terms of the dead conformity of the life which they saw all around them, and of the threat to themselves as individuals and artists of the all-powerful commercial machine, it seemed to make sense. If practically ineffective, it at least had a positive human validity. What I enjoyed in their company was the mixture of sophistication and innocence. In a sense, they had learnt everything; in a sense, they had everything still to learn.

One evening, straying into Café Society, I met a lady of fashion, a lady, that is, working on a fashionable magazine. Sipping only a little champagne—if she sipped more, she explained, she would become at once a mass of allergies—she talked to me of the art of 'modern living,' known still to so few but exemplified by her air-conditioned apartment. During the day, when she and her husband were both out at work, it was kept at ice-cool temperature, summer and winter, for the sake of the flowers and plants which lived in it, its air thus remaining pollen-free and so allergy-free; and in the evening, when they returned after a busy day's work, it automatically warmed itself up for them. While on the subject of the New York social hierarchy, I asked her if she often met artists. 'One doesn't meet them much,' she said. 'And when one does, one nearly always finds there's some *Democrat* behind it.'

Most of the artists, she said, congregated down in Greenwich Village, where they made a cult of Marlon Brando, and rebelled, without of course a cause, against most things American. 'Against what in particular?' I enquired. 'Against success mostly. They're known as the hipsters. You ought to do a piece on them.'

Had I fallen among hipsters? Or were these the 'beat' boys? I thought not. For their spirit of protest was positive: it was based on ideals. Gerrit was at heart a serious scholar. Howard had a deep love of literature. Harry was seeking to find himself as a painter. Ellsworth had already done so. Their values were European, though, paradoxically, they hardly knew Europe. They would not conform. Yet they were not of the breed who, as Harry once put it to me, are 'beat' and declare that nothing matters and then go on to *make* nothing matter. They were neither negative nor destructive. I was contented among them.

After a week or so, Harry invited me to stay with him, offering me the bed in his sitting-room. I accepted and checked out of the Algonquin Hotel with relief. Ironically enough, as Ruth remarked, it is the poor in New York, with their several haphazard rooms, rather than the rich with their immaculate, well-planned apartments, who can more conveniently invite their friends to stay.

To Constance I wrote:

'Like a boy at his first school, I am finding my feet. This great impersonal city has suddenly come alive for me, in personal terms. There is nowhere, except possibly London, where you need people as much. Paris and Rome give you life, *as* cities. You don't have to be in love to love Venice. Not so New York. It was draining the life out of me. But now I have friends and back it flows. Intimacy, I suppose because of the inherent loneliness of the place, comes quickly if it does come. Hearts are worn on the sleeve. They may not always be hearts and there may not always be much up the sleeve, but if they are and there is then you get an immediate and rewarding response. And the City itself falls into perspective. You belong.'

◦ 4 ◦

A Race of Telephones · Sun-bathing off Wall Street—
Riverside Life

NEW YORK, for all its immensity, now came quietly into focus for me, developing a coherent personality in terms of neighbourhood life. Harry's tenement stood at the corner of a dead-end street which looked on to the river across the swift unceasing roundabout of the East River Drive. It was a neighbourhood inhabited by many Czechs, refugees from the Germany of the nineteen-thirties, some of whom, like the tailor who repaired and cleaned and pressed my clothes, could barely speak the English language. There were Czech restaurants and delicatessen shops, and a few doors off from us a bar plastered with the photographs of boxers and baseball players, and frequented by labourers, loose-limbed and swaggering, who kidded one another with horseplay and mock-tough backchat, speaking a Czech-American jargon which was hard to understand. I grew familiar with its patrons, listening to them as I stood, drinking ice-cold beer and eating freshly cooked hot-dogs at the bar, and accepting an occasional drink from the barman; familiar too with the Chinese laundryman down the street, strange in his ways and often speechless, perhaps under the influence of opium, but always retaining a practical grasp of essentials.

When I remembered to have my shoes cleaned—which, accustomed as I was to English habits, was all too seldom—there was a neighbouring parlour of negro bootblacks, with knockabout ways, whose talk ran interminably on the problems of car-parking. I bought whisky at the local liquor store, and my ten-cent cigars at the local cigar store, and my groceries at the local supermarket—wheeling around a 'pram' to collect my chosen purchases, and coming to enjoy picking quick-frozen and packaged foods from the pernicious deep-freeze machines. I never learnt, however, to enjoy American bread, which is not only pre-sliced but made, unlike most American manufactures, to last—in the refrigerator. With this in view, certain ingredients are removed from it and other, less desirable ingredients, put in, giving to the bread the texture—and indeed, in a sense, the taste—of wadding. 'Where do you get your bread?' was a common question among those who disliked this stuff. The answer might be, 'From the Jewish bakers on Fridays,' or, 'I know some Swedes,' or, 'The Ouspensky people have a bakery of their own, down at their place in the country.'

One American lady replied to my question indignantly, 'But *I* make excellent bread.' Somehow, in such a civilization, I did not feel that this should be really necessary.

My neighbourhood had an intimate atmosphere. It had even a village church, the chapel of St. Wenceslas, where on appropriate Saints' days crumpled flags were put out for a church bazaar, with a jumble sale and sideshows, as at some village fair in the heart of Central Europe. It was a relief now to dress casually in sweater and slacks—staying far from the madding skyscrapers for days at a time, enjoying that sense of ease and human proportions which the broad streets and the low buildings afforded. The streets themselves were far from clean. We had to carry our garbage downstairs in paper bags and deposit it in the garbage cans, ranged along the kerb, taking care to shed the dry rubbish in the trash-cans adjoining. My English friend, Anne Fremantle, unfamiliar with this ritual, once confused the two cans, just as one was being cleared, and received the reprimand, 'Hey, sister, I'm trash, not garbage.'

In the neighbouring flat lived an old man who subsisted largely by scavenging. I would hear him stirring at four o'clock in the morning, then padding quietly downstairs to do the round of the trash-cans, with a sack over his shoulder, before the collecting carts appeared. Long before breakfast he would be back, pricing his treasures and laying them out in neat piles; for his flat was kept scrupulously tidy and clean. At night, water would be sloshed over the street, from trucks, while pillars of steam would pour up through gratings in the roadway, suggesting mysterious happenings underground.

The mails were less regular than in most villages; the postman might call at any time between midday and two o'clock in the afternoon, and there was only one delivery a day. But this was typical of New York, where the telephone services are better and the postal services worse than in most cities in the world. I have known a letter take two days to reach one part of New York from another, while letters to Boston or Washington, only a few hours away, may take three or four days. Yet the Post office is alive enough to modern methods. On Lexington Avenue there was a talking post-box, which answered questions put to it. Once, on my expressing some doubt, it apologized to me for giving the wrong information about the postage due on a post-card to England.

But the Americans are essentially a race of telephoners. In Harry's flat the telephone would ring, not only through the daytime, but at all hours of the night—an inconvenience for me, since it was beside my bed. Friends would not hesitate to call him for a chat before going to bed at the lonely hour of three o'clock in the morning. During the daytime he would have long conversations, from which, hearing only one end, I would deduce that his friends were in chronic trouble, whether of love or money or alcohol or a combination of all three.

'You mean you're too drunk to get to the psychiatrist's alone,' was a characteristic remark.

Listening to these long conversations, I reached the conclusion that in America telephoning is not necessarily a prelude to personal contact, as in Europe, but a substitute for it. Harry would often ring off with an air of having seen the person concerned and of not requiring to see him again for a week or so. Americans are at ease on the telephone. Perhaps, it occurred to me, the impersonality of the instrument reassures them. Certainly telephone operators throughout the States are more polite than shop assistants, faced as they are with the spectacle of a flesh-and-blood human being.

*   *   *

The Spring was now belatedly on its way, after a month of alternate gales and sea-fogs. The skies became higher and bluer, and the sunlight poured down into the streets and over their horizons with a buoyant, insistent glitter. There were, alas!, few trees down the avenue to burst into bloom; and New York, like London, offers few facilities for eating out of doors. But there is an open-air cafeteria in the Central Park Zoo, and here Harry and I would often go for lunch, usually walking but sometimes taking the cross-town bus, which started at irregular intervals from the corner of 72nd Street. I had grown used to the New York buses and to their deadpan driver-conductors, obliged ambidexterously to drive with one hand and issue tickets with the other, their consequent taciturn ways casting a spell of awe-struck silence over the passengers. Once I heard this silence broken by a girl, talking in accents even stranger than those normally heard about the streets of New York. I moved up behind her, hoping to hear some outlandish Southern or Western dialect. I recognized the accent at once. It was broad Glasgow.

In the Park we would fill our trays at the cafeteria, then sit out in the sun, eating our luncheon and looking out at the sea-lions posing and disporting themselves about a fountain, like bronzes by Brancusi. Sometimes Ellsworth would join us, dejected by the sale of a picture to some unsympathetic client, and we would cheer him up by taking him to visit the leopards, slinky as hostesses, in their cages. My favourites, with two cages discreetly between them, were labelled, respectively, Mr. and Mrs. Ernest C. Jarvis. In a cage outside was a polar bear which had—so I was told— torn the arm off a débutante.

Children around us were eating ice-creams and buying balloons, which men were inflating from cylinders like jet-rockets. Often I would walk on down the Mall, never ceasing to be surprised by its very English Victorian statues of Shakespeare and Scott and Burns. I liked, too, to watch the chess-players, on their open-air pitch—the most silent and intent of all New Yorkers; and the far from silent children whisking in baroque cavalcades around the gay Carrousel. But above all I liked the grey squirrels, with fur tippets for tails, now scampering everywhere and preening themselves unabashed on the seats reserved for visitors. With the Spring, Central Park had acquired for me an identity.

Ellsworth had a studio at the top of an old dilapidated building downtown, between Wall Street and the River, and here we would sometimes go at weekends. I had seen Wall Street on a weekday when it bustled with the money-making crowds, visiting an acquaintance in a lush office, hung with modern paintings, lunching with him off cherrystone clams and rare roast beef in a lunch club, done up in *eau de nil* green, with Audubon prints of birds on the walls. Afterwards I had visited the Stock Exchange, with its continuous uproar of voices and its falling snowdrifts of paper and its farrago of figures for ever clacking up and down on mysterious boards, while men shouted and signalled from booth to booth with the agitated gestures of bookmakers. Standing by the portico of the street's Doric Treasury and looking up between the skyscrapers to the black church spire, I had been surprised by its shortness and its relatively intimate air.

Now at weekends it was silent, and seemed cosier still. But its towers bounded up into the sky above Ellsworth's roof like some abstraction of Babylon. We sat there beneath them, sun-bathing and looking idly through a packet of letters which he had found, by accident, thrown out from the office below—that of a mail-order firm which published books of an equivocal character. They were a series of ill-written scrawls from dissatisfied clients:

Herewith is your book *Marriage Mischief* with which I am not satisfied. Kindly forward your book *From Freud to Kinsey* in lieu of cash refund.

I'm returning your wonder book to you I have been wondering for two days what it is good for but can't find a thing couldn't read it so please send me my money back.

Have remitted $1.00 for a copy of your book *Bedroom Manners*. Please rush this to me at once. I need it bad.

I received your book, title *How to Get Along with Girls*. The fact is I had the book from you years ago. But because of a different title I didn't know it was the same. I don't want my money refunded. I would like you to send me the book *How to Get Along with Boys*. Yours truly, Henry.

Then we went out and bought foot-long 'Hot Hero' sandwiches and cans of beer, and had a picnic, squatting on a deserted wharf where an artist was painting the Brooklyn Bridge with, oddly enough, his back to it.

I grew to love this East River, lapping at the banks of the city from the Battery Park in the south, with its row of Victorian houses like those at some English seaside resort, to the equally Victorian frontiers of Harlem in the north. From the Battery I once made a curious expedition by the ferry-boat, a craft with an agreeably 'period' character, across to Staten Island. It was organized by a friend, Gretchen Green, who had once taken a herd of racing camels to Timbuctoo for Lord Wavell. We travelled in a hearse, which a friend of hers had resourcefully converted into a station wagon, and our objective was a Tibetan Lamasery on the island. This turned out to be a villa, furnished in the Buddhist style by a rich lady interested in such matters, with a library of oriental philosophy, its books bound symbolically in orange for Tibet, red for India, green for China, grey for Japan, purple for comparative religion, and black for the occult. An adjoining temple contained a large variety of Chinese idols.

On the river, I loved especially the Queensboro' Bridge, soaring high as a skyscraper from Fifty-ninth Street across the foot of York Avenue, then dipping gracefully over the water, three broad swags of steel between pointed spearheads, the spires of the skyscrapers thrusting above it, like spearheads too. Before them arose the cold glass precipice of the United Nations building, and around them, huddling shabbily at their feet, the low brick tenements, now fast disappearing, of an earlier New York. Before, I had been disturbed by these disorderly incongruities of size and style; now, I began to enjoy their dramatic effect, symbols as they were of the city's essential, unceasing fluidity.

I found it a romantic experience to venture across this Queensboro' Bridge in a tram, stopping half-way over it to descend in an elevator on to Welfare Island, and there to visit an old friend, Eugene MacCown, in the City Hospital, an old foundation still equipped with iron staircases and vaulted ceilings of a massive nineteenth-century pattern. I loved to stroll up from the bridge by the welling grey water, through a poor neighbourhood to a rich one and then to a poor one again; along the waterfront where 'dead-end kids' in tartan shirts roistered around with an affectation of toughness, and where one old couple, seedy as a pair of characters from Dickens, seemed to live on a bench, with all their frowsty worldly possessions, day and night throughout the year. Then I would walk up beyond to the elegant gardens of Gracie Square, where the Mayor of New York lived in a nice Georgian house, towards Harlem and to a footbridge which led me across to Ward's Island, again with a hospital upon it but with a park as well. Here, one summer afternoon, I stripped off my shirt and lay back on the grass, in unaccountable solitude, with the tideway dividing to either side of me, the ocean ships bearing down on me from a misty mid-town skyline, and the roar of the traffic beneath it reduced to a murmur as of distant bees.

∽ **5** ∽

Manners Makyth Madison Avenue · Fish are so Relaxing · Unbrave New World? · Problems of 'Communication' · A New Friendship · Irma the Body

MY new way of life, in the basement of this pyramid of the impecunious and unsuccessful, added point to my upward excursions into the pyramids of the successful and rich. When I left London a friend, versed in the ways of the city, had said to me: 'You'll need a fixer. I know the ideal man for you. He'll fix you anything from theatre seats to TV appearances or introductions to Café Society. He's the "inventor" of Public Relations.'

It was thus that I came to meet Benjamin Sonnenberg. My letter of introduction, sent through the post, took as usual two days to reach him. On the morning of the second day, there he was on the telephone—a Saturday morning, a mellifluous voice full of old-world courtesies. He had a book of mine in front of him, he said, a book about Turkey: it didn't tell him much about me. What was I doing here? Whom did I want to meet? What plays did I want to see? He could fix anything. He poured out a flow of invitations for the weekend; a theatrical supper-party for Gladys Cooper, lunch with some millionaires, a dinner for Alastair Cooke before his departure for Europe, with the preview of a film in his private theatre afterwards. Unluckily, having a full weekend, I had to refuse these attractive invitations, so we compromised on an interim appointment for tea on Monday. This seemed rather an anti-climax. Fearing that I might have disappointed Mr. Sonnenberg, I added as an afterthought—indeed rather in jest, so impossible did the request seem—'I suppose you couldn't manage a couple of seats for *My Fair Lady* tonight?'

'I'll have my secretary call you back,' Mr. Sonnenberg said.

She called me back, saying two house seats would be at my disposal at the box office that Saturday night—for the show which New Yorkers were waiting years and paying fortunes to see.

On Monday, at 4.30 punctually, I rang the brass bell of Mr. Sonnenberg's house in Gramercy Park. The house had a brass plate on the door and a pair of coach-lamps outside it; the square looked not unlike Portman Square. Inside there were lush Turkey carpets on the floor and a portrait of Millicent, Duchess of Sutherland, by Sargent, on the staircase. The room in which I awaited my host was at hothouse temperature, cretonned and panelled and glowing with a richness of polished brass. A visitors' book, lying on a table, revealed that it was the Streatham Castle Room. Beside it was a brass inkstand, presented to Viscount Castlereagh by the Seaham Harbour Conservative Association. Projecting from the walls were polished brass carriage-lamps, and in the corner of the room a library ladder with a brass pestle and mortar on the first step, a brass flat-iron and a brass cigar-box on the second, and a Guardsman's brass helmet on the third, all stepping up, not to a bookcase, but to a luxuriant rubber-plant in a handsome brass pot.

A butler came in, bringing tea in a silver teapot on a silver tray, and Mr. Sonnenberg presently followed him. He looked like a character from *The Forsyte Saga*, or from a drawing by Daumier, short and immaculate and spherical, with a well-kept walrus moustache, a short cutaway jacket buttoned high at the neck, neatly pressed drainpipe trousers and highly polished buttoned boots. Offering me a cigar with my tea, he expatiated, eloquently and shrewdly, on New York society, confirming several of the impressions which were already forming in my mind. In London, he said, everyone knew everyone; in New York no one knew anyone. One of the functions of such people as Mr. Sonnenberg was to bring people together—business men with scientists, financiers with permanent officials, advertising executives with senators, writers with theatrical producers, university professors with newspaper publishers. He was a power in Madison Avenue, the centre of the Public Relations world; and Public Relations, now increasingly and significantly called Human Relations, covered Private Relations too. As the psychiatrist helps Americans to get to know themselves, so does the Public Relations man help them to get to know other Americans. In a community without Old School ties, he enables them to get on to an Old Boy basis, and thus to rise on the road to success. Such was this expansive Benjamin from Central Europe.

Before I left him, he gave me a number of invitations and made me a number of promises. He showed me his wife's drawing-room, with the panelling from Cassiobury and the Grinling Gibbons carving from somewhere else, and his Victorian room, with the portrait of the dear Queen above the chimney-piece.

Entering a room done in a more contemporary style, he introduced me to his daughter. He referred philosophically to his son, who was going through a rebellious phase, wanting Ezra Pound to run for President, but would get over it. In the hall he bade me an old-world farewell, and the linkman showed me out.

Thereafter I got communications from Mr. Sonnenberg almost daily—invitations, cuttings which might interest me, letters of introduction (presenting me, I was gratified to see, as 'an extremely attractive personage'), telephone calls from his secretary asking me which play I would like to see next. Some weeks later I met him again on a gastronomic occasion, the twenty-fifth dinner, at the Waldorf-Astoria, of the Lucullus Circle, held in honour of the two-hundred-and-fiftieth anniversary of Benjamin Franklin, 'a great citizen of the United States and an Honorary Citizen of France.' We sat down to a banquet, Roman in character and proportions, with rare orchids and tropical fruits banked down the table, a set of priceless French tapestries decorating the walls, gold plate to eat off, and before each plate nine goblets of golden glass engraved with purple grapes. The menu, printed in French on the finest parchment, offered seven courses, including an *Intermède*, a *Dorure*, and an *Apothéose*, with caviar and *pâté de foie gras* in profusion; and ten wines, including two white Burgundies and six vintage clarets, to say nothing of a preparatory *Amuse Bouche*, with a choice of five wines more.

The guests came, for the most part, from high in the pyramids of big business, publishing, the theatre and sport. I sat between two millionaires, one the owner of a chain store who, with a wink, slipped me a gift under the table—a plastic pocket figurine of a girl, nude but for a hula-hula garland. The millionaire on my right touched none of the wines. 'They do not much interest me,' he explained, adding, with a touch of irrelevance, 'You see, my business is tea.' When we rose, the millionaires took sprays of orchids from the table, to take home as corsages for their wives, and we were each presented with a jeroboam of Burgundy tied up with blue ribbon. I gave it to Harry, who gave a party on it a few nights later—a party of a rather different kind.

Among those American Nights, I remember one more contemporary in its setting: a fashionable dinner-party, given for an exhibition at the Museum of Modern Art, in a house, consisting only of a single room, belonging to some Rockefellers. Its walls were of rough brick, whitewashed and decorated with substantial masterpieces of non-objective painting and sculpture. The room was divided into three parts by walls of plate glass, the second part being a pool of water across which it was necessary to trip insecurely by stepping-stones in order to reach the bedroom—converted for the evening into a sitting-room—and the usual offices beyond. From here, seen and magnified through the two glass walls and across the sheet of water, the guests in their modish dresses had the air of creatures sequestered in an aquarium, swimming and gesturing and mouthing to each other amid the strange shapes of the sculpture, like fish from the more exotic tropical depths. This spectacle, being silent, was strangely soothing, and I was reminded of the remark which a lady, a busy public relations executive, had made to me at luncheon a few days before: 'I can only relax,' she said, 'in the company of fish.' Hence, doubtless, the popularity of those aquariums introduced into fashionable New York apartments as a form of interior decoration—though the Hollywood tropical fishmongers, as I later observed, purvey specimens so unrelaxing as a black shark from Borneo and a man-eater from the Amazon.

More rarefied still, but in the baroque manner, was a party given by the rich cosmetician, Madame Helena Rubinstein, in her 'triplex penthouse' on Park Avenue. Here the hostess was wearing a necklace of outsize raw pearls, and the guests consorted with an assembly of African idols, while tapestries by Picasso glared down at them, cross-eyed, from the walls. Wandering in a daze through marble halls adorned with busts and planted with tropical foliage of the variety known as 'plastic,' we found ourselves in an Indonesian bar, with a counter of black glass beneath purple and amber mirrors; then in a dining-room painted by Salvador Dali, with the hostess's profile, built into a cliff, covering one wall; then in her bedroom, its great glass double-bed floodlit from the floor, with a biography of Madame Lupescu on the bedside table, glass chairs surrounding it, and a galaxy of pink opaline ornaments ranged along the walls between pink-lit, pink silk curtains.

Upstairs, holding its own with the surrounding rooftops, we found a long picture gallery, about to be converted by Mr. Cecil Beaton from a medieval banqueting hall into an Edwardian conservatory, and containing among its works of art a portrait by Tchelitchev of Madame Rubinstein's daughter, her face composed entirely of tissues of the brain, as in a medical diagram. It was, I think, at this party, or perhaps at another the same evening, that

I met an American-born peeress who deplored the lack of education throughout the United States.

'Nowadays,' she lamented, 'people are becoming so ignorant that they don't even wear collars and ties.'

More austere were the soirées, high up on Fifth Avenue, given by Mrs. Murray Crane, the last of New York's intellectual hostesses, a tall, gracious lady in rimless spectacles and a pale blue satin gown which swept right to her ankles. We were invited for 8.30. At nine o'clock precisely, after an interval for drinks, the hostess announced not dinner but Mr. Aldous Huxley. For the invitation had read—'Discussion—Supper,' in that order. For an hour Mr. Huxley, with eloquence and charm, lectured us on the 'Brave New World,' and how very much worse it was turning out than even he, in his darkest forebodings, had ever imagined. 'Soma,' his tranquillizing drug, had indeed been granted to us, and was now on sale at every drugstore in the form of Milltown and Equanil. But his imagination had never conceived of such amenities as automation, and the atom bomb, and the fact that more and more people were being born and moreover staying alive. The outlook for the future, we inferred, did not seem to him all that brave.

When the lecturer had finished, the hostess rose to her feet and, in a melodious, challenging voice, said: 'Well, I am sure we are all very grateful to Mr. Huxley for his interesting talk, and that we all disagree profoundly with almost every word he has said.'

She then called upon a number of distinguished Americans to voice this disagreement, and for the next hour they did so, at length and only a trifle less eloquently, most of them expressing the opinion that the world was, on the contrary, becoming a better and better place all the time. At eleven o'clock punctually we went into the best of all possible suppers.

At another of these parties, at which the lecturer was a Harvard professor and his subject 'The Anatomy of Revolution,' I was shocked to hear, suddenly, a trumpeting snore, and still more shocked, on starting up at the sound, to realize that it was I who had snored it. The hostess, with delicate tact, pretended not to have noticed this. Later she called upon two English guests to express their views on this subject. But neither of them—such, to my relief, was her consideration—was myself.

Parties in New York tended to run in cycles, conditioned perhaps by the arrival and departure of some V.I.P. I remember a whole week of them, at which I had the pleasure of meeting, and going on meeting, Miss Rebecca West. I remember especially one, the forerunner of others which I was to attend with pleasure, given by Leo Lerman in his house uptown on Lexington Avenue, lovingly crammed with Victoriana and Edwardiana, for an imaginative selection of guests to whom, in a welcome un-American style, he gave only red wine to drink.

Then I reverted contentedly to the V.U.P. ways of the cold-water world, where evenings were unplanned and spontaneous. Someone would call up and say, 'What are you doing tonight? Come over to my place and eat;' or we would go down to Green-wich Village, that free-and-easy quarter between the two belts of skyscrapers, compounded of Soho and the Chelsea of the 'twenties, with just a dash of Montparnasse; or we would go over to the West Side, where Gerrit lived, a world outwardly more bourgeois than the East Side, but with a mixture of races which gave it an underlying rawness and vitality, as of some foreign town.

Evenings here, after a round of the bars, would end in his chronically disordered apartment, with books and magazines and gramophone records and pieces of clothing and strange curios discovered in junkshops, all strewn untidily around. He was for ever on the point of moving to another apartment, but it was still furnished only with a hookah and a pack of tarot cards. Mean-while cans of beer would come out, and the conversation would flow, young and uninhibited and irreverent. I remember an evening when spirited reminiscences followed the question, 'Which did you dislike most, your father or your mother?' But after one o'clock in the morning the talk would drift off into metaphysical speculation about the Nature of Truth and the Meaning of Life. This was the moment I would choose to slink home to bed.

New York, like Paris, is an all-night city—it is possible even to shop in it all night—and Harry and his friends would not often be in bed before three or up before eleven. But I was doomed by habit to awake early in the morning—often the radio in the opposite flat, as luck had it a radio repair shop, would wake me —and I would thus wilt early in the night. It was, I found, a myth that the New York air is so stimulating as to make fatigue un-known and sleep superfluous.

Howard, who lived also on the West Side, ordered his life in a more deliberate way than Gerrit. His apartment was roomy and orderly, containing a library of books, methodically arranged, a small collection of modern American paintings, mostly by his friends, and, adding a touch of fantasy, a pair of Japanese lanterns to light the sitting-room. Here he would move around among his guests, distributing Bourbon and beer and diffusing affection, creating a relaxed atmosphere and prompting talk which was serious without ever becoming too solemn.

Underlying it, on these and other occasions, was an introspective trend, reflecting a personal problem which is perhaps characteristically American—that of 'communication', not between one place and another but between one person and another. One evening, at Harry's, I remember creating some surprise by the suggestion that it was possible really to get to know and to understand another person, and that I had, during my own youth and since, sometimes achieved this. Imprisoned, as many of these young men were, in varying degrees of isolation within themselves, they laughed with cynical incredulity. They were human beings who wanted human understanding, but had not yet learnt how to achieve it.

There were others who had not yet learnt to want it. Harry once wrote to me, when I had returned to England: 'I went to a party last night chez some friends of Ellsworth and came away feeling dissatisfied with the lack of concern everyone showed for human beings. The party was a rather impromptu affair assembled to watch a display of fireworks over the Hudson. The rockets exploded into huge, fiery globes looking like the rose window at Chartres, and created an electric night that was sadly let down by the people, who drifted off into their own personal darkness. My lovely image of England is of an island where people talk, communicate with a high degree of articulateness, and *do* care for each other.'

When Ruth gave a party, it had just this personal flavour. Working all day long in her murky little kitchen, she would create goulashes and pastries which smelt and tasted of Central Europe, and provide pitchers of red Californian wine to wash them down. The guests were few, but they were her friends, chosen each, from a diversity of worlds, for his own individual quality—for who, not what, he was. Her affection acting as a solvent, and her ideas as an astringent, soon made them friends of one another, creating a European atmosphere free from all such 'communication' problems.

One figure stood out as a dominant influence among this group of friends. He was John Latouche, a Broadway writer well known as a librettist for musical shows, a man in his late thirties, of combined Irish and Huguenot origin, who had risen from an obscure family background in Richmond, Virginia. His life was busy and varied, and it was some time before I met him. I had heard much of him, however, both good things and bad but never anything commonplace, from Ruth and Gerrit and especially from Harry, who was one of his closest friends. John, I knew, had influenced him strongly, meeting him when he was still at college in a formative stage, and in Socratic fashion—he was ten years older—teaching him to live and to seek human values, to discover and to develop himself. This influence, I knew also, had its destructive side, since John was dominating in his friendships and, moreover, lived at a turbulent pitch such as few human beings can sustain for long. He would work and talk all day, and drink and talk all night, carrying along with him, irresistibly, his small court of adherents, of whom Harry was always one. Drawn into so immoderate a life, always at John's beck and call, Harry had neglected his career as a painter, and eventually his health had broken down. Recovering, then making a trip to Europe, he was now less closely involved with John than before.

Eventually, I met John at an exhibition of paintings by a mutual friend. He was stocky and short and was becoming rotund. But his impact, like that of many short men, was compelling and positive. Once or twice in America, on looking around a room or a bar or an office, I have had the sharp, sudden sensation of setting eyes, among a cast of anonymous lay figures, on a Person. John stood out in this way. Black eyes ablaze with awareness, voice resonant and quick with curiosity, personality vital, he combined the energy of a dynamo with an eager human sympathy. My response to him was immediate. We went out and had some drinks on Lexington Avenue, and a few nights later he and Harry and I spent an evening together, which I remember in terms of expansive warmth and resounding laughter.

After an ample meal downtown at Luchow's, a sumptuous German restaurant of the eighteen-eighties, we went to the Bon Soir, in the Village, a night-club run by a negro, with an edge to its entertainment in the form of a sharply satirical cabaret. It was only in such cabaret turns, written often by Jews, that irony seemed to flourish here in New York, scurrilously flaying the absurder aspects of modern American life. So astringent a spirit seemed sadly absent from the revue stage and the movie screen, and above all from the Press, with its cautious conformist ways.

Hence our laughter, whetted when one of the singers, who knew and recognized John, improvised a verse at his expense. Hence, hour after hour, round upon round of whiskies, while John's talk grew more vehement and his manner more challenging and his eyes more consuming. Mercilessly he nagged at me, bent on bullying me into agreement with some premise, alcoholically-inspired, on the Meaning of Life—on the relative significance, I think it was, of Being and Doing, for it was a theory of Harry's that John was a Do-er, while he himself was a Be-er. 'You know it,' he hammered away at his point, 'you know it. You know it.' But the mists of incoherence became such that I took in barely a word of what he was saying. We were the last to leave the restaurant. The long avenues, as we drove up them homeward, were empty of traffic, but for the garbage carts now beginning to emerge; for dawn was breaking. Thus started a new and stimulating friendship.

*   *   *

Negro night-life, at this sophisticated level, has now shifted from Harlem to the Village. New Yorkers tell the visitor that Harlem itself is not worth visiting, now that the Negroes have grown so prosperous; moreover, they warn him inconsequently that he is liable to be knifed there. But Harlem can still stimulate. At the time of the Presidential election, later in the year, I went up there with Ruth to a bar called the Baby Grand. Prosperity was evident enough, with the coloured ladies all slinky from the pages of *Vogue*, and the coloured gentlemen all swagger in tweed caps and hacking-jackets, perching on bar stools like English race-goers on shooting-sticks. But the coloured singer, in his morning coat, sang in a political vein so highly irreverent that it would have been banned anywhere else in New York as *lèse majesté*.

He sang of 'Our Father which art in Washington' and of his great love for Peace—the Peace in his blood, the Peace in his bones, the Peace in his soul, the Peace in his brain. But, in a sacrilegious spirit, he expressed doubts as to where and how this Peace might be found, thumbing through the Manhattan telephone directory and tearing the pages to pieces as he sang, in a vain and frenzied search for it. Peace and Prosperity were then an article of American faith, both Republican and Democrat, which few dared question.

On another evening, with Harry and Howard, I went up there to the Savoy Ballroom—a place famous in the 'twenties for its wild Bohemian ways[1]. We found that a charity gala was in progress, an object-lesson in decorum, at which the guests, all of them coloured, sat in parties at numbered tables by the ballroom floor, with bottles of Scotch and champagne on their tables, talking and smiling at one another politely, and getting up gracefully to dance, with faultless rhythm, to the hottest of New York's bands. The dresses and jewels of the ladies, to say nothing of their figures, were as chic as any normally to be seen at El Morocco, the smart haunt of Café Society.

Towards one o'clock in the morning there were speeches, followed by a solemn coronation of a chosen 'King and Queen' of Morningside, the district of Harlem in which this charitable enterprise, a housing project for the workers, was situated. The Queen wore a tiara and a simple white frock, the King a green satin robe, fringed with gold. They were crowned by a parson, in a clerical collar, then charmingly, primly, swung around in an old-fashioned waltz. Soon the band changed its tune to the Charleston, and all took the floor with them, dancing gravely at first, then relaxing involuntarily, bodies kindling to the hot music with an atavistic but decorous excitement.

The lowest form of entertainment, the Burlesque or strip-tease show, is now banned from New York. But it may still be seen near by at Newark, over on the mainland of New Jersey, and here one evening we went. Across its river New York came to an end with startling abruptness, in a waste-land of bogs and litter dumps and rank, neglected vacant lots. Strange fires burned in this wilderness, as we drove across it in John's car. The tentacles of neon-lit roads and shining railroads reached out across it over a network of bridges, all curving and intersecting and careering one above the other like switchbacks until, after about half an hour, the lights of Newark, the first centre of civilization, appeared, puncturing the sky in a myriad points as on the board of some giant game of chance. Lights more garish than the rest showed off a street or so of theatres, where the All Girly Revue enjoyed a monopoly of entertainment.

In one of these we sat, transfixed by the antics of Irma the Body, a lady, it seemed, deeply engrossed in herself, admiring and stroking and manipulating each of her limbs as she unveiled them, with gestures at once provocative and comic, and with a general air of amused delight in her own body. The audience was, unexpectedly, a mixed one—indeed, largely a family audience,

[1] It has since been destroyed.

composed of husbands and wives, seated comfortably and intently together as though picking up a few tips for the relief of suburban marital monotony. The strip-tease, it seemed, was no longer a mere furtive entertainment for the licentious male. It had perhaps its own part to play in this age of 'Togetherness', of which I was always reading in the advertisements ('When Pop pitches Junior a slow one, that's fun—and togetherness. . . . When the whole family pitches in to give the house a good spring-cleaning, that's fun—because it's togetherness.'). Indeed later in Texas I came upon a notice of it: 'Bring the family (adultwise). The Burlesk cabaret is a place where you can take the ladies or get up a party for the Convention or sales meeting and go out and have yourself a real ball.'

We went to more serious entertainments too—*Waiting for Godot*, for example, of which Harry became an addict. One of the successes of Broadway was *The Middle of the Night* by Paddy Chayevsky, a domestic drama disturbing to one of my age, since it concerned an 'old man' [*sic*] of fifty-three, played by Mr. Edward G. Robinson, and the vital things he could no longer do. He got so distressed, worrying about this, that one evening he actually *walked* the forty-two blocks from his office to the garage where he kept his car, instead of taking a taxi to it, and as a result of this aberration, returned home fearing that he might be going out of his mind.

Another success was Tennessee Williams's *Cat on a Hot Tin Roof*, featuring similar frustrations in the heart of a family whose members behaved towards one another with a venom which I found hard to credit. When I expressed this incredulity to Harry, he said:

'How ingenuous you are! That's just how all American families act.'

NEW ENGLAND

6

Stately Homes of New England · Books on the Grass · America
at its Best

SUBURBS spread far and wide around New York. It is here that
most New Yorkers live, commuting into the city, countless
millions of them, from homes often as far away from it as Oxford
is from London. They are suburbs, for the most part superior
in their aspect to those of Britain, suburbs such as would not, on
the whole, displease the Georgian Group. For America, going
back in her architectural style no farther than the period of the
Mayflower, has been generally spared the half-timbered whimsi-
ness of 'Tudoresque' and 'Jacobethan.' These suburban villas
tend to preserve the traditional colonial style, their Georgian
windows and fanlights and weather-boarded fronts suggesting,
in their setting of lawns and trees, how a Regency garden suburbia
might have looked, had this way of life developed in England a
century earlier. When a lady on the *Queen Mary* had said to me,
'We have beautiful suburbs,' I had suppressed a cynical smile.
But I now began to see that her remark had meaning behind it.

What these suburbs lack, however, is privacy. The lawns,
wandering away among the houses without the interruption of
hedges or palings or garden walls, give an agreeable sense of
space to the general design. But they reveal a manner of community living antipathetic to the Briton, whose home is his castle.
For in America no man, lest he be dubbed anti-social, will shut
off his house and garden from that of his neighbour. Nor, in a
similarly sociable spirit, will he draw his curtains or lock his front
door. Here in the suburbs is the epitome of American group-life,
moreover so strictly graded as between one income group and
another that few Americans live in a single house—or even a
single district—for more than a few years at a time. A move upwards professionally means, inevitably, a move upwards geo-
graphically and domestically. Here, I began to see, was one reason
for the lack, in New York, of an urban society on the European
model. It was a city decentralized. The Americans, never countrymen, are now ceasing also to be oppidans. America, as I travelled
across it, became increasingly a United States of Suburbia.

I now began to make trips around New York. From Grand

Central Station, sumptuous in style as some neo-baroque cathedral, warm as a Roman bath-house, where music played and there was never a sound, far less a smut, from a train to defile the precincts, I now travelled north-eastwards along the coast into New England. The suburbs gave place to provincial towns, to harbours like those on the estuaries of England, and to their own suburbs in turn, so that, between New York and Boston there was hardly a stretch of open country—only tangled woodlands running down to the grey Atlantic, with houses scattered among them. So the train drew into Boston. My taxi-cab, passing the Catholic Chapel of Our Lady of the Railways, was in a few minutes bearing me along Arlington Street, into the heart of an elegant brick-built Georgian city, like the capital of an East Anglian county.

Steeples of city churches, built in the manner of Wren or the Greek Revival, rose around me. Brick terraces, with porticoes and fanlights and balconies as graceful as those of the Adam brothers, contemplated a park, called a Common, laid out with picturesque lakes and well-grown trees in the Romantic manner. Its garbage cans, I observed, were discreetly disguised as tree-trunks. Behind, streets with brick pavements led away into spacious squares, like those of eighteenth-century London. In the churches were box pews, and pillared galleries, and pre-Raphaelite windows, and in one of them the choir was singing an anthem to the tune of 'God Save the Queen,' but with American sentiments.

In the larger houses the old Boston families had lived. But, with a few exceptions, they did so no longer; they had moved out to the suburbs, making way for offices and clubs and apartment blocks. In the smaller ones, resembling those of Westminster or Hampstead, they lived still, and here, in a friendly and informal way, I was entertained to cocktails, proceeding afterwards to dinner at a large hotel, with Roman décor, where the tables circulated gravely on a platform designed to resemble a merry-go-round. Eating on this roundabout I remember a solemn conversation with a college girl, who assured me that the young generation in America were evolving on different lines from the old. They were concerned especially with people, she said, with 'the study of mankind,' whereas their elders had been preoccupied too much with things.

In one of these houses I met a gentleman who claimed to have fathered the English National Trust. Here indeed, in New England, is a respect for the past putting older England to shame. When the city authorities tried to replace the brick pavement of one of these streets with concrete, the ladies inhabiting it banded together and did a sitdown strike before the doors of their houses, preventing the workmen from carrying out the task, and finally achieving a change in the state law to preserve such amenities in perpetuity. The Stately Homes of New England draw reverent crowds of visitors, admiring the Chippendale and the Sheraton furniture which the eighteenth-century American craftsmen faithfully reproduced. In the less stately homes more modest treasures—old prints and pewter and pieces of Lowestoft —are displayed with pride, while throughout the Eastern States of America, in suburban and weekend houses, 'the New Early American Look' (as defined by one of the magazines) prevails, in converted barns and in kitchens with wheel-backs and porringers, gridirons and girdles, revolving spits and copper pots. Here 'the old-fashioned spice shelf is as popular as the power blender, and we expect the new refrigerator to harmonize with a 200-year-old highboy.'

Through the city of Boston itself I did a tour by bus, on which a guide, with the solemn incantation of a Baptist pastor, showed off with pride and no prejudice the site of the Massacre and the Tea Party, the Riding Academy for the King's Men, the Lion and Unicorn still emblazoned above the Queen Anne State House, and in the house of the revolutionary Paul Revere leaded window-panes from England, a toddy-warmer, a bed-warmer, an English piggin for measuring grain, a wallpaper copied from a London church and, in a Bible and Prayer Book, the signature of George II himself. Finally, before an obelisk (fifteen minutes' walk to the top and no elevator), the guide called for a minute's silence as a tribute to 'the men who gave their lives in back of this bus at the Battle of Bunker Hill.' (The command on that occasion was not, he told us, 'Don't fire till you see the whites of their eyes,' but 'Fire low and pick out the whites of their eyes.')

But the guide-book could not resist its dig:

'According to tradition, Boston is the hub of the universe, its cultural and intellectual centre, populated by superior individuals, all derived from one country, one single stock, and at least one Mayflower ancestor. According to statistics the country's fifth largest city is one-third foreign born, and three-fourths un-English descent . . . the city today is largely run by its pre-dominantly Irish population.'

Certainly, as I wandered through the streets and down towards the harbour, smelling the Scotch sea-fog which seeped in from the Atlantic, I sensed a strong foreign atmosphere, predominantly Italian, with grocery stores selling all kinds of *Pasta*, and stalls bright with fresh vegetables, and a group of old men, sunning themselves on a bench outside a church, smoking pipes and gossiping away about their neighbours in the Italian language. But I enjoyed especially the Common where, in the Puritan tradition, Bostonians would congregate in small groups, as they do at Marble Arch in larger ones, to dispute on Biblical matters with religious eccentrics and pastors, black and white.

An atmosphere distinct from that of Boston envelops its 'suburb,' the city of Cambridge, which Harvard occupies. It is a red-brick university built in the style of Queen Anne, laid out in quadrangles with immaculate lawns and immemorial trees, but so spick and so span as to retain an irredeemable 'new look.' Nevertheless, for all the newness, even the lushness, of its air-conditioned lecture-halls and its streamlined laboratories, the university, from the reverent 'shrine' to Keats in the Harvard Library, where the first editions were handled like sacred books, to the Fogg Museum, where students were sedulously copying the noughts and crosses of abstract paintings, had a comforting aroma of civilization. Here was a place clearly capable of being all things to all.

Its students lounged on the grass with every appearance of ease, but always with books—not only portable radios—beside them. They strolled casually through the streets, but with books —not only magazines—under their arms. 'You see, we are here to study,' they seemed defiantly to be implying—as the Oxford undergraduate, bookless in public, would defiantly imply the opposite; and in the air-conditioned libraries, sprawled though they were face down on sofas or legs up over the arms of deep armchairs, they were indubitably doing so, for the books lay open before them. Here was at least an appearance of earnestness, foreign to the lackadaisical ways of Oxford or Cambridge; an appearance too, equally foreign, of conformity, for all looked alike, their heads closely shorn into crew-cuts, their lower limbs tightly sheathed in workmanlike khaki drill pants.

Were they in fact all alike? Most of them probably aspired to be, knowing just what they were here for, what jobs they hoped to get from what courses of study; seeking no unforeseen truths, no revelations of a life beyond the job. Such at least was the assessment of a friend, a young and perhaps disenchanted Ameri-

can lecturer in English literature, with whom I sat over a cafeteria
luncheon in his House dining-hall, smelling the familiar canteen
smells and looking around at his students, thus shaven and clad,
as they drank their milk and ate their Hamburgers and talked,
perhaps, of their studies. There were altogether too many of them,
he said, fifteen thousand already, and the university authorities, in
a spirit of mass-production, aimed to increase this number,
whereas in fact they should halve it.

The House, where we lunched, and where the students lived
several to a room, was built, in this neo-Queen Anne style, around
a quadrangle, and resembled a college but, having none of its
traditions, had little of its community life. Nothing corresponded
to a high table or a common room, and there was, my friend told
me, relatively little social contact between professors and students.
When his own students visited him, it was usually to give vent to
a general sense of insecurity, regarding their jobs in the future,
or to pour out their troubles to him regarding their girls. He had,
he avowed, little patience with such confessions. In their courses
of study, few chose the humanities, though some aspired to
graduate, without too many tears, in Classical Civilization, known
familiarly as 'Classy Civ.'

Another day I lunched at the Faculty Club with Arthur
Schlesinger, the lively and distinguished professor of political
history, and his wife. He brought with him a bulging brief-case,
and led me swiftly down into a room in the basement, where he
opened it to extract a bottle of Bourbon and three glasses. From
these, after he had secured some ice from upstairs, we drank out
of sight of his colleagues, for whom no liquor was obtainable on
the premises. Arthur was a provocative companion. A close
associate of Adlai Stevenson, and a liberal of outspoken opinions,
he talked of 'the miseries of this age of abundance,' of the need
for his countrymen to awake from their mood of smug, quantita-
tive prosperity, and become individuals, with a sense of qualitative
values once more.

Everyone played safe; no one attacked anyone; no one mocked
at anything. There was no longer any spirit of invective, as in the
great days of Mencken. There were no longer any rebels. In two
or three years, perhaps, America would begin to stir from its
materialist dream. But not yet. I spoke to him of my friends, who
would have agreed with his views, and he said: 'I'd like to see a
lot more of these young men driving taxi-cabs.'

From Harvard I went to Yale, which has fewer students and

relatively more teachers, and is built, by contrast, in a medieval style. Here I spent an evening of civilized relaxation, staying with a professor and his wife, Beecher and C.-C. Hogan. Their white, weather-boarded house, which they had built themselves, combined English taste and American comfort with a warm personal atmosphere. Their garden, created with art and husbanded with love, provided pleasure for the senses and, moreover, a welcome privacy, for they had so planted it as to shut themselves off from their neighbours without, of course, appearing to do so. Food and wine and guests were discriminately chosen. Talk was stimulating, effortless and varied; and after dinner there were two-piano duets, played with an informal gusto.

These were people of humanity and an eclectic culture, bringing American warmth to play on European wit, American vitality on European wisdom, and American flexibility on the English tradition, to create an environment cosmopolitan in a true Greek sense. Here, in this university city, was surely America at its best.

7

The Georgian Look · The Pennsylvania Dutch · Edwardian Life on the Hudson

IN Boston, the saying goes, people ask, 'What do you know?' —not 'What do you do?' as in Chicago, or 'What have you got?', as in New York. In Philadelphia they ask, 'Who was your father?' Here I stayed in the heart of the city, on Rittenhouse Square, with Henry McIlhenny, a hospitable, cosmopolitan American friend with a discriminating collection of Impressionist paintings.

I found a community of rich families, all proud of their ancestry, who still live, not in apartments, but in Georgian houses, and give dinner-parties in an open-handed, pre-war style now becoming rare in New York. At one of these parties a charming lady, pointing a finger around the table, tactfully 'briefed' me on the names of the guests and on the origins of their families.

Here on the left was a mere nineteenth-century couple, here on the right a nineteenth-century lady talking to an eighteenth-century gentleman. Stacked around the table was Old Money, New Money (Radio Money, to be exact, but a face, was it not, with the refinement of a Princess?), and here even a touch of

Glamour Money (Mdivani). She herself, she modestly confessed, was eighteenth-century only. But her husband was seventeenth and, according to an old diary lately unearthed, their respective families were on calling terms for two whole centuries before she married him in the twentieth. But the *Pièce de résistance* was a decorous and elderly couple, conversing together just as two of their distinguished ancestors had conversed after each had appended his signature to the Declaration of Independence.

'It is nice to think,' she said, 'that they have been talking to each other, at dinners just like this, for the past two hundred years—just like the families in your English country houses.'

Naturally, another lady remarked to me later, I was aware of the fact that Abraham Lincoln was not his father's son. 'His real father,' she said, 'was from here in the East. Otherwise how could he have spoken such beautiful English?'

In Independence Hall I inspected, with appropriate awe, a quill pen with which the Declaration was signed and an ink-pot into which it was dipped, together with innumerable other relics and records of this momentous occasion. The building provides a graceful example of that American architectural style which might be defined as 'delayed William and Mary'; and the same applies to the other halls and red-brick churches, with white plastered steeples, which embellish Philadelphia. For the colonists, Conservative in spirit and moreover remote from the home country in its latest developments of taste, were as a rule some two generations behind, in the design of their buildings and of their furniture too. This time lag, disguising Regency as Georgian and Georgian as Queen Anne—even, at a later period, Late Victorian as Early Victorian—gives to the Eastern seaboard of America a look much older than its actual period; a look, generally speaking, of eighteenth-century England, all too rare in the England of today. This applies in particular to Mount Pleasant, one of the old houses, scrupulously preserved, in the romantic Park which graces the banks of the winding Schuylkill River. With its tall chimneys and its high-pitched roof and its monumental pediments, it might have been built by Inigo Jones. But its date is 1761.

Not far from Philadelphia is one of the Stately Homes of America—Winterthur, the seat of the du Pont family, which is now a museum. Called after an ancestral village in Switzerland, built in 1817 and enlarged at different periods, it is now intended 'to help show modern Americans how earlier Americans lived,' and contains probably the largest collection of American furniture in existence. Here, designed and made by colonial craftsmen, are signed pieces of Philadelphia Chippendale and New York Sheraton, often holding their own with their English prototypes. I drove to Winterthur one day, encountering car-loads and motor-coach-loads of ladies from all parts of the Eastern seaboard, flower-hatted and tight-skirted and bespectacled by the thousand, their chests ticketed to show who, what and whence they were— Home Makers of Baltimore, Garden Lovers of Birmingham, Parents Educational of Norfolk—with sometimes a male or two following in their wake. It took all day long—with a pause in the cafeteria for a box-lunch and a carton of milk and a chatter about homes and gardens—for the ticketed hostesses, graduates in furniture, to conduct them around the mansion.

I myself, with a single guide, was able to do the tour in a morning, but even so became satiated by the unending procession of strictly period rooms—from the Upper Salem Stair Hall to the Eagle Room, the Morattico Hall and the Flock Room, from the Montmorenci Stair Hall to the Marlboro Room, the Chinese Parlour and the Baltimore Room, all so faultlessly furnished with these 'Highlights of American Craftsmanship' as to appear more English than anything English. A friend, who had stayed in the house before it became a museum, told me that, to preserve its immaculate period quality, all the possessions of the guests, left lying around, were scrupulously tidied away in drawers, leaving the bedrooms free from tell-tale traces of modern occupation. The gardens likewise, dazzling as they were in their infinite variety of rhododendrons and azaleas and other flowering shrubs, planted in soil specially imported for the purpose, bloomed a little too gloriously to seem true.

More characteristically native was a New England bedroom, suggesting that a talent for gadgets, so conspicuous in the Do-It-Yourself civilization of today, was an Early American trait. Here, dating from pre-Victorian times, were such 'tuck-away,' fold-up, space-saving furniture and double-duty devices as the deception bed folding into a bureau, the desk serving also as a perspective glass, the Windsor chair serving also as a desk, the folding wash-stand fitting into a two-foot space, the combined wrought-iron shoe-horn and boot-puller, and—a foretaste of the mechanical devices of the Bar Mart—the combination corkscrew, bottle-opener and brush.

*   *   *

Another day, Henry drove me out into the countryside of Pennsylvania. The dogwood was all abloom, the stars of its white flowers scattered profusely over branches, still wintry and bare, for the spring was late. The pastures, rolling away beside the straight broad highway, were freshly green, moreover scrupulously tended, for this was the country of the Pennsylvania Dutch, for whom the tilling of the soil is still closely linked with Biblical teaching. They are 'Peculiar People,' belonging to the Lutheran sects of the Mennonites and the Amish who originated in the Netherlands and spread eastwards through Germany and Russia. Here they were at first welcomed for their skill in farming undeveloped lands. But they were subsequently oppressed and driven to emigrate, in groups, to the New World, many of them finding tolerance and peace and the opportunity to work here in the Pennsylvania of the Quakers.

Thus around us, contrasting with the streamlined highway, was in effect a landscape of eighteenth-century Europe. For these Pennsylvania Dutch have kept their exclusive identity and have barely changed their way of life since first they settled here in Lancaster County. Their farmsteads consisted of clean, white timbered buildings, well-grouped, shaded by ample trees and commanded by spacious high-pitched barns. Their villages were trim, with a Sunday-go-to-meeting appearance. The older men still wore the beards and the black clothes and the black wide-awake hats of the early Puritans, while many of the women wore white-lace caps at the backs of their heads. They drove along the roads in hooded buggies, and ploughed their fields with teams of horses. A God-fearing people, aspiring to live in literal obedience to the text of the Bible, they farm their lands on a small-scale co-operative basis, with the family as the unit, providing its own system of social security and reluctant to conform to the demands of the State in such matters as children's education. Many of them are still trilingual, speaking English, High German, and a Pennsylvanian Dutch dialect, resembling the German of the Palatinate.

It was market day when we drove into Lancaster, a place with the atmosphere and, indeed, the architecture of an English country town. In the big covered market fresh-faced, mob-capped peasant women sold local home-made delicacies—shoofly pie, schmeercase cheese, apple butter, and pretzels, fresh from the oven. Samples of these lent an agreeably Germanic flavour to a picnic luncheon, eaten with a friend of my host in the garden of

his antique shop hung with pictures by Demuth, one of the outstanding American painters of the early twentieth century.

*   *   *

But I was lingering for longer than I had meant in and around
New York. Now it was time to go south, where the weather
would soon become uncomfortably hot. Before I left, Harry and
I spent a weekend up at Rhinebeck, overlooking the Hudson,
with Alice Bouverie, that friend whom he and I, at our first
meeting, had found in common, and of whom both of us were
fond for her unusual qualities and her unpredictable ways and
that refined, sallow beauty which was, in its way, so strangely
oriental in cast. We had seen her once or twice, when she could
find a free moment, lunching with her at the Gladstone, where
Tennessee Williams once joined us, or in her comfortable and
casually elegant house, linked to the house next door, for the
two young daughters to whom she was a loving and assiduous
mother.

Alice had been a close friend of John's and, for a long time, the
two of them with Harry had formed an intimate trio, spending
much of their time and engaging in various enterprises, artistic
and otherwise, together. But the cycles of their respective lives
had since changed, and Alice saw them seldom. She was pleased
to see Harry again, and talked to me with a certain concern for his
future.

Her life at this time was a harassed one, overburdened with conflicting obligations to family and friends and acquaintances, and
her slanting dark eyes had always a perplexed, distracted look.
Born to money, and impulsively generous in its use, she had
been reared in a worldly American society, and had sought ever
since, in her elusive way, to be free of it, marrying and living
in Europe and especially in England, where she had created her
own hospitable world, gracefully Bohemian, surrounded by
beautiful possessions, and loved by friends with a variety of
talents and interests. The war had brought her back to New York
where for a while John, at once rousing and tormenting her, had
swept her away into his own restless rhythm of life.

At Rhinebeck she had created a country house subtly English in
its atmosphere. It stood in a well-tailored version of an English
park, belonging to her millionaire brother, Vincent Astor. Here
he and his wife lived in a house whose façade resembled the Grand
Trianon at Versailles, but whose interior consisted of two squash

rackets courts, ingeniously converted into elegant reception rooms. There was also an indoor swimming-pool. All along the river, in other such parks, stood stately homes, lavishly built in a variety of Georgian, Victorian and Edwardian styles, where families with honoured American names—the Roosevelts, for example, the Delanos, the Ogden Millses—still lived, or had lived until recent years. There survived here a life of Edwardian luxury and social exclusiveness, with tea served on lawns, from silver teapots, and butlers handing sandwiches; with dowagers refusing to receive neighbours who had been divorced, who drank, or who were Democrats.

But the charm of the Hudson lay rather in its earlier, stuccoed houses, built above the river in the Greek revival manner, and each competing with the other in the grandeur of its portico, like a series of Palladian villas along the banks of the Brenta. In one of them, boasting the noblest portico of all, we spent a relaxed hour or so drinking and talking and playing Chinese checkers with Gore Vidal, an intimate friend of Alice, who had come to live and write his books here, at her instigation. In style, these houses were more sophisticated, more European, than the old colonial homes like Washington's Mount Vernon, which I was later to see on the banks of the Potomac. In the villages behind them, were the stern white steeples of the Dutch Reformed Churches contrasted with the more fanciful traceries of 'carpenter Gothic' village homes, the countryside had once been rich in fruit farms. But large-scale economic competition had usurped their markets, and now their orchards were derelict—a scene of wastage all too familiar in America, where land is plentiful and the farmer ready enough to move on to pastures new.

Alice knew and loved all this neighbourhood and, while Harry played tennis with the MacEwen brothers (one of whom was later to marry her daughter Romana), drove me around it on Sunday, seeking out the lesser-known villas and other specimens of architecture to show me. It was for her, in a sense, a substitute for the Europe to which, in spirit, she belonged. She confessed to me that she looked forward to the day when she would settle in the country in England, among all her English friends. But for the present she was tied to America, largely by the illness of her mother, whom she attended with daily devotion.

We talked of John, whom she now saw seldom, and also of Peter Watson, that other mutual friend of Harry and myself, of whom tragic news had just arrived from London. He had died

suddenly, it was thought from a heart attack. Alice had known
him better than either of us, and spoke of him with sadness. I was
to remember our conversation six weeks later.

Now I set off for Washington, en route for the South and the
West. Harry, dreading the long hot New York summer when, in
any case, his taxi earnings dwindled, agreed to join me in Santa
Fe, New Mexico, towards the end of June. John had written the
libretto of a new ballad opera, which was to have its first performance around that time, in Denver, Colorado. They would
perhaps drive out together. I thus looked forward to a journey
across the continent in which I would not be altogether alone.

A Sitting of Congress · The British Adlai

A SUCCESSION of broad muddy rivers, between tangled banks,
crawls down into the Atlantic across the plains of the Eastern
seaboard. After the Hudson comes the Delaware, then the
Susquehanna, then the Potomac, on which Washington stands.
It is a city Roman in style and conception. Laid out in the classical
manner, beneath its Capitoline hill, with spacious parks and
broad avenues and long stretches of ornamental water, its government offices are sumptuous Roman palaces, its monuments
temples, erected at points of vantage to the memory of Republican
gods and heroes.

Big Brother Lincoln is a seated marble Zeus, thrice life-size,
in square-toed seven-league boots and a marble armchair, with
fasces at the front of it and a flag draped over the back of it. A
Parthenon shelters him, with two tripods to guard it and broad
marble steps to approach it. Its floor, I was told, is of pink Tennessee marble; its walls of Indiana marble; its panels, engraved with
his orations and adorned with eagles, of Alabama marble 'satur-
ated with melted beeswax to produce translucence'; its ceiling of
bronze, ornamented with the emblems of laurel and pine. Big
Brother Jefferson is a standing bronze Apollo, equally heroic in
size, dressed in a well-tailored greatcoat and waistcoat, and posed
on a pedestal of black Minnesota granite. He stands within a
rotunda of Vermont marble, its dome lined with Indiana limestone and its walls with panels of Georgia marble. His orations
are recorded on them in bronze, beneath crowns of laurel. Before

him spreads a lake and around it gardens, planted with the traditional but still middle-sized elms of the Homeland, and a grove of barren but blossoming cherries, the gift of a Japanese mayor. From these monuments classical vistas spread away through the trees, in geometrical symmetry, to the Capitol on the one hand and the White House on the other, while from the centre, commanding and challenging, there leaps up a giant Pharaonic obelisk.

Over five hundred feet high (this time with an elevator inside it), it is the memorial to Big Brother Washington, his disembodied eyes looking down from the points of it over the parks where, such is the industry of his sons, hardly a citizen strolls or reclines.

The White House, under the British a Brown House, and in fact rather a grey house, where the Big and lesser Brethren have lived and reigned, is 'a lovely old colonial home,' adorned in relatively Spartan simplicity with marble and gilt, containing a Blue Room, a Green Room, a Red Room and a ballroom, with a piano whose legs are golden eagles. 'You sure could chase around here with a ball all right,' remarked a gaping young citizen as the guide took us round.

The Capitol stands crowned by a dome like that of the Pantheon, with a stained-glass eagle for a skylight—'The light,' we were assured, 'that never fails.' Around its imposing premises, in the wake of the guides, flowed wave upon wave of young citizens, great-grandsons and great-granddaughters of the American Revolution, close-cropped youths and pony-tailed girls, white-skinned and black, clad as brightly as birds in ballerina skirts and bobby socks and shirts of many colours, with, on one or two heads, at a rakish angle, a comic cardboard bowler hat, emblazoned 'Washington D.C.' Cameras around necks and bangles around wrists, badges and fetishes on chests and gum in mouths, they looked and listened, then, at a sign from their guide, moved obediently on.

This, he instructed them, was no mere exhibition but the Shrine of their Liberties. Let them then listen attentively. Lest they obstruct Senators or Congressmen, let them form a column of twos and keep to the right. Lest they get separated and lost, let them stay within touching distance of the rank in front. Thus in orderly fashion they walked through the marble halls, admiring vast historical murals, including one by an Italian artist who had 'found his freedom' here; a portrait of Washington in a robe of imperial purple; three formidable American ladies of the Revolution, carved from a single block of marble, in the basement; and various traces of the burning of Washington by the British. ('I knew we'd burned St. Joan,' was the crack of an ingenuous Britisher, 'but I never knew we'd burned *him*.')

We swarmed into the galleries of the Chambers themselves, that of the Senate, then that of the House of Representatives, staying five minutes in each. In the House, beneath an array of busts ranging from Lycurgus to Edward the First, a Congressman stood at a lectern, reading into a microphone what appeared to be a lecture on scrap-iron. A shorthand reporter hovered around him, scribbling alertly. In the other place Senators, sitting two by two at their desks like classmates, were answering a roll-call from a dais with a marble desk and a tilting leather throne. In both Assemblies, pages circulated freely among the legislators— brisk, blue-suited boys, strolling at ease through the Chamber, lounging like prefects in leather armchairs by the bar, serving draughts of cold water in cardboard cups, answering telephones on the steps of the throne. In Supreme Court, says the cynical Congressman, they write the judgments.

*   *   *

In Washington I stayed with an old friend, Kay Halle, in the elegant Georgian suburb of Georgetown. Here were leafy Chelsea-ish streets and gardens, and slopes of grass, running down to a river, where on Sundays the residents—politicians, diplomats, columnists, generals, civil servants—lay sunbathing like corpses in a canvas by Hieronymous Bosch. Here was a society more integrated than that of New York, relaxed and informal but almost exclusively occupied with the topic of politics. All morning Kay, lying open-eyed, blonde and cool in her large white bed, with the breakfast tray beside her and the daily papers strewn over her counterpane, talked politics into her ivory telephone in her slow, wondering voice, commenting on the remarks of the columnists and the commentators, enquiring after the President's health, hearing the latest cracks (Dulles, 'The man with the grey flannel mouth'), extracting a morsel of inside gossip from one friend, passing it on to another, checking up on it with a third, until at midday the postman arrived and the negro maid brought up the letters, with more news which she sat down to discuss with her until it was time to get up for luncheon. It seemed that only the birds in the trees outside the Georgian windows talked no politics.

Just now the Presidential election lay six months ahead, and the primaries were raging, that strange series of pre-electoral battles for the selection of a candidate, in which, in State after State, Democrat fights Democrat and Republican Republican with more apparent venom than, in the final resort, Republican fights Democrat. This time they were shadow battles, for the final election of Mr. Eisenhower seemed certain enough. But they were none the less violent for that. If Republican Ike was to be elected President, what Democrat was not to be? The Opposition had put up, in hot mutual opposition, two candidates for non-election—Mr. Adlai Stevenson and Senator Estes Kefauver. Democrat against Democrat, dog against dog, they battled fiercely with one another in this primary Wonderland, a worried Adlai who did not much want to be President and would not be, a bland Estes who very much wanted to be President and would not be. Together, on the TV screen, they faced an invisible audience of Georgetown drawing-rooms, where the ladies of Washington worried away.

Adlai, their favourite, nervously tugging at the knot in his tie, had all the brains, hence few of the answers; Estes had fewer brains, hence all the answers. If only, the ladies sighed, dear Adlai could contrive to be just a little less intelligent, a little nastier to his Democratic colleague, a little less polite about his Republican enemies! If only he would bore people a little more, use a few more clichés, repeat himself more often, make jokes against others instead of himself! If only he would look as though he were *enjoying* it! His ways were all right the first time he was not elected. But 'you can't be a virgin twice.' Meanwhile, just in case of some accident to Ike, the friends of Estes campaigned for Adlai, and the friends of Adlai for Estes.

One day, into the midst of the Wonderland, another star dropped. Mr. Gaitskell, leader of the Labour Party, appeared on the TV screen. Meeting the Press in the guise of a Social Democrat, Continental style, he was as fresh-faced as Ike, he wore a nice foulard tie, he smiled like a schoolboy, he had not too few yet not too many brains, he knew some but not all of the answers, he was polite, but not too polite, about Sir Anthony Eden. With Kay I went to the Sheraton Park, 'the largest suburban hotel in the world,' where Mr. Gaitskell glided down a red carpet to address a concourse of thousands of lady garment-workers, lady cleaners and dyers, laundryladies, all permanently waved and expectantly seated at blue-silk table-cloths, beneath banners and exhortations and Big Brother photographs of Union officials, Hollywood size. Mr. Gaitskell captured the hearts of them all, and became, to the scribbling columnists, 'the British Adlai'.

'If only,' sighed the ladies of Georgetown, 'we had some like *him* to run for President!' And around them the birds laughed away in the trees.

Meanwhile, each week in the White House, the President in person received the Press—an occasion which, under a Constitution without ministerial responsibility, largely replaces the British ritual of the Parliamentary question. They sat before him, crowded together in a Corinthian saloon of the late Italian Renaissance, beneath a ceiling of stars and within walls of porphyry, observed by eagles and cherubs with eagles' wings, and cooled a little by a pair of electric fans. Spotlights shone upon the President, TV cameras whirred at him, camera-plates clattered as, with an easy avuncular freedom, he replied to their questions.

Aware that he had lately not been well, and being in any event politer than their scurrilous transatlantic neighbours, they were content with such homely and colloquiel replies as, 'Just as in your family that every difference or spat doesn't result in going to the golf—er, the divorce courts, well in the same way here, you can't take any one idea or any one act on the part of another government and say "That's the end, that's that!," anything, I mean, short of something absolutely inconsistent with your own safety and security.' One, asking considerately after his health, his capacity, for example 'to withstand long physical and mental fatigue,' was referred to the favourable reports of his doctors. So the Republican citizens of America relaxed with relief: there was no call for a change of masters: Ike would be elected again.

◦ **9** ◦

Colonial Williamsburg Inc. · To the South

IT is curiously hard to get a drink in America. Prohibition, in some form or another, dies hard. I first discovered this in Washington, where it is not permissible to drink at a bar but only at a table, served by a waiter or waitress; nor is it permissible for the drinker to carry a drink from one table to another: the waiter or waitress must do this. At Washington Airport it is possible to buy only wines and beers, since, to the inconvenience of travellers, it happens to be situated in the State of Virginia, and here the sale of all spirits, except at the State liquor stores, is prohibited. No such handicap, however, prevails in the country houses of Virginia, where the whisky, I found, flowed free. To the friendly ridicule of my American hosts I preferred to drink it not 'on the rocks,' finding whisky to be stronger if there is not too much ice to dilute it.

Here I stayed with an old English friend, Tony Wilson, and Emily, his American wife. They had a white Georgian house which looked out over undulating pastures, lined with white wooden palings, to the Blue Ridge Mountains, a landscape for ever changing in its lights and colours. They had an adjoining farm, where they bred sleek cattle. In Virginia, among the commuters and the retired businessmen, there are still gentlemen farmers. In the evening—and indeed far into the night—we drove around the countryside, paying visits to neighbours in houses as glossily English in their furnishings as in any illustrated magazine, but more feminine in their style, the smoking-room of the male, with its hunting prints and foxes' brushes, being upholstered, if not with cretonne, then with well-polished leather in a variety of bright smart colourings. Nor was there any male untidiness, the impedimenta of the hunting field—whips and boots and spurs and such—being all neatly arrayed in centrally heated cloakrooms.

Emily had promised to drive me down to Charleston, in South Carolina, and we had agreed to take the journey easily, spending two nights on the way. So we took to the road, becoming enmeshed in that network of highways which envelops the American continent from north to south and from east to west. No Roman ever envisaged such roads, six-hundred-and-seventy billion miles of them, highways and flyways and expressways and thruways and freeways, defying all natural obstacles, plunging into tunnels through mountains, soaring above the treetops of forests and the rooftops of towns, crossing bridges which span rivers and bogs and lakes and stretches of ocean.

This highway to the South ran, straight and interminable, hundred mile upon hundred mile through a flat unchanging landscape, the monotony of its acres relieved only by belts of tangled woodland. At intervals there were motels, neat conglomerations of dolls'-house châlets, built in the colonial style and resembling miniature suburbs, where the motorist might stay, from one coast to another, snug and secure from the unfamiliar outside world. Otherwise this was a landscape—as New York had been a townscape—of words, battering away at the traveller. There was only the unending literature of the roadside to divert us: 'Gas. Beer. Coke. . . . Jumbo Milk Shakes . . . Live Bait . . . Don't be a Litterbug. Keep it Beautiful. Trash can ahead . . . "Tiny" Condon for Sheriff. A Big Man for a Big Job.' Emily declared that, outside a filling-station, she had once seen a notice, 'Eat and Get Gas.'

Miraculous inventions measured our progress: 'Speed checked by Radar . . . Speed Electrically Timed . . . Resume Safe Speed'— and this meant, curiously, driving faster, at fifty-five miles an hour instead of thirty. Poets had coined lines for our protection: 'Safely Drive, Arrive Alive . . . Slow Down and Live . . . If you *must* drink and drive, Drink Milk and Stay Alive.' Piling up an atmosphere of suspense, hoardings announced to us, at tantalizing intervals, 'Big Blue Tube . . . is like Louise . . . You get a thrill . . . From every Squeeze'. Similarly spectacles were announced for our diversion: 'Monkeys $5\frac{1}{4}$ miles . . . Monkey Theatre. Singing Jackass—4 miles Alligators. Animal Farm' . . . and finally, with breathless imminence, 'SLOW DOWN. WILD ANIMALS 200 yards.'

Once or twice, at a level crossing, we encountered a freight train, so long that it held us up for ten minutes or more, reading the romantic names emblazoned on its trucks: the Route of the Rockets, the Way of the Zephyrs, the Route of the Hiawathas, the Orange Blossom Special.

On the first evening we reached Williamsburg, the pride of Colonial America. The capital of the Virginian planters in the reign of William and Mary, which gave place to Richmond and declined towards the end of the eighteenth century, it has been restored and reconstructed, as good as old, at a cost of some sixty million of Rockefeller dollars. As Colonial Williamsburg Inc. it is lovingly maintained, with the aid of further such subsidies that 'the Future may learn from the Past.' Here we received exceptional hospitality, the chairman of the concern having placed at our disposal the eighteenth-century guesthouse used on his visits by Mr. Rockefeller in person. Reconstructed exactly according to period, it had nevertheless such modern conveniences as plumbing, air-conditioning, electricity and telephones, discreetly concealed; toothglasses in the bathrooms hygienically wrapped, and beside them packets of the 'New Two Ply Charming Facial Quality Tissue.' More important, two bottles of Scotch whisky were laid out for our use—a notable asset in this non-alcoholic State.

In Williamsburg, says the guide-book 'trim carriages once more roll along Duke of Gloucester Street'—and indeed they do, driven by coloured coachmen in cockaded tricorne hats. For the place is in effect a stage, and the people tripping out of their neat, white weather-boarded houses, through Jacobean cottage-gardens, fragrant with edgings of box and 'authentic' medicinal herbs, are in a sense merely players—ladies in farthingales, gentlemen in ruffles and breeches and hose—for the diversion of an audience. For here again were the spectacled, flower-hatted, be-ticketed Colonial Dames of the United States, escorted now by sons and sires. 'Hi!' proclaimed the label attached to one of these males, 'My name is Sids B. Hooe, Houston, Texas.'

Dawdling and chattering through the past, they buy eighteenth-century bread at the Bakery; note that the Shoemaker has 'taken the post to Yorktown for jury duty,' and that he now makes 'shoes for elves in the latest styles and as well made as from Ireland'; toy with perruques at the Wigmakers; buy plaster busts of Lord Botetourt, the last Governor but one, 'done in the genteelest manner'; gaze upon the Blacksmith working away with his seventeenth-century tools. The Milliner supplies them with kerchiefs and toilet waters and fine French perfumes, fans and plumes and boudoir caps; the Apothecary with a good wintergreen toothbrush, slippery elm for sore throats, pomanders for foul and stinking closets, bay-scented shaving soap, or the finest domestic leeches. They are photographed with their heads in the pillory (for those gossiping or kissing in the street) and in the Public Bath try out the earliest indoor toilet. They are served at the King's Arms Tavern with foods 'prepared by the oldeft and moft approved Recipes'—Efcaloped Oysters, Chicken Pye, Sally Lunn and other hot Breads, with afforted relifhes, a Salad of Frefh Garden Stuff and Herb Dreffing, and Tipfy Cake to end with.

'Would you like to have your napkins tied round your necks?' the costumed maid enquired obligingly.

Scanning the public notice-boards, the visitors read proclamations, in facsimile, signed by the last Governor, the Earl of Dunmore, together with other more mundane notices:

'A gentleman is in want of a good Cook who can be well recommended of either sex but would prefer a man. A good price would be given for him or her.'

'Whereas my wife Lucy hath behaved in a very unfriendly

manner to me, this is to forewarn all persons from trusting
her on my Account, as I will not pay any debts she may
contract.'

'Whereas it has been reported by certain sly and malicious
persons that I have kept Filmer Moore from his wife and child
whome he placed at my house, I do here declare that the said
remove her to any Place of Peace and Safety where he shall
think proper.'

A lady guide—a retired actress, but not, as it happened, in a
farthingale—was allotted to us, that we might see all under the
best possible auspices. She conducted us around the College of
William and Mary, with its dignified, well-restored buildings by
Wren, and the lamented Lord Botetourt's statue before it. She
took us into the parish church, on Prince George Street, named
after Bruton in Somerset, where we sat for a moment in Mr.
Jefferson's pew and cast a wistful eye upwards to the slave
gallery. She showed us, with disapproval, the one renegade
Victorian house near the Capitol, which its owners, defying the
Yankee invasion, had refused to allow to be pulled down and
rebuilt with the Rockefeller dollars. Finally she led us to the
Governor's Palace, inducing us to shed a tear for the Royal
Arms carved above the gate; reminding us, salutarily, that America
thrived for almost as long before Independence as after it;
evoking nostalgically Lord Botetourt's elaborate balls, which
reduced him to bankruptcy, and pausing for a reverent moment
beside the bed the good lord died in.

'To be invited to the Palace,' she explained, 'was to be invited
to the Court of London.'

And the spectacled ladies and gentlemen sighed.

*　　　*　　　*

Beyond Williamsburg the landscape grew gradually more
Southern in its atmosphere. The light skies gave place to a colour-
less haze, the woodlands and fields to large plantations of tobacco
and maize, which negroes raked with a listless air. The negroes
swarmed thicker on the ground, and it seemed darker in hue, their
wooden houses and bungalows, with unkempt porches, strung
along the roadsides and around the tall slatted tobacco stores. But
they looked empty, their inhabitants all hard at work on the land.
Cafés 'for Coloured People' began to make their appearance. The
words by the roadside began to cater not merely for the body but

for the soul: 'Fine Food. Quick Loans. Jesus Saves,' read a series of notices. 'A Man with God is always in the Majority.' Beneath a Cross was the injunction 'Get Right with God'; on the back of a taxicab, 'Now, more than ever, go to Church.'

We spent the night in a town named, appropriately, Wilson, in North Carolina, where a notice by my bedside advised 'Relax and enjoy yourself on the Long Distance Telephone.' Next day, having searched in vain for a café where it was possible to obtain a meal with a glass of beer—an insistence for which Emily justly rebuked me as the English rebuke Americans for demanding iced water—we turned off the road to lunch at Myrtle Beach, by the ocean breakers. It was a straggling seaside resort, still out of season, but it promised such entertainments as the Miss South Carolina Beauty Contest, a two-mile-long Shrine Parade, preceding the Spring Ceremonial of the Omar Temple, and a Baton Twirling Contest in the High School Gym. On Sun-Fun Day, when all must wear bathing suits on pain of being 'fined a buck by pretty lady cops and/or jugged in a special barred jail parked down town,' there would be a jousting tourney on the Coastal Speedway Track, and on the Pavilion Terrace a Human Checker Game, as first played four hundred years ago before the castle of Marostica, Italy.

Driving now through a forest of a sub-tropical aspect, we reached the Lord Chesterfield Motel, and beyond it a notice: 180,000 Hospitable People Welcome You.' A long bridge soared over an estuary like a sequence of switchbacks, and led us into Charleston. We were to stay with friends of Emily, at the Naval Base. Within its gates we were greeted by an outsize two-dimensional girl in a bikini, announcing, 'Mrs. U.S. Navy Contest. Nominate your wife before 15 June for the Navy's most outstanding wife.'

SOUTH

In Charleston a picture postcard from Harry awaited me, portraying a young orang-outang from the Central Park Zoo: 'I'm sorry,' he apologized, 'not to have a photo of Mrs. Jarvis instead of limp-wristed Andy. Ellsworth's show opened last evening, attended by a host of admirers, family, children and an endearing dog. Their comments were confused. These are strange times: people distrust what they see and hear (recall "Godot") and seek instead some inner, *real* meaning. As Bridey Murphy, in her pre-birth period, comments on communication beyond the pale: "We want to talk to them but they never listen." Yours, Lucky.'

Charleston seemed, and indeed is, a long way from New York. Above all other settlements on the Eastern seaboard, it retains the atmosphere of a self-contained colony. All but an island between its two converging rivers—named the Ashley and the Cooper, after its lordly English seventeenth-century founder—it bore indeed less affinity to the American continent than to the West Indian islands which, rather than New York, are its neighbours and moreover its contemporaries in terms of colonial history. The tropical June heat which now enveloped it—for I had indeed lingered in and around New York for too long—aggravated the illusion of remoteness, and created also a stillness foreign to the America I had seen. Most of its gentry had left for cooler places, and the streets, slow in rhythm beneath the torpor of the day, had an agreeable muted air. When, however, I later referred in an article to Charleston as 'nostalgically asleep' between its two rivers, I was severely scolded for so un-American an epithet by 'Lord Ashley Cooper,' the author of a column in the local *News and Courier* entitled 'Doing the Charleston with His Lordship.'

Belatedly Adam in style, the architecture of the Charleston gentry was so revolutionary, it was said, as to surprise Virginia, interest Pennsylvania and infuriate New England. The climate imposed on it an unfamiliar feature: pillared, two-storeyed verandahs like those of most tropical countries but of a more elegant, Georgian design, shading the façades and the sides of the houses. Charleston is assiduous in self-preservation, looking back to its past with pride. To the local antiquarian, Mr. Sam Stoney, a discursive and erudite guide full of love for the place, this past was still alive, in terms not only of its buildings but of the families —many of them Scottish country gentry—that had lived in them. So indeed it was to all the ladies and gentlemen of Charleston, living, in their graceful houses, lives of cultivated ease and refinement suggestive of some American Cranford.

Wearing a pointed beard and sandals, Mr. Stoney showed us, as we strolled down the shady side of a street, here a nice piece of ironwork, there an unusual fanlight, here a church with an early pulpit, there a rice-mill built in the Palladian manner. He treated us, with a touch of Scots inflection in his voice, to a flow of reminiscence, which might well have been personal, of eighteenth-century days gone by: of the Kinlochs of Gilmerton, who had lived in this house, of the Nesbitts of Dean, who had lived in that; of the old local battles between Presbies and Piscies; of Dr. Alexander Garden, who gave his name to the gardenia; of the Lady Anne Murray, a pillar of the Kirk, who alone kept her head when a lesser young lady fell into the fire as she dropped her a curtsey. He himself was a Piscie, who had worshipped each Sunday for seventeen years in a church bearing the arms of George I. Stung, I am sorry to say, by a reference in my article to his beard and his sandals, he later broke into the *Courier*, at my expense, with a crushing lampoon, 'On a Visiting Nobleman.'

On Sunday our hosts took us for a picnic in the Admiral's launch—out across the torpid bay to the toy Fort Sumter, where the first shots in the Civil War were fired, then back up the Ashley River for luncheon. Since the refreshments, dispensed from an early hour, included a quart of Martini cocktails freshly mixed, a certain torpor had descended also on the guests by the time we reached the river banks. Along them Charleston's country houses stand amid woodland gardens, planned with taste and imagination by America's earliest landscape gardeners, and flowering with a profusion of magnolias, camellias, azaleas and sub-tropical shrubs.

None, alas!, were in flower, but the woods and the waterways in themselves conjured up around us settings of a romantic, dreamlike fantasy. For here and throughout the South the live-oaks of the forest are draped with the diaphanous 'Spanish moss,' festoons and wisps of it sagging and trailing from the branches like tattered veils of weird grey crêpe. As strange are the cypresses, their tall buttressed trunks standing in lakes of dark transparent water with, as an aid to 'breathing,' groups of 'knees,' gnarled products, it seems, of abstract sculpture, arising in a phantasmagoria of conflicting shapes and sizes around them. Such are the gardens of Middleton, planned in the eighteenth century, with their Cypress Lake and Azalea Pool, their alleys of camellias and magnolia walks and bamboo groves, their broad terraces looking down to the river over sunken gardens and ornamental lakes and a marsh with a disused Georgian rice-mill which, in the heyday of Charleston, was a lush, productive rice-field.

The house itself, Middleton Place, home of the Middleton family, was destroyed in the Civil War and has only been partially restored. But Hampton, amid ghostlike woods to the west of Charleston, survives intact as a rambling, decaying country house of the colonial period, inhabited still by the descendants of the family that built it. The stairs creak ominously, the paint is worn, the plaster flakes from the walls, but the proud classical portico still stands forth from the head of its broad flight of steps, confronting a moss-draped patriarch of a tree solemnly declared to be seven hundred and fifty years old. The ballroom within still flaunts its Delft-tiled mantelpiece, once doubtless the envy of the less affluent planter families.

An aged Coal Black Mammy from the outside kitchen quarters, whence slaves, so she told us with relish, once carried all meals across to the big house, invited us to call her Aunt Sue, and showed us the path through the wood, where a notice read: 'Down this path rode the Swamp Fox to elude Colonel Tarleton.' By the foot of it sprawled the sluggish river, sinister and tropical in aspect, its banks overgrown with reeds which surely harboured serpents and alligators. Here the Deep South, unmistakably and a shade uncannily, enveloped us.

11

Land of Perpetual Motion · Way down Yonder · Arty-Crafty and Honky-tonk · On the Mississippi

'WALTERBORO, Yemassee, Pocataligo, Savannah, Brunswick, Jacksonville . . . .' The amplified voice, like that of a disembodied pastor reciting a litany, droned on, on its single note, dropping mournfully at the end of each line—a voice incomprehensible, I felt, to any but a churchgoing people. Some passengers rose from the benches where they had been listlessly sitting, and filed out to the bus. Others, from the coloured persons' waiting-room, followed them. Emily, marvelling that anyone could travel in so primitive a way, said goodbye to me, a little apprehensively. This was the start of my journey by the Greyhound Line from one side of the American continent to the other.

The bus, silver and streamlined, sped southwards along the highway, as comfortable and smooth as a railroad coach. Air-conditioning cooled me, my well-upholstered seat tilted back as in an aeroplane. To my delighted surprise I could read at my ease. Since the landscape was monotonous, I read my way into Savannah, Georgia, where I spent the night. This was to be my regular programme. The hardened traveller had the habit of sleeping in the bus night after night, very likely from New York to Miami, enjoying with his fellow-passengers the companionship of shared discomfort. Unhardened to this, I planned my journeys in a sequence of day hops, stopping off each night at some suitable stage—and thus, as it turned out, became a creature somewhat aloof from my fellows.

Savannah was a Southern city, well shaded with trees and agreeably designed in a succession of dignified squares, with monuments in the centre of them and Georgian houses and churches grouped around them. One church recalled in its design St. Martin-in-the-Fields; in another John Wesley had preached his first sermon. This was a godly city—or so it seemed from the church services, listed on a board in my hotel, offering a choice between Baptist, Catholic, Christian Science, Christian [sic], Presbyterian, Episcopal, Jewish, Lutheran and Methodist.

My second night's stop, at the end of a twelve-hour journey through a monotonous flat landscape, was at Tallahassee, a town with apparently no more than a single street, which I was surprised to learn was 'the capital city of Fabulous Florida.' That we were already in the State I had gathered only from a notice announcing the fact at the frontier, above a row of picnic tables, with outdoor fireplaces for cooking, set amid palm trees and hedges of scarlet hibiscus.

'Opportunities for profits and for happier living,' I read, 'abound in Tallahassee'; and indeed on this street the offices of realtors and bankers predominated, offering 'Money on your Name Only.' Apart from borrowing money, there seemed little to do here, and I went to bed early, diverting myself with the alternative greetings telegrams inscribed by my bedside for use on the approaching Father's Day:

> 'When I (we) picked a Dad
> I (we) picked the very best they had.
> All my (our) love on Father's Day.
> Mother was smart as she could be
> In picking a Dad like you for me.
> For your generous ways, all you've done,
> And always being so much fun,
> Thanks a lot, Dad.'

I sat down and wrote to Constance:

'Here I am, a tiny anonymous speck in the huge anonymous South, heading west. No more of New York and the East— the "English" America, for a while. Some of it's been boring, much of it interesting. The misleading thing about the East is that it *is* so English, so European, in so many outward ways. But it isn't at all underneath. It has an English past but not an English present. I guess one only begins to understand America when one stops expecting it to be like Europe. But in the East —in New England especially—so much of it is *trying* to be like Europe that this isn't easy at first.

'What's the difference, really? There's the rhythm of life, of course. One can exaggerate this. It isn't such a whirl as all that, not for the ordinary American and not outside New York. Still, there is all the time the urge for action, as opposed to reflection. Quite a civilized woman said to me, "I always feel guilty if I read a book during the day, when I ought to be *doing* something. At night, in bed, it's different." There's the vulgarity, the stridency of the advertisements, the showiness of everything. But we're getting plenty of that in Europe. Look at Italy. There's the conformity, the fact that every-body's trying to be the same. But look at the English suburbs and provincial towns. There's the money-worship and the success-worship. But then this is a businessman's country, and you'd find the same if you did a journey through the English Midlands—or through the Surrey hills, for that matter.

'It's a middle-class country without an aristocracy or a peasantry (farming is simply a form of business, not an attach-ment to the soil). And as it hasn't the traditions of the one and the earthiness of the other, it's essentially fluid. That's the first difference from Europe. There's perpetual motion, perpetual change. Nobody stays in the same house or in the same job or with the same wife very long. Change is welcomed and respected as a way of living. They've the instincts of a nomadic people still.

'But the big difference, I think, is in terms of human relations. In Europe everything begins and ends with the person. Here it isn't so. Things matter more than people. The boys at the universities don't study the humanities. There's a strong strain of Methodism everywhere, which is against human—to say nothing of aesthetic—values. The proper study of mankind isn't man, it's a lot of other things first—though I suppose you might say it is, to some extent, men, in the plural. People matter collectively, more than individually—in terms of the group rather than of the person *as* a person. There's hospitality because there's warmth and a desire for company, but it isn't selective. Everybody's a grand guy. Nobody really knows what anyone else is really like—or really wants to know. And nobody knows what they're really like themselves.

'When I say nobody, of course, I don't mean nobody: there are all sorts of exceptions to prove the rule. There are my own friends in New York, the opposite to all this—the rebels against it. There are all those highly civilized people living in and around the universities mostly, and in provincial art galleries who combine the best of both worlds and have a splendid all-roundness and open-mindedness, which is almost Greek. They can take anything from Beethoven to baseball and Marlon Brando to Bellini. They touch life at every point. They know just where they are and where other people are, as human beings. But they're the élite and they stand out in very sharp relief against the mass.

'For them—the mass—it's each man for himself, with a second loyalty to the community, usually some local community, but not much room for the other person in between. They want to be loved, because it gives them a sense of security. But not to love, and they haven't learnt to understand. They're emotional—or, rather, sentimental. (They're more Germanic than British in this way—and in other ways too; their fondness for theoretical conceptions, for instance, which don't fit in with practice: thought without action and action without thought.) They're very uncynical and uncalculating about marriage. All is romantic bliss until something goes wrong, and then there's an end to it because there isn't this capacity for understanding —or the patience for it.

'All this is glib generalization, of course, but it'll do to be going on with.'

*   *   *

From Tallahassee it was a long day's journey to New Orleans, with the steamy skies of the Gulf of Mexico rolling up from the west to envelop us. We travelled for the most part in silence. Greyhound passengers, it seemed, were not a talkative race, and for this on the whole I was thankful, preferring to read. Two only, sitting in front of me, chattered monosyllabically. One was a hillbilly farmer from the Tennessee foothills, the other a nursery gardener from the Florida plains—worlds utterly separate one from the other. After listening for a while, the man of the plains remarked, 'I ain't never seen a mountain. Two thousand feet? No, *sir*, that's too high for me to get up.' They left the bus at Pensacola and their seats were taken by a soldier, sprawling across them, with a pile of magazines by his side. Looking over his shoulder, I read the headlines: 'Your Mysterious Sex Glands . . . The Truth about Paris Prostitutes . . . How to join a Nudist Camp . . . Why I strip for a living . . .'

The motels had begun to affect a Spanish architectural style. Everywhere the gasoline was GULF. We reached the Gulf itself at Mobile, in the State of Alabama, a place oppressed by the heat, with an air of bleariness and fatigue about its weather-boarded houses, but with a fine avenue of live oaks to give them shade. Thenceforward, crossing into the State of Mississippi, we followed the sea, breaking sickly and sluggish on the beach at Biloxi, the summer villas of the New Orleans gentry withdrawn discreetly behind tropical trees, and a sequence of piers striking out into the shallow grey water, one of them devoted, it seemed, to a 'Sea-shore Methodist Assembly.' So we reached New Orleans. In its bus station was a slot machine, promising me relief of nervous and muscular tension. 'Step up for a pick-up, for new pep and energy.' I needed it, put a dime in the slot, and received a mild shaking.

We were now well into June, the wrong season for New Orleans. Grey, sultry clouds hung heavily over the city, bursting two or three times a day into a ferocious tropical downpour.

'This rain,' my poor host, Dick Orme, exclaimed, 'drives me out of my mind. I'm a sun-worshipper.'

I was fortunate, however, to be staying in his well-shuttered apartment in the Vieux Carré, shaded from the heat by a broad verandah of ornamental ironwork, which formed an arcade sheltering the pavement below. In the apartment above his, Tennessee Williams had written *A Street-Car Named Desire*, its title inspired by the predecessor of a trolleybus, which ran by the street corner every few minutes en route for the suburb of Desiré. This was the old French quarter, with French-named streets and historic French houses. But the ironwork had an English Regency flavour, suggesting Old Brighton more than Old Orleans.

On the morrow of my arrival, a hospitable lady took me off to luncheon, in the courtyard of a smart new restaurant which had been until lately the city's oldest bank. The menu offered, among more substantial delicacies, the following:

CANAPE LORENZO
Hot lump crabmeat zestfully seasoned and anchovy crowned

OYSTERS ROCKEFELLER
With an unforgettable dressing of spinach, exotic herbs, anchovies and absinthe

BRENNAN'S LUNCHEON SALAD BOWL
Colorful and refreshing—strips of ham, turkey, Swiss cheese and beets with mixed greens, tossed with French dressing and garnished with quartered tomato and hard-boiled egg

FRAISES FLAMBÉES
Louisiana strawberries on sliced pound cake, covered with meringue peaked to hold an egg shell which is filled with brandy and brought flaming to your table.

But this was nothing, as I discovered later, to Diamond Jim's, advertised as the most expensive restaurant in New Orleans, whose proprietor considered himself naked without a quarter of a million pounds' worth of jewellery on, and whose specialities were Irish stew laved in brandy and pork-chops stuffed with sea-food.

The guests now seated around us, in this more refined establishment, were for the most part ladies, alert-eyed and voluble, wearing orchid sprays and fashionable hats like inverted basins and chattering gaily away in their soft Southern voices like tropical birds. My hostess entertained me with anecdotes in the Kentucky dialect—for she was not herself from the South—and with reminiscences of the Civil War, whose history is a source of vivid and often scholarly interest to these Southern American ladies. Then she walked me down the street, stopping every few paces to exchange greetings, often in French ('Bonjour . . . tiens, comment ça va?') with other such ladies, or to look into the antique-shops and gift-shops and tea-shoppes ('Psychic reading from tea-leaves gratis,' read a notice) which many of them ran, or to take a peep into the patios, somewhat Spanish in character, of the picturesque houses in which they lived. One of them kindly invited me to a 'brunch' party, at ten o'clock on Sunday morning. Not at my best at such an hour, I refused as politely as possible, renewing the refusal when, around four o'clock on Sunday afternoon, a series of brunch-drunk voices urged me to change my mind.

Art in the Vieux Carré seemed ubiquitous. American Bohemia tends to form into groups, settling in a series of artists' colonies from Greenwich Village to Monterey, California. New Orleans was, as it were, a colony of Montparnasse in the 'thirties. A popular highbrow resort was its *Petit Théâtre*; another was Napoleon House, for classical or operatic readings. Along Dauphine and Bourbon and Toulouse and Chartres Streets, French-named establishments—Antoine's, Broussard's, Arnaud's, the Lafitte, the Café du Monde—served 'French' Creole dishes, French bread and French wines (or alternatively American milk to the majority who preferred it). There was a touch of English too—in Aunt Sally's Old-Fashioned Candy Shoppe, for instance, in the scones (called biscuits) which were served in the tea-rooms, in the Livery Stand, next to the taxi stand, where a Victoria plied for hire, with a coachman in a top hat and a horse in a sun-bonnet.

'The Petite Shoppe' displayed, in its name, a commendable spirit of Anglo-French compromise. But beneath the French veneer lay an essentially American core, Models of Coal Black Mammies guarded the doors of the Shoppes. Lucky Pierre's had an Ante-Bellum Room. The Old Absinthe Bar served also Daiquiris, Pink Squirrels, Grasshoppers and Zombies. An American idiom pervaded *The French Quarter*, the gossipy weekly news-letter: 'RAMONA, well known in Quarter circles, had an extended haggle and frassle with another Quarterite . . . Mrs. Cameron, mother of Louise the Printer, has been receiving gardenias regularly every week. Now, now, Mrs. C. . . . What Quarterite has SUSZANE JOLYN, that attractive model and artist, been spending so much time with? . . . That old-time auto collection of Jack's at the Bookshop is growing fast past all expectations.'

The painters congregated with their easels beneath the arcades of the Louisiana State Museum on Jackson Square, drawing portraits of anyone who came along, for three dollars and upwards. They set themselves up behind shop-windows—'Dot's Art Saloon', at the sign of the 'Two Starving Artists'—where they painted them in oils for a little more, luring customers in with arch invitations: 'Come up and let us show you our etchings. Y'all come in and browse. Give us the brush and we'll do the rest'. On St. Peter Street stood 'Gipsy Lou', dressed as a gipsy and purveying 'water-colours with charm.' On the street corner was a notice-board proclaiming 'If you're lost or want to get lost, tack what you wish on this board.' Tacked on it were a number of advertisements for Gipsy Lou, and a pencilled note, 'Milton. Waited 3 hours at Pat O'Brien's. Not nice. Jan.' Nearby was the Coffee Club, where I breakfasted each morning beneath shelves of 'personalized' coffee mugs, painted with the names of its patrons—Bebe, Sallie, Tito, Sexy, Freckles, Satana, Van. One of them, breakfasting earnestly with another, was saying: 'He's too much in conflict with himself to tell whether he really likes me or not. . . . He keeps on punishing himself for things he has done, and takes it out on everybody else. . . .'

At night honkey-tonk reinforced arty-craft. The streets of the Vieux Carré were ablaze with garish lights and agog with the music of jazz-band and juke-box. Pin-table saloons catered for restless crowds, together with photographers' shops where they might be photographed jitterbugging, riding pigs, disguised as monkeys, or emerging from gaol. Burlesque shows vied with one another in nudity. Bohemia thronged bars designed for a variety of sexes, wearing blue jeans and pony-tails, bangles and ballet-skirts, corduroy shirts and leather jerkins. From midnight onwards all together, reinforced by clusters of débutantes and their escorts, thronged Bacino's Back Bar, whose barman, Mr. Candy Lee, the 'Little Jewel of America' and 'Queen Bee of the Mardi-Gras,' entertained them coquettishly in a high falsetto, wearing panties and a brassière and a single paste earring.

In the midst of all this it was easy to forget that New Orleans is on the Mississippi River. For it stands with its back to this sprawling monster, the river banks providing sightseers, mile after mile, with a formidable array of docks and machinery and warehouses, but with little else to please the eye.

*   *   *

Here I heard from Harry. He had evolved the plan of driving John's car out to the West for him, since John would be travelling by air. But nothing was yet decided.

'Our plans,' he wrote, 'are still contingent on the jingle of the telephone, which will tell me about John's latest attempt to rehash my simple proposal. Schemes of this sort must emanate from John, so when I called him Friday and lucidly suggested that his trip, my trip, and the convenience of the car all added up nicely, he was vague and unable to fasten on the simplicity of it all, meanwhile milling over in his mind ways to complicate it.'

'I told John,' he wrote again, 'that I wanted to meet you in Santa Fe on or about the 23rd, but the conversation soon began to sound as tedious as an Aristotelian explanation of metaphysics, so he rung off promising to talk to me further about it tomorrow.' Later: 'I just called John but never succeeded in penetrating his mother's jasmine tones and Southern comfort to get directly to him.' But finally: 'At last the telephone! I just spoke to John and everything has worked out superbly, i.e. I am to take the car out to Colorado this week. So I will be in Denver by Sunday. It is 400 miles north of Santa Fe, a day's drive away. Alors, you must try to get to Santa Fe as soon as you can.'

I must therefore press on, cutting short my visit to New Orleans. Anxious, however, to see some more of the South, I made a brief return journey a few months later.

⌐ 12 ⌐

Black and White · The Ku Klux Klan · Integration
in the Heavens · At the Johnny J.

THIS second time I flew down to Atlanta, in the heart of the cotton lands of Georgia. In this nondescript city a street called Auburn Avenue runs down from the central business quarter, and it was here that I spent much of my time. On the surface it looks much like any other American street, with drug-stores and cafés and churches and commercial buildings, and a long line of sleek cars parked by the kerb. It has indeed only one difference. It is inhabited entirely by negroes.

Supplied with introductions, I called on the President of an insurance company. He was neatly and discreetly dressed, with a pearl pin in his tie. His offices were streamlined and air-conditioned, as an American businessman's should be. He spoke at length of his insurance activities, and referred also to his trip to Europe, remarking how much he and his wife had enjoyed Madame Tussaud's and the Tower of London. I called on a bank manager, in a smart modern bank, equipped with venetian blinds and contemporary furniture and pots of tropical greenery. A glamorous secretary showed me into his office, where he greeted me with an expansive 'Hiya!' and talked of banking, and of his Cadillac, and of his beautiful home. I called on an editor, busy in shirt-sleeves and horn-rimmed spectacles, who talked in the vernacular of his trade; he was writing a leader on agriculture and called my attention to a work on his desk of George Washington Carver, the great agricultural scientist. I called on a political agent, resplendent in a bow-tie in the Old Harrovian colours, with a photograph of the President in one buttonhole and a diamond IKE in the other, and an office resplendent with an extra ration of bunting in Red, White and Blue. Later I attended the meeting of a luncheon-club, at which ladies in basin hats and mink stoles, with smart accessories, listened to a lecture and took part in a discussion on Human Relations. All these were negroes—and all a hundred per cent Americans, closely wedded, it seemed clear, to the American Way of Life.

My last call that morning in Auburn Avenue was on a lively old gentleman, in a checked tweed shirt with an IKE button in his lapel and a golden watch-chain across his waistcoat, whose bright eyes danced behind gold-rimmed lenses. He was a Grand Master Mason, his name was John Wesley Dobbs, and his father, he assured me, had been a slave, who had not been allowed to learn to read and write, so had learnt to play the violin instead. But 'I myself,' he remarked, 'missed that institution by seventeen years.' In a whirlwind of enthusiasm he swept me through his Masonic Building, from its radio station, where I met a half-negro disc-jockey, to its dental clinic, where I met his daughter, a child receptionist; from its playrooms to its libraries and its offices concerned with welfare, all the while throwing out bright disconnected remarks: 'Victor Hugo said "Remove ignorance and misery." You remember? . . . Don't you just love that old tune they're playing?' and he hummed, ' "Me-an to Me" . . . America started a new kind of democracy, like the Greeks and Romans. What's become of it? . . . Have you heard my other daughter Mattiwilda? She sings at Covent Garden. God gave her her vocal chords.'

Miss Mattiwilda Dobbs gets a good welcome when she comes to Auburn Avenue, but must be careful not to stray beyond the end of it into the hotels and the restaurants where the Whites have chosen to segregate themselves. Their newspapers, in recording her visits, are tactful enough, so I learnt, not to refer to her colour or to divulge the extent of her international reputation. At which the negroes of the Avenue laugh.

Altogether it was a gay morning. Underlying it, however, was a deep concern with the racial problem, of which we talked at length. For the States of Georgia, Alabama, Mississippi and South Carolina were the hedgehog of White resistance to integration with the negroes in schools and professions and social life. They imparted their views, on the whole, with moderation. Time was on their side, and above all the Federal Law, declaring segregation in schools illegal, which the States could not resist for ever. Their present resistance, said one, was like that of children with one foot tentatively in and out of the water, reluctant to take the plunge.

When I came to leave Auburn Avenue to return to the White world, beyond the end of the street, I hailed a taxi, but was told with polite embarrassment that it could not take me: it was a negro-driven taxi, plying for negroes only; if I didn't mind waiting, my friends would telephone for a White one, and this they did. That evening I should have liked to return to the Avenue, which seemed to promise some liveliness in its bars and dance-halls, while the rest of the city was dead. But I refrained, for fear of causing embarrassment: the negroes were not supposed to serve a white man, and preferred not to do so for fear of causing trouble.

Meanwhile, up in the State Capitol building, beneath that Roman dome which is reproduced in varying sizes, in emulation of Washington, in capital cities throughout the continent, I had talked with Georgia's Attorney-General. Tight-lipped and unsmiling, he spoke of the necessity to prolong segregation. 'If we throw in the towel,' he said, 'then I might as well go to Russia.'

The negroes, in his opinion, could never reach the white level of culture. Twenty-five per cent of them were bastards (in the literal sense), fifty per cent of them had syphilis—or used to have. The right of the white child to go to a white school must be protected, and that of the black child to go to a black. The Supreme Court decision threatened an inflammable situation, such as occurred following the release of the slaves at the end of the Civil War. 'The whole State may go haywire,' the Attorney-General said. For this reason he had given his official sanction to the revival of the Ku Klux Klan.

I had seen the Charter of this branch of the Klan, and had heard something of its activities. 'A secret fraternal organization,' formed 'for social and charitable purposes,' its aims were 'to promote the Christian faith, to promote a better way of life among its members and to uphold the Constitution of the United States.' In a Georgian paper, the *Columbus Ledger*, I had seen an advertisement:

WANTED: 500 more Law Abiding, Freedom Loving, Gentile American Men from 18 and up to join the Knights of the Ku Klux Klan. Columbus Klan Number 21 meets every Monday Night at Lodge Hall corner 24th and Hamilton. Charter in Washington, Legal in 40 states. A clean, one hundred per cent American Organization.

In pursuit of these declared aims, the Klan distributed propaganda against integration: an anatomical leaflet, for instance, with an ape on one side, and a negro, all but identical, on the other; a ballad beginning:

'When a white girl marries a negro, the sun of her life goes down,
And glaring spots of sin appear on her white wedding gown.'

Its Knights dressed up in robes and hoods and helmets. They waved flags and brandished the Bible; they roared through the cities in motorcades of expensive cars; they made speeches and burned Crosses to symbolize the Klansman's Flaming Zeal. The negroes, I gathered, no longer took such performances very seriously. Once they had struck awe into the hearts of the liberated slaves; now the children laughed away at them gaily as at some new entertainment. One of their elders remarked to me, 'It's the last twitchings of a dead beast.'

The head of the Klan, its 'Imperial Wizard,' was a Mr. Eldon Edwards, by religion a stern Baptist, by trade a paint-sprayer employed by General Motors ('Hitler could at least use a brush,' remarked a sardonic negro). I rang him up on the telephone, asking permission to call on him. He would prefer, he replied, to visit me privately at my hotel. I gave him my name, and the number of my room, where I would await him. When he failed to appear I went downstairs, and there I found him, looking lost before an equally lost room-clerk, having forgotten both name and number. He was a man in his late forties, with glazed brown eyes and a mottled complexion and a nostril slightly swollen. Making sure that my bedroom door was locked, he began in a slow, low voice to tell me of the objects of the Klan.

'Mongolization,' he said, 'yes, *Mongolization* stares us all in the face. It is Russia's intention to Mongolize the world, to mix the White Race with the Black so as to bring it under Communist control; we all know that. The Catholics are behind this too, and so, of course, are the Jews. Both have their own secret societies for the purpose of stirring up the niggers. There are evil elements working in this country, and we must search and dig them out.'

The Catholics had their Knights of Columbus. Could he spell the name of the Jewish society? He could not. But he tried to pronounce it again. 'It is the Jewish Gestapo,' he exclaimed. 'We don't want to see the white blood vanish. We're out to protect the White Race. We'll give our blood to protect Christ and the Constitution of the United States.'

Ninety per cent of the niggers, he said, were entirely content. 'Everyone wants to beat on the South as crucifying the nigger. But it is the South, not the North, that has advanced the nigger to where he is today, and that's farther than any other nationality in the history of the world. He has better schools and opportunities than the white man. But God created the races and segregated them. The Bible teaches segregation.'

'In what passages exactly?'

The Wizard hesitated. 'Well, the Bible is a big book.'

The Klan is one of a number of such Fraternal Orders—the National Association for the Preservation of the White Race, Inc. is another—which dislike not merely negroes and Catholics and Jews, but such threats to their interests as income tax, water fluoridation and polio vaccine.

After 'marching through Georgia,' I 'drove through Alabama,' still by Greyhound bus. The landscape, with its interminable flat plantations, had a tired, dispirited look, as though it had never come altogether back to life since the Civil War had ravaged it; moreover in some men's minds the war still raged. The cities had little to offer. From Montgomery I wrote to Harry: 'This place lacks life. Every evening I look out on to negatively ugly buildings and identical streets and silly pretty lights flashing out about LIQUOR and LAUNDRY and LOANS. There is nothing to look at with pleasure, no entertainment but stale movies (I saw *Treasure Island*), no aliveness except possibly in the negro quarter, and there is segregation for whites, and I have nothing left to read. The little black elevator girl said today, "Do you have one of them novel books? I don't like the murder kind." So I gave her my last, *Chéri*, by Colette, which I didn't feel in the mood for anyway. I hope *she* did.'

I remember, however, a restaurant, with excellent cheap oysters from the Gulf, served either in their shells or in oyster stews, and a waiter who took an enlightened view of the negro problem. Pointing to his head, he said, *sotto voce*, of his rulers: 'They've nothing up here. They don't accept that they have to change. The last will be coming first, what with time and education.'

The taxi-driver who drove me out to call on the protagonist of the segregationist Citizens' Council, spoke less liberally: 'As sure as the Lord made little green apples there'll be war and murder. I wouldn't mind declaring war on 'em. Send 'em back to Africa, I say.'

Reaching my destination, I found a Senator, a country gentleman as solemn as the Georgian Attorney-General and with the blank brown eyes of the Imperial Wizard, but a man even slower in his speech and with a soft Southern brogue. He confessed to me that he and his organization were having some trouble with the Radicals.

'They want to go for the Jews as well as the negroes,' he explained. 'But in my opinion, we need everyone with us, even the Jews. We've got to whip this thing.'

The negroes, he continued, were a people with no character, no morals and no brain-power. Their only qualities were physical. I asked him about their universities.

'One of the biggest rackets the negroes work,' he replied. 'If a negro Ph.D. was sittin' here, he'd be talkin' in English, just like you and me. But get him back among his own people, and all of a sudden he'll get mad at someone and act like an animal.'

That evening I went in search of a negro Ph.D. He asked me to call on him at his house near the negro 'university,' a training college for teachers. My taxi-driver was ignorant of the address

'We don't get much call,' he said, 'to go to these coloured neighbourhoods.'

With my host was another young Ph.D., and a friend, a professor, joined us later. They might have been a group of friendly young dons from Oxford or Cambridge. The Cellophane covers were stripped off the armchairs, glasses of Bourbon were poured out for all, and we talked easily and lightly of the negro problem. The heart of it, said one, was the vote, in a State composed in effect of a number of white 'rotten boroughs'. Every obstacle, including long questionnaires, was placed in the way of the semi-illiterate negro, trying to record his vote.

'All the negroes want,' he said, 'is to be good Americans. Give them their rights, and they'll vote just like any other American, regardless of colour. In Chicago they rather prefer white candidates.'

Here, as among those educated negroes of Atlanta, was more patience than anger, more humour than recrimination. It became an evening of jokes—Jim Crow jokes among them. In Alabama there is integration in the heavens alone. When they descend from their aircraft, Black and White separate, and go to wash off the grime of the journey through doors marked respectively 'Men. Women. Men Colored. Women Colored,' with one marked 'Janitor' keeping them apart. In the railroad stations it is the same. My host laughed reminiscently.

'The other day,' he said, 'a friend and I had to take an early train from Montgomery station. The Janitor wasn't on duty yet. The man at the desk was busy, issuing a ticket to my friend. Needing a wash, I took the opportunity to walk through the door marked Men—not the Colored one. It was the first time I had been inside one of these places. Frankly I was disappointed. I had expected something in the nature of silver cuspidors and golden stools. But it was rather a crummy sort of place, with shabby woodwork and a lot of plaster peeling off the walls. While I bought my ticket my friend went in. He thought the same about it as I did. And afterwards we had a good laugh together in the train.'

They spoke of the recent bus boycott. In the Montgomery buses Whites used to sit in front and Blacks behind. Then one day a black lady, a Mrs. Rosa Parks, refused to move back and give her seat to a white gentleman, because it meant she would have to stand.

'She was an ideal type to become a popular heroine,' said the

Ph.D. 'Attractive and quiet and a churchgoer, looking just like a symbol of Mother's Day.'

Three days later she appeared in court and was fined—and from that moment the negroes stayed off the buses. All day long they stood at street corners, laughing as the buses, all but empty, drove by. After an hour or so of this, my host told me, the Mayor of Montgomery got on the telephone to a prominent member of the negro community, demanding, 'Will you please stop your people laughing? The bus-drivers don't like it.' At which the negroes laughed all the more.

Now they were back on the buses, pleased to have gained their objective by legal and non-violent means.

*   *   *

Leaving Montgomery, I drove in succession, by bus, through three separate states—and in each segregation took a subtly different form. Through Alabama the negroes were confined, crowded together, to a few rows of seats at the back, while the Whites occupied the rest of the bus at their ease. Through Georgia it was the Blacks who sat at their ease, while the Whites were crowded into a few rows in front. Tactlessly, I motioned to a negro, who was standing, to sit beside me, about half way down. The driver immediately separated us, not sending him back but bringing me forward, and thus leaving him alone in comfort. Through North Carolina there was no segregation, Black and White, back and front, sitting together. We were approaching the civilization of the North.

Meanwhile, I had spent the night in Augusta, Georgia, a city whose streets and bars and cafés swarmed with troops. In the centre of it was a dignified classical monument, commemorating the Civil War and inscribed with the lines:

'No nation rose so white and fair
None fell so pure of crime.'

Following my usual practice, I chose the hotel nearest to the bus station. Its name was the Johnny J. To my surprise, the man in charge of it was a negro. To his surprise, I had a bag, which I asked him to carry upstairs for me. Mislaying the key he forced open the door of my room with a coat-hanger. It was a small room, unkempt and carpetless, with thin partitioned walls, and a hard, high double-bed, and tattered lace curtains, black with grime, covering part of a window which looked out on to a wall.

For amenities so spare it was expensive. Presently I understood why. Scrawled over the wall in an illiterate hand were the words, 'I want get girl but ten dollars is to much.'

Outside a trim little negress tripped down the corridor and knocked at an adjoining door. A white soldier opened it and admitted her. Here, without a doubt, was desegregation—of a kind.

◦ 13 ◦

Suburbia for the Millionaire · The New American Nights · Beyond the Greco-Roman Frontier · A Golden Calf in Banknotes · Evangelists of Success · Dream Homes · Uniforms of Mink · Luncheon among Blackamoors

BEFORE leaving New Orleans, I had a long-distance call from Harry. He had arrived in Denver, Colorado, and would meet me in Santa Fe a week hence. So I said goodbye to my host and took the bus into Texas—a country (no mere State) which, in the eyes of its inhabitants and in maps supplied to visitors, occupies all of the North American continent but a fraction set aside for the United States, Canada and Mexico. Texas has capitalized bombast as Aberdeen avarice. If all its steers were one, he could stand with his front feet in the Gulf of Mexico, his hind feet in Hudson Bay and his horns in the moon; if all its hogs were one he could dig the Panama Canal with three roots and a grunt. Its cotton crop would make a mattress on which all the world could lie at once; the juice of its tomatoes could float a battleship and leave enough for all America to drink to the health of Texan garlic (the strongest in the world). And now Texan farmers were complaining that when they drilled for water they kept striking oil—which the cattle couldn't drink.

Ahead of us stretched a flat flooded landscape of dead trees and oil derricks like small Eiffel Towers, with orange smoke rising in coils from the horizon. This was the frontier. A single Texan waggered on to the bus, wearing a ten-gallon hat. He was tipsy and he carried a mandolin. Instead of playing it, as he might well have done, he flung it up in the rack, and sat down beside me, though the rest of the bus was now almost empty. (Texans, I assumed, needed no such modest means of transport.) He proceeded, with some incoherence, to tell me of the technical processes involved in the extraction of oil from the Texan earth. We reached Houston at ten o'clock in the evening. In its all-but-empty bus station was a rocking horse, offering a ride for a dime in the slot. The streets seemed deserted. On the street corner newspapers, untended on an 'honor rack,' were selling themselves for a nickel. In the few bars which were open, only beer was available. I ate a dozen oysters and went to bed.

This emptiness, at night, of the cities of Texas reflected the trend to Suburbia which I had observed in the East, and which was to strike me more forcibly as I moved farther West. The richer the States, the emptier of life were their cities, the more lively their suburbs. The Mayor of Houston—a city, said its guide-book, of six hundred millionaires—looked forward, he told me, with pride to the day when its suburbs would spread for fifty miles in all directions, harbouring a population of some two million people. Already they were a millionaires' paradise, their one-storeyed houses, family size, standing discreetly Georgian, Spanish-American or Contemporary, with garage space for three cars (one for Pop, one for Mom, one for Junior, that he might drive himself to school), amid communal lawns, spreading down to a glossy black four-lane highway and a well-trimmed parkway beyond.

Such houses can cost as much as a million dollars to build, as I learnt later from an architect who was designing one. This was to include two garages—one for sporting and one for everyday cars—a trophy room, for heads of big game, forty thousand dollars' worth of central heating and air-conditioning, a twenty thousand-dollar kitchen, and fifteen outdoor barbecue grills. The pride of the house, I gathered, would be the kitchen. Lately the ladies of Dallas, anxious to raise money for their local symphony orchestra, had organized, in aid of it, not a garden tour, which is popular for such purposes, but a kitchen tour, on which it was possible, for three dollars, to visit a selection of the best kitchens around the city. Gone—or going—are the days when Texan millionaires lived permanently on their Wild Western ranches. Today, as a rule, they merely fly to them, on weekend or holiday trips.

I visited my first oil millionaire next day, in his office. He was dressed in white, with blue-glass spectacles and a yellow pleated silk shirt, and he sat at a streamlined desk, clear of papers, with television screen on the opposite wall. 'Do you drink?' was one of his first questions; and he seemed pleased by my affirmative answer. 'You must meet my squaw,' he went on, and that evening accompanied now by a Russian prince who had lately joined his staff, he drove me out in his air-conditioned Cadillac to his air-conditioned 'ranch-type' house, worth two hundred thousand dollars, where she received us cordially. We had a few drinks, and my flamboyant host soon grew as warm, and even affectionate, in his demeanour as an expansive child at a party. To him millions were clearly toys to be enjoyed.

The suburban way of life in America caters little for entertaining in the home (or indeed as a rule for putting up guests). So we drove along the road to the neighbouring River Oaks Country Club, a building conceived on a Hollywood scale, which costs its members an entrance fee equivalent to £1,200 and a subscription of ten guineas a month. Shining plate-glass windows, Texas-size, looked out on to a golf course. The lights, like stars on the ballroom ceiling, were reflected outwards in perspective far into the night, creating a looking-glass landscape which mirrored the rooms, converting trees into Christmas-trees and greens into starlit carpets. In other rooms, discreetly opulent, families fresh as though from the bandbox, their complexions, coiffures, clothes more immaculate than in the glossiest advertisement, proclaimed their togetherness. In decorous intimacy they talked and played, consuming Bourbon and malted milks and ice-cream, while High Fidelity music swelled softly and from an invisible source around them. Afterwards, that I might feel at home, we went to the Red Lion Inn, a 'tavern' run by an Englishman in a scarlet hunting waistcoat, done up in a Texan-Tudor style, and offering its patrons, on a Bill of Fare printed in Gothic lettering, such English refreshments as Bass, Guinness, Black & Tan, 'Alf and 'Alf, or a glass of home-made blackberry wine.

A few evenings later the party was repeated, when my new but now lifelong friend drove us down to Galveston, by the seaside. The car this time, the world's largest model, was his wife's. Unluckily it broke down (as cars do not in America) on the brand-new four-lane freeway (the world's fastest: forty miles in half an hour), its battery exhausted by an excess of air-conditioning and other electrical amenities. This was a situation unprecedented, moreover apparently insoluble, since who would build a garage on so short a stretch? Besides, nobody yet lived on this freeway. For half an hour we stood there, while two cars a minute drove contemptuously past us, and my host, with a child's petulance, berated his wife: if the car had been his, this would never have happened. She received this in patience, explaining to me only, with un-American understatement, 'He does get so worried.' Finally a vehicle, humbler than the rest, drew up, and a schoolmaster at its wheel gave us an undignified tow.

At Galveston we dined amid the Balinese décor of a casino, jutting into the khaki-coloured gulf, with the rocks around it painted in pastel shades. Here turkeys were cooking, impaled on flaming spears, and mammoth birthday cakes were borne to the tables lit with spluttering fireworks. But my Pasha-like host ordered T-bone, Jumbo-size steaks for us, each overlapping the edge of the plate. Afterwards we adjourned to the gambling rooms, where the stakes, at poker and craps and roulette, were unexpectedly modest. We drove back to Houston, the car now repaired, through a landscape lit by pillars of fire from the oil-fields.

*   *   *

Already I had been introduced to the mysteries of the oil world, first over a convivial luncheon at the Petroleum Club, a place decorated in the manner of a Chinese palace, and later in a yacht and then an aeroplane placed at my disposal by another friendly millionaire. He himself was away, but his chief executives—only one of whom was a Texan, the others being Yankees of German, Swedish, French and Italian ancestry—seemed to have little to do but entertain me, and this they did in hospitable style.

In the yacht we sailed down the Houston River, Texas-made and converting the city into one of America's largest ports, admiring the oilfields and refineries, the factories and mills and chemical plants now gracing its grassy banks and for the most part painted in a variety of gay colours. Our objective, where we lunched, was the tallest monument, an obelisk five hundred and seventy feet and five inches high, commemorating the Battle of San Jacinto in 1836, one of the world's most decisive, which under Sam Houston won Texas, to say nothing of large tracts of America, from Mexico.

In the aeroplane we flew down south in the heat, over a patchwork landscape, towards the Mexican frontier, landing at Corpus Christi. Here we lunched in a dark and ice-cool restaurant, decorated like the bottom of the sea. We were joined by a soft-spoken lazy-eyed Texan, with a puckered brown face, and by an expansive red-faced Yankee, of Irish origin, with whom we drove through fields of maize and cotton, as rich as those of Egypt but with oil pumps rising among them, until we reached the million-acre King Ranch, the largest in the world. Here the largest steers enjoy harems of cows, rounded up for them by the swiftest of horses, to make in due course the dearest of steaks. Mountainous in form and aloof in demeanour, broad in the brisket, full in the loins, deep in the flanks and long in the rump, with a low sagging dewlap and a trace of a hump on the back, they stood silkily and squarely before us—Brahmans crossed, through generations, with Herefords and Shorthorns to make the Santa Gertrudis breed. As buzzards and vultures wheeled overhead, a young man with an equally thoroughbred look, lean-limbed in yellow boots and a wideawake hat, showed them off to us, calling attention in passing to a few of the three hundred miles of tarmac roads and eighteen hundred miles of unbarbed fencing which spread away in every direction across this self-contained 'country' towards the Mexican frontier.

Driving back to the airfield at Corpus Christi, we stopped for a number of beers in a jovial bar in the village of Kingsville. Emerging, our soft-voiced Texan companion insisted on taking the wheel, drinking more beer as he drove, and promising us that he would cover fifteen miles in three minutes—a promise left, fortunately, unfulfilled. We gave a lift back in the aeroplane to the Vice-President of an insurance company who clutched, and periodically poured and drank from, a bottle of Bourbon.

'Call me Toughie,' he urged me, with childlike affection, and proceeded to talk, grasping my arm, in a language almost without consonants, hence hard to understand. I understood him nevertheless to be singing the praises of an English friend, the loveliest man in the world, a lovely Limey, with an equally lovely wife. He lived in Fort Worth, and I must at all costs stop over on my westward journey to see him.

From the airport he offered to drive me to the house where I was dining, and we set off in his wide green-and-white car, with white upholstery, weaving a little from side to side of the highway, jerking abruptly at traffic lights, and finally losing ourselves in our search for the house. We eventually reached it, an ultramodern building by a famous architect at which he looked with an air of bewilderment. Its outer walls were mostly of glass; there was a pond inside it, among tropical plants; the inner walls were hung with Picassos and Chiricos and Braques, and there was a Renoir above the bar. My hostess, a European, and the wife of a civilized Frenchman, poured out more Bourbon for him and listened sympathetically while he, in his turn, poured out, in a confiding and ingenuous flow, the story of the death from

sclerosis, a few months ago, of his much-loved adopted child.
Her own children, alert-eyed and solemn, stood around surveying
him with silent surprise, failing to respond when he rumpled their
hair and punched them playfully in the chest and went through
the motions of the ball-game. When he had gone, and she had
bidden him a sympathetic farewell, she turned to me and
remarked:

'We had a French friend who came here the other day. He
said, "*Ici, c'est la fin du monde Greco-Romain*".'

*   *   *

Certainly we had passed the frontier of Greek civilization. But
there was a certain neo-Roman splendour about some aspects of
Texas life. Next day I attended the gala opening of a vast new
bank, a skyscraper without windows, the Bank of the South-
west. 'Our family of some 500 friendly people joins me in
extending to you a warm welcome to our new banking house,'
the invitation ran.

From the great façade of polished porphyry, with its soaring
tower of silver and glass, only one adornment was missing—a
symbolic and monumental sculptural relief. Having paid the fee
for it (fifty thousand dollars) the directors had discovered, only
just in time, that the sculptor had Communist leanings. Beneath
this empty space twenty huge glass doors swung open into a
rotunda. Thence a ramp of swift and silent stairways moved up
into the great pillared Olympian precinct, rich with multi-
coloured marbles from all the world: Negro Marquina and Rose
Alhambra from Spain, American Imperial Black, White Georgia,
Tennessee Filetto Rosso. And here, 'painted by one of the truly
great artists of our century—perhaps all centuries' (a Mexican
better disposed, it seemed, to the capitalist system) was a mural,
Texas-size, symbolizing the abundance of America and the
melting—in the flesh less familiar—of the American and Indian
races.

Beneath it hostesses, hand-picked for their glamour and
groomed to perfection, received and guided guests and clients
with the welcoming smiles and caressing phrases of those well
versed in charm. To the soft strains of 'Music while you Bank,'
the longest line of tellers in Texas, behind glass, served their
material needs, together with smiling executives, seated in chairs
of scarlet and black at desks of the rarest inlaid woods, each
adorned with a vase or a golden urn of exotic tropical flowers.

A tropical plant was indeed given away to each housewife who opened an account, together with '1003 Household Hints and Worksavers' to help her beat the high cost of living.

Eager customers were shepherded by hostesses down the aisles and into the offices, gazing into the Trust Department, with the largest carpet in the United States; the Directors' Conference Room, built of creamed Italian marble, with lemon-yellow curtains and white kid sofas, and chairs upholstered in the softest white hand-woven wool. Its artificial windows were flooded with artificial daylight, its folding doors concealed a cinema screen, a pair of scales on its table weighed silvered pineapples and scarlet lilies against blackened grapes and white ones. We visited also the drive-in bank, where motorists could drive up to the first floor and cash cheques and make deposits without leaving the driving seat. But the main centre of pilgrimage was a tall glass case, placed in a position of honour and surrounded by a rail, with the citizens crowding around it in solemn, wide-eyed wonder. Within it was a tower, some ten feet high, composed of a million dollars in notes. Discreetly covering it was a machine gun, concealed in the ceiling.

*   *   *

FIDELITY, UNION, LIFE was the illuminated message which rode the sky as I entered the city of Dallas. It was the motto of a great insurance company housed in the newest skyscraper, close to another where in the daytime cars were parked up to the fifteenth storey. At night Dallas seemed even more dead than Houston. As in all parts of Texas there was nothing to drink in the bars but beer—served, however, in the bar opposite my hotel by ladies, slender as models, in Voguish slacks. But the liquor stores were open day and night, and there was one in the hotel lobby, enabling visitors, if they so desired—as many did—to drink all through the night, in their bedrooms.

Next evening a hospitable friend drove me around the suburbs of Dallas, showing off to me houses so air-conditioned that the women no longer wore summer frocks in them, but light mink stoles specially designed for indoor wear, while the men, coming in, shirt-sleeved, from the sun-heated air, would involuntarily reach for their coats. One lady said that she often lit a log-fire in her drawing-room in August. My guide showed off to me also, with far less enthusiasm, those suburbs, as trim to my eyes, and likewise with Cadillacs parked by their doors, on which, to his stern disapproval, the negroes had encroached and were encroaching further.

A member of an old Texan family, with the slow, soothing vowel-sounds of the South in his voice, he regretted the days, not so long ago, when quail could still be shot in these districts. Besides houses, he showed me churches as smartly new, including one which the Baptists were building for two million dollars. It was designed to hold three thousand worshippers but, in perhaps an unworldly spirit, no space had been provided to park their cars. Here the churches were rich, none richer than the Presbyterians of Houston, who had sold their church for a million dollars to the Five and Ten Cent Store, and were now building another. Godliness indeed seemed general. On the flyleaf of the telephone directory was a notice, 'Dial-a-Prayer. TE 2146. A prayer there 24 hours a day.'

I lunched with a man to whom I had received an introduction —a lunch somewhat at cross purposes, since he thought I was an oil expert and I thought he was. Half way through the meal I discovered that he was, in fact, a manufacturer of cooking utensils, and especially of a machine for grinding salads into shreds; and indeed he was wearing a sapphire-and-diamond tie-pin, designed to resemble a salad bowl. He took me to his office where, proudly displayed, was a ten-foot bear, which he had shot in the Rockies, and a six-foot shark, which he had caught in the Carribbean.

After luncheon I went to a convention of Alcoholics Anonymous, at a neighbouring hotel. 'Anonymous' was hardly the word since we were all given tickets, with our names and addresses to pin on to our breasts, and it was with embarrassment that I observed some of the delegates peering at mine with unabashed curiosity. They were a cheerful crowd, with eyes feverishly bright and an animation which gave them the air of being slightly drunk—from lack of alcohol. A panel of ten alcoholics, of both sexes, with a parson among them, each in turn recited a kind of confession: 'My name is . . . . and I am an alcoholic. I have not had a drink since November 18th, 1946 . . . I have been sober twenty-four hours a day since April 9th, 1952 . . . By the Grace of God I am sober today . . .' Each then proceeded to recount the circumstances of his conversion ('Before I sobered up in 1949,' began the parson), and to answer relevant questions put to the panel by the audience. It mistrusted psychiatrists ('the damnedest bunch of liars on the whole earth'), trusting rather religion ('God wants each one of us to be sober more than we want to be sober'), though one questioner protested, 'Lots of guys have attained their sobriety without any high-sounding talk about the spiritual angle.' Others stressed rather the community feeling: 'Attendance at meetings strengthened my feeling of belongingness.' Throughout the discussion, members were rising restlessly to go out for a cup of coffee, letting in waves of convivial, indeed almost deafening chatter from the buffet outside.

The Convention, whether of alcoholics or otherwise, is an important feature of American life—and this was the convention season. Wherever I now travelled whole hotels had been given over to this form of entertainment: conventions of air hostesses, of barbers, of Daughters of the American Revolution, of Young Judaca, of 'the Supreme Council of the Mystic Order, Veiled Prophets of the Enchanted Realm'. Later, in Denver, there was a convention of the Dale Carnegie Courses for making friends and influencing people, becoming more successful and happier, getting better jobs with bigger incomes; and this I attended, receiving an invitation from Mrs. Dale Carnegie in person to try one of the courses later on, in New York.

It was introduced by a smart young man with the breezy speech of a Billy Graham and the dexterous legwork of an Elvis Presley. Dancing, as it were, on his toes, with brisk springy steps up and down the aisle, turning the head of an assured *jeune premier* to left and to right, swinging his lines perceptibly, he wooed an audience of both sexes, bent on persuading them to invest a hundred and thirty five dollars in themselves, through Mr. Carnegie, and draw dividends for the rest of their lives: 'Now make yourself comfortable. Be among friends. I've a better idea—say "Hello!" to the person sitting next you'—and a few of the audience shyly did so.

They must uproot their inhibitions and shed their fears. 'Why didn't you get that promotion? You must get along better with people, develop more skill in communication, conduct yourself better in front of groups, get excited about things and show it, learn to think on your feet. Now, how many of you would like to make a little talk, here and now?'

He opened his arms wide and, as among the alcoholics—and indeed the converts of Mr. Graham—Carnegie graduates came up, one after another, to make their confessions: 'I wasn't pleasing to people,' admitted one. 'Fears kept creeping in.' But now a fearless success was his, as Assistant Campaign Director of the United Cerebral Palsy Association.

'I was more gloomy, more fearful than the Prince of Denmark,' confessed another. 'The world was out of joint. I blushed, I stammered, I shuffled my feet, I sneaked out of the door. And then like a bolt from the blue the truth came to me. There was something wrong right here.' He thumped, for some reason, his chest, and went on to relate just what it was.

'What makes these graduates run up and down this aisle?' queried the evangelist. 'It's that they want to move things. They better had.'

'Now I can get before anyone, tell anything I want to, and they'll believe it. . . . Now my husband and I have a deeper understanding with each other, a richer, fuller, happier life. . . . I've faced myself, and now I've a better chance of attracting and holding the kind of guy I'd like to have.'

The last word was with a Jap: 'I had difficulty in human relations,' he said in perfect American, 'in getting along with my boss. I read Confucius but he didn't work. Then I tried Carnegie. He's up-to-date, and he did work.'

'Now there's a success story,' the crooner crooned.

Back in New York, I was privileged to attend the first of ten sessions in a course for women. The sympathetic smart lady in charge of it explained: 'This is not a charm course. You can pick up the fundamentals of charm by reading the magazines.' She handed round the curriculum, inscribed with a quotation from *How to Help your Husband Get Ahead*, by Mrs. Dale Carnegie: 'Learn to love; respect and enjoy other people.' The lessons designed to this end included, 'How to remember names and faces; Human Relations; How to make introductions; How to get along with men; How to extend your horizons.'

For a start, by way of practice, the ladies were invited to come up to the platform and there to describe their homes and the homes they would like to have: 'I've a home with a patio and a barbecue pit in Albuquerque. I'd like a home with a man in it. . . . I'm a tree and a flower and a grass girl. I'd like to have a home with tranquillity. . . . My New York apartment reminds me of many happy years spent in English hospitals. . . . I've a colonial-type house in Westchester with a dear little girl and a sweet little boy. I couldn't hope for anything better. . . . I live in my mother's apartment, but it lacks a desk. I'd like a place where I could get things straightened out. Just one little room. I'd call it my junk room.' All spoke with fervent conviction and apparent self-confidence.

Then the lady, to my consternation, called upon me to describe my home and dream home. In some confusion I advanced to the platform and stammered out, rather breathlessly, a description of a small Early Victorian house in Paddington. 'I couldn't hope for anything better,' I murmured. I smiled awkwardly and, feeling shamefaced, returned to my seat.

But I was reassured when the lady rose and said: 'Well, you came here to overcome fear, and I'm very very proud of you all.'

*　　　*　　　*

Meanwhile, here I was in Dallas, Texas. On Sunday I went out to lunch in a house larger than the rest, moreover furnished with a distinguished collection of modern pictures. Frank Lloyd Wright had done an initial design for it, but as he insisted on a house without a roof a more conservative architect was employed in his place. By the swimming-pool, where we lunched, I was given a 'V.I.P. towel,' interwoven with golden thread. One of the guests, in a spirit of competition, invited me to visit *her* swimming-pool, on the banks of which was an ice-cream soda fountain. Another, introducing himself, said, 'I own three oil companies.' A third recounted how, at a recent baseball game, he had counted two hundred and fifty seven private aeroplanes. My host, Mr. Stanley Marcus, was the proprietor of the fabled fifty-and-hundred dollar department store of Neiman-Marcus, which has become part of the mythology of Texas. I visited it next day.

First I was shown a vitrine, containing a million dollars' worth of diamonds. At Christmas-time, as a front-window display, they had been hung around the neck of a tiger, with the addition of a ruby on his nose and a half million dollar solitaire between his eyes. (The tiger, it seems, was stuffed.) The jewels remained momentarily unsold but a small boy made an offer for the tiger. His letter read:

'Dear Mr. Neiman-Marcus,

How much is your Tiger? Not the diamonds. I am a tiger collector, not diamonds. I am seven and have 5 tigers. Not real. Just play. I love tigers, especially yours. Please send the letter —the how much it cost without the diamonds letter—right away. Also, can you charge it or do you have to pay right away. I have my garden money, so please send letter right away before I lose it.

Your Friend,
Jinky Robinson.'

He was sent a mounted tiger head from Mr. Marcus's big-game collection, and replied as follows:

'Dear Mr. Marcus,

Thank you so much for the wonderful tiger head. Its the best-est tiger or any thing I have ever had. You will be glad to know I am over the chicken pops. I mean I think you will be glad to know I am over the chicken pops. Least I would be glad to know if you were over the chicken pops. I have ten tigers but yours is biggest. Tigers can swim. Tigers hunt alone. Tigers are fierce!! You are very nice. Someday I will send you something.

Your Friend,
Jinky Robinson.'

Texans, window-shoppers in the literal sense, like to save themselves trouble by buying whole window displays outright. One, sentimentally inclined, fell in love with a child wax model, and week after week bought all the clothes off her back to give to a favourite grand-daughter, exactly her size. Another bought a mink coat, as a Christmas present for his wife. Anxious to present it in style, he had an entire display window reproduced in his own house, exact in detail, with a wax mannequin in the centre, posed in the priceless coat.

Mink, I was soon to discover as I went round the store, is the basic uniform of the Texan Pasha's lady—mink coats up to the equivalent of £15,000 apiece, mink stoles for a mere £1,000; a wardrobe of maybe twenty-five pieces of mink, for all Texan occasions. Devotedly, throughout the length and breadth of America, these little animals are reproducing their species to gratify her, in an ever-changing variety of colours from brown to black and white to silver, from Cerulean to Sapphire, Pastel to Palomino, Desert Sand to Autumn Haze. Less prolifically, alas, a rare Peruvian llama is doing the same, that the soft wool of its underbelly may provide her, and her Pasha, with an annual vicuna coat, downier than cashmere or camel-hair.

Thanks to oil and gas and cotton and cattle and Neiman-Marcus, the Pasha's lady may deck herself out in £1,000 brocaded gowns, £100 hats glittering with semi-precious stones, glass slippers at £30 the pair. She may sleep beneath mohair blankets at £25 each, eat off an embroidered set of table mats at £120, carry a £1,500 white-calf handbag, travel with £1,500 worth of alligator luggage, ice the drinks of her friends from a leather bucket on wheels costing £125, supply her pet lion with an electric comforter, and collect charitable donations from fellow-millionairesses in a golden pomegranate, studded with semi-precious stones.

She dresses her Pasha meanwhile in silks and satins; smooth silken jackets for the evenings, with satin facings and satin cummerbunds, 'bosom-fronted' shirts pleated and embroidered and ruffled from the finest lawns and Sea Island voiles; jackets of rough tweeded silk for the golf course, leisure coats of many colours, and a 24-carat gold neck-tie, hand-loomed from the thread of gold and scarlet silk in the Indies. For their homely suburban family Christmas there may be 'a gigantic brandy snifter containing several gallons of frothy lingerie, cashmere sweaters and jewelled blouses,' or a 'Christmas cocktail constructed out of a huge champagne glass holding a £10,000 mutation mink coat frosted with a necklace or two and a bottle of perfume.'

And so it goes on. An old-time banker remarked to me sceptically that his pile of bad cheques had lately risen from half an inch to three inches. But Texas laughs at such conservative doubts.

*   *   *

The banker drove me to Fort Worth, the neighbouring city of a hundred and twenty millionaires, where I spent the night in a hotel as the guest of the 'lovely Limey' of whom my acquaintance 'Toughie' had spoken with such warmth. He soon came up to my room to greet me, bringing a bottle of Scotch whisky and calling for a bucket of ice. Fortunately a local reporter arrived a few minutes later, to interview me, and helped to polish it off. My host talked still with an English accent, but in an American idiom. He liked America, but much of its life, he considered, was make-believe. As for the language, he commented:

'Well, do you elevate your hat in a lift or lift your hat in an elevator?'

He took me off to a night-club for dinner, producing the key of his private locker, from which the waiter extracted another bottle of whisky. The emptying of this created a convivial atmosphere, in which my host positively refused to allow me to leave early in the morning, as I had calculated I must, in order to keep my rendezvous with Harry at Santa Fe. I must at all costs stay until after luncheon, and he would arrange some means of getting me to Santa Fe, whether by road or by air. I could count on him.

Next morning I visited him in his office, where I was effusively greeted by a high-powered female secretary. She had never met an English writer, she said, but she had read the works of one, which had made her think; his name was Nevil Shute.

'When they hear her voice,' her employer remarked concerning her, 'my friends think they've been bitten by a mosquito.'

His office was hung with framed certificates of membership of the various groups to which he belonged (and to which it was socially and commercially necessary to belong) here in Fort Worth: the Ancient Arabic Order of the Nobles of the Mystic Shrine, the Rotary International, the Business Forum, the Lions' Club, the Kiwanis, the Knights of Columbus. He was also, it seemed from an especially flowery certificate, an Admiral in the Texan Navy.

He took me to call on a friend of his, in another office, embarking on a discussion with him as to whether a deep freeze was really necessary in the house, and at what temperature it should be kept.

'Grace says 92°.'

'Betty says 80°.'

'D'you know how much coke my two kids drank from the freeze last month?'

'How much?'

'Five hundred and twenty-seven bottles.'

Some concern was expressed by both at the report that it was intended to ban cars, to relieve traffic congestion, in the centre of Fort Worth, a measure which would oblige them to walk some hundreds of yards from their offices to the City Club. We now drove there for luncheon in the Blackamoor Room, where real blackamoors waited upon us, without apparent embarrassment, amid baroque effigies, gilded and stylized, of their eighteenth-century forbears.

After luncheon my host dropped me back at my hotel and said goodbye. He was leaving for Oklahoma City that afternoon. There was no further mention of the promised transport to Santa Fe, which was indeed some five hundred miles away as the crow flew. Fortunately I was just in time to catch a bus which took me as far as Lubbock. Here I spent the night in the Lubbock Hotel, diverting myself next morning by sending post cards of it, with appropriate comments, to a number of friends at home whose name was Lubbock.

To Constance I wrote a letter:

'It's all rather like one huge children's party. Endless fun and games and expensive presents for all. They love their toys, a children do. They love showing them off to each other and to the grown-up visitor—their cars and their gadgets and their TV sets and their refrigerators and all the other machines. They love their games. In every house there's a playroom, called a rumpus room, where Pop and Junior play together and are allowed to make all the mess they like. But the real games are outside—building bridges and striking oil and making millions, all of which they do with enormous gusto.

'They love you, too, as children do—for the moment. They've forgotten you next day—and you've forgotten them. And they're extrovert children. For every mixed-up introvert —and they're mostly in New York, which is a hybrid city— there must be nine hundred and ninety nine perfectly good Americans who are perfectly content with their material blessings and never think of going near a psychiatrist. They've a great sense of enjoyment and good animal spirits. They're often boring, of course, just as children are boring. They've not much idea of conversation, apart from telling you about their own affairs—often confidingly. A woman I sat next to at lunch started straight off by telling me she had cancer; her doctor had diagnosed it last week. They like information and instruction— lecturing and being lectured to. At one rather sticky party I tried to get a conversation going by producing an idea out of a hat—the idea that the Americans are more Conservative than the British, I think it was. I threw out a few observations and then there was a short pause and somebody said, "Well, it's very interesting to hear you talk"—and that was the end of that. Just as though I had given a little lecture, and I suppose I had. Like children, they want to learn, and this is refreshing. All this adds up to a quality of innocence, which is endearing. I wonder if all the West will be like this.'

WEST

14

*Into New Mexico · A Cock to St. Peter · Little Lurking
Buffalo · The Art of Santos · Mortifying the Flesh*

THE West properly begins half way across Texas. Wide open spaces now lay ahead of me. But they were to afford little solitude. This was the holiday season, and as I emerged from Texas on to the main westward highways, I seemed to enter a world made exclusively for the car. I joined henceforward in an endless procession of these stream-lined wonders, insulating American families behind glass and enamel in their soft, deep upholstery. For America is a nation on wheels: the car is the national pet.

Love and understanding are lavished upon her, more perhaps than on a mere human being, during her all-too-brief spell of life. Hers is the Body Beautiful, dotingly admired and caressed and primed and preened and pampered. 'Sculptured in steel and shimmering color with crisp flowing lines,' endowed with 'a beautiful opalescent pearl body . . . that assumes the color and the light playing on it,' the loved one has a 'great, deep-breathing engine' and a 'live, lithe luxurious action'. The 'deep hush' of her interior may be 'smartly different,' with upholstery of unborn calf.

Fifty-eight million of these pets were now conveying a happy three-quarters of America's families hither and thither at will. ('The more you drive, the less it costs.') Often, on holiday bent, they drew satellites behind them—speedboats on wheels or gleaming trailers. Some of the millions indeed, such is the instinct for wheels, seemed to live permanently in these trailers, often in 'mobile home parks,' ready to be up when the fancy took them. Even houses may be moved, without too much difficulty, on wheels. I was once held up on the road by a frame-house changing its site in this way; while in Los Angeles, on a recent occasion, one of these broke loose, careering down a steep hill and obliging a motorist to claim damages because his car had been run into by a house.

In the design of the cars there was already a certain confusion of elements, as I had seen in a motor show in New York: there were corvettes and clippers, streamlined and tapering like ocean cruisers; the Astra-Gnome, with a silver aluminium body and a Plexiglass dome covering a cockpit like an aeroplane's, and such astral-sounding amenities as a celestial clock and an automatic planetary gear set.

Americans like sometimes to torment themselves with the thought: What if one day, suddenly, all these automobiles were to vanish? Ten million Americans would be out of work, twenty-five thousand American cities would be cut off from the world, and millions of American families from their supermarkets; half the schools would be empty, the pace of work would slow down by half, and there would be little to do but roller-skate over the disused parking-lots. An American nightmare—which might, for a few, prove an American millennium.

As it is, each car must die, since man kills the things he loves. There is no pet like a new pet, so after a year or so it is off with the old, for a few hundred dollars. And who wants a used pet, save perhaps for a year or two more? Around these American cities stretched acres of land, wide open graveyards strewn with thousands upon thousands of unburied vehicles—abandoned Loved Ones, some still looking bravely, uprightly new, others gaping obscenely on their backs, rusting away into scrap-iron. 'Federal Auto Wrecking,' the notice read; and men browsed among the remains like vultures, picking here and there a choice bit from the entrails. Soon, doubtless, with the march of progress, they would be joined by superannuated gas-cookers, refrigerators, television sets, washing-machines, slowly and steadily encroaching on the wide but not unlimited open spaces. Only another war, it seemed, could absorb or destroy the Forgotten Machine, as the Forgotten Man.

Meanwhile here they all were, these glittering painted things, bowling westwards on their springy, unburstable tyres, and I, on the more cumbersome wheels of my Greyhound bus, among them. Cities, one after the other, competed, with hoardings and figures inscribed on them, for the number of their victims: 'Auto Fatalities. July. Last year 50. This year 71.' In one city the killer itself was exhibited, battered but unbowed, like a human in the stocks, in the public square, before an awestruck populace. Familiar now, on the outskirts of a town, was the drive-in-movie, where a film might be seen—or not seen—in the balmy night air without moving from the car. These were especially popular, not always only for the sake of the film, among teenage couples. Similarly I had noticed the drive-in supermarket, the drive-in liquor-store, the drive-in church, the drive-in Post Office, and the drive-in cafeteria, with a plugged-in telephone to call up the waitress. One Californian even designed a drive-in home for himself and his car, the garage built into it like a living-room.

Across these wide open spaces I drove through towns which seemed to have no identity except in relation to the car: places consisting of little but garages, parking lots, gas-stations, car marts, used car marts, motels and perhaps a liquor-store for the master. Strung out between them were establishments by the thousand, existing only to serve the car, to feed her and doctor her, bath, spray and shampoo her. Garage hands handed out Wheelburgers and Hubburgers, or perfumed her with the gift of a Car Cutie ('A pin-up with a purpose. Freshens the air in your car'). For a two-dollar gas purchase her masters were lured with such competitive sops as a pepper-shaker, a kite, a ball-point retractable pen, or the chance of a Californian dream house.

Meanwhile, 'Welcome to New Mexico, the Land of Enchantment.' The bar at frontier was El Corral; its Hamburgers were Mexican Burgers, served with a hot chili sauce. There was something Spanish in every eye, moreover an agreeably listless tempo. We drove on across a broad yellow prairie, with a violet ridge on the skyline and a suggestion of mountains beyond it. As we drew closer they materialized beneath a bank of indigo cloud, the evening sunlight seeping down through it in white liquid rays. They were the first mountains, the first 'scenery' indeed that I had seen since leaving Virginia, two thousand miles back.

Harry arrived an hour after I did, on the bus from Denver, where he had left the car with John and his friend, Ken Elmslie. He looked robust, well tanned by the Western sunshine. We had something to eat, while he told me of his long monotonous drive out from New York—a monotony broken only by a fine of fifteen dollars for speeding somewhere in Indiana, which had left him short of funds. He was impressed and a little over-awed by the size of his own continent, having never come West before. After a few days in the Y.M.C.A. in Colorado Springs, sketching the mountain scenery around, he had met John in Denver and had left him absorbed in rehearsals for his ballad opera, *The Ballad of Baby Doe*, which was to open in ten days' time at the festival of Central City.

After dinner we went out, seeking life in Santa Fe. But to his astonishment there was none. In daylight, too, it disappointed us. A single square and a few streets, self-consciously flaunting the native adobe style of mud construction, it was a city for the

tourist—'the City Different'. There was a museum, showing
Indian and Mexican folk art; there were shops, selling souvenirs
and Indian bric-a-brac—fetishes, head-dresses, drums, beads,
blankets—shops run by artistic ladies, and one by an artistic
gentleman from New York, wearing a silver belt around his
jeans, silver bracelets on his wrists, a turquoise amulet above one
of his moccasins, and about his person a few becoming turquoise
brooches. There was a shop called Qui Na Ma Articrafts and, in
its courtyard, a restaurant where another such gentleman, in a
tartan apron, served well-cooked Mexican dishes. There was an
adobe gas station, adorned with stags' antlers. There was also a
Drive Ur Self car-hire place. So at the first opportunity we drove
ourselves away into the surrounding desert.

For Harry it was the first sight of a desert; for me a wistful
reminder of Eastern deserts, long familiar. Rejoicing in its space
and its dryness and its golden-pink lights, we crossed the muddy
Rio Grande, and sought the shade of some poplars, picnicking
with a bottle of red Californian wine by the banks of an irriga-
tion canal, which ran cold and clear and brown. After a siesta
we drove on through dry silvery brush to the Indian village of
San Domingo—like any Arab village with its haphazard mud
houses, its thick, indeterminate smells, its wandering, dusty, un-
paved streets. Here, we had heard, there was to be a fiesta, for
it was St. Peter's Day. The village at first seemed deserted; but
sure enough, on a flat stretch of desert beyond it, we found its
people assembled. Sallow and chink-eyed and corpulent, the
Indians squatted along the bank of a ditch, in the ample shade of
a tree fit for worship, flaunting bright, barbaric colours, and pig-
tails threaded with beads and shells. Besides ourselves, only two
other car-loads had come from the city to watch.

Before us was a rough clean whitewashed church, and within
it, as an offering before the altar, a loaf of bread, and a live skinny
cockerel, with its legs trussed. In the arena there was soon a
mustering and a milling of horsemen, all brightly shirted and
jockeying for position by the wall of the church. Presently another
live cock was flung into the mêlée, and they stampeded to snatch
it one from the other, hooves pounding and dust flying as they
tore at it, limb from limb. Eventually, one horseman grabbed
the lion's share of the cock and galloped away with his trophy
across the desert and through the streets of the village, closely
pursued by the field in trailing clouds of sand.

Several times the sacrifice—to St. Peter ? to Aesculapius ?—was repeated. Then a final cock was tied by its legs to a tightrope, between two tall poles, and the horsemen cantered beneath it, leaping up to reach it, one by one. Inch by inch, crowing and somersaulting in a macabre dance of death, the bird was lowered until it came within reach. First a wing was torn off it, then a horseman with a last great leap grabbed the rest of it, galloping off with it into the desert as before.

At that moment we heard the sound of a melodious siren, and a silvery train, from another world, sped by on the Santa Fe track, all sleek and shining and streamlined. Antiseptic and humane in their roomettes and drawing-rooms, the passengers turned a blind eye to the happy birthday of St. Peter.

Having little inclination to remain in Santa Fe, we took the bus next day up through a leafy valley, between mountainsides speckled with juniper, to Taos. The bus-driver was communicative. 'Here on the right, folks,' he said, 'is the ranch at which Eddie Anderson spent a vacation, shooting elk, two years ago. He will be familiar to you all as the talented TV artist in the Jack Benny show. . . . This is Taos, folks, one of the largest art colonies in the world. It contains sixty-five resident artists and fifteen art galleries.' All sixty-five of them, from Arello and Berminghaus to van Vechten and Waters, were listed alphabetically in the guide-book, including seven poets (one the lady Poet Laureate of New Mexico), eleven writers (one of mystery novels), a ceramist in masks, a designer of peasant dishes, a designer of Spanish colonial furniture, and a luminous painter on glass. A whimsical map showed their residences, including that of 'Tony & Mabel'— Mrs. Mabel Dodge Luhan, a lady writer who 'willed' D. H. Lawrence to come to Taos, and is married to an Indian gentleman.

The town was smaller, and in its arty-craftiness more concentrated than Santa Fe, boasting an adobe supermarket, an adobe ten-cent store, and an adobe bus station, art gallery and hotel combined, in which we stayed. In the afternoon we walked out of it along the road to the Indian *pueblo*, described as 'the oldest apartment house in the world.' Numerous cars, driven by tourists, drove past us; then a turquoise-blue station wagon drew up beside us, and its driver offered us a lift. He was an Indian from Albuquerque, plump and prosperous, on his way to the *pueblo*, where he was vacationing in his family home. He had fought in the war, and had married an English girl—but she did not care for *pueblo* life, and had gone home. This was not entirely surprising.

The *pueblo*, baked by the sunlight, with the bare mountains rising behind it, was certainly old: a hive of mud-built, flat-roofed houses, piled haphazardly one on top of another, like some confused organic product of the earth. Cleaned up though it had been for tourists, it was primitive still, and there were parts of it which they were not permitted to visit. Nor might they photograph or draw the Indians, except on payment of a statutory fee. Harry put his sketch-book away. In the town, standing around on the street corners in all their finery of feathers and beads, they were ready to be photographed for nothing. But beside one of them a notice read, 'If tipped, the Indian will dance.'

In the evening we strolled out to the Stagecoach Park on the Santa Fe Trail, where there was a performance of dances. Children from the motels clambered precariously about on a property stagecoach, while in the arena, to the flash of cameras and the wail of a microphone, the Indians stomped and twirled for a minute or so each. Here, announced one after the other, were Ben Marcus ('You'll often have seen his picture in the magazines'), in a 'nice fast war dance'; Little White Parrot ('He has often danced on the TV') coming 'from the Blue Lake singing' to do a hoop dance; the even littler Lurking Buffalo ('There is something very beautiful about the innocence of children') showing a precocious mastery of the steps which would be needed to make him a star of the studios.

It was Saturday night, and in the bars of Taos was a hybrid assembly of cowboys, Mexicans and Indians, loping unsteadily about to the Spanish twang of a juke-box. At a table sat a character from a Western film, wearing a Stetson hat with a bandana around it, and sharing a bottle of whisky with an Indian, weather-beaten and wrinkled and pigtailed, of considerable age but indeterminate sex. Alcoholically amorous, they drank blearily to each other, then, arms twined around necks, staggered precariously out into the night.

*   *   *

We decided to hurry northwards, into the lustier atmosphere of Colorado. Here the road led us up among Alpine pastures grazed by cattle, and grey-capped mountains thrusting out fortress walls of limestone. This was the beginning of the Rockies. The crags of Pike's Peak pencilled the horizon to the west of us—goal of the '59 Gold Rush, when 'Pike's Peak or Bust' had been the slogan scrawled over the hoods of the covered wagons. Colorado Springs emerged beneath it, a mountain city with broad clean streets and a Germanic air about its architecture. We had to hurry to get a drink before the bars shut at eight o'clock, as they do at weekends in the State of Colorado.

Next day we visited the well-built modern Museum of the Fine Arts Centre; and here for the first time I became fully aware of a form of Christian art unique in the States, of which Harry had spoken with enthusiasm. It was that of the Santos, the wooden carvings of the Spanish colonists from Mexico of the eighteenth and early nineteenth centuries. In Santa Fe we had seen a few of them, not shown to the public but locked away in a store in the museum basement. But here they were all around us, shown off with pride and imagination and taste—Christ and the Virgin and a hierarchy of Saints, moving to see in their curious blend of sophistication and naïveté, their creative invention and simple religious feeling.

The *conquistadores* came here to New Mexico—then embracing Colorado—with the sword in one hand and the Cross in the other. The priest as much as the soldier, usually a Franciscan Father, was the dominant figure among them; the Church, as much as the family, was the focus of their lives—lives fraught with hardship in the struggle to extract a living from an unyielding, alien soil. The churches themselves were primitive adobe structures, with ceilings of pine beams and saplings and willow branches, bound by mud. New Mexico, moreover, was so remote from the main stream of Spanish-American, to say nothing of European, civilization that the colonists had to rely on themselves, expecting nothing but levies and taxes from the central government in Mexico, and obliged to make, from local materials, their own weapons, tools, furniture and clothes.

They were obliged to make also the ornaments for their churches, and it was thus that the art of the New Mexican Santos came into being. These were images of Saints, derived from the Spanish word *Santo*, and were the work of *santeros*, makers of images. Their craft developed especially from about 1750 onwards, when communication with the outside world was increasingly interrupted by hostile Indians, and at times ceased altogether. The *santeros* were sometimes local villagers, sometimes (as in the New England colonies of the East) travelling craftsmen. They worked in the soft woods of the country—pine and cottonwood—and a form of *gesso*. Having no paints, they used the local vegetable dyes, brilliant and pure in colour—yellow from sage, brown from nuts, red from the cochineal insects which fed on the cacti of the New Mexican deserts. As a rule—and especially after the missions were obliged to withdraw, leaving the Christian communities to themselves—Santos were made without the supervision of priests. Sometimes indeed they were commissioned not for churches but for family homes. Hence perhaps their freedom of expression, unfamiliar in the more stylized Christian folk art.

Various observances were centred upon the Santos. The most dramatic were those of the Penitentes, who brought out their figures of the bleeding Christ each year for the elaborate ritual of the Passion. They were a secret Catholic Order of a primitive and austere character, who did much to keep the Catholic Church alive during the period when the missions had all but withdrawn. Worshipping in small windowless chapels of their own, they practised flagellation and other extreme forms of penance, designed to exorcise the spirit of sin and, less consciously perhaps, to achieve release from the hardships and frustrations of their mundane lives. By drawing their own blood, they sought to identify themselves with the Christ who had died for them in the flesh, attaining through ecstasy to a sense of spiritual liberation and fulfilment.

During Holy Week they marched in procession up to a hill they called Calvary, bent beneath the weight of heavy, ten-foot Crosses, and pausing on the way by piles of stones which marked the Stations of the Cross. As they walked they whipped their bare flesh with cactus plants, bound into balls, chanting and playing weird airs on the flute as they did so. With them went a realistic life-size figure of Christ, which was hoisted on to the Cross. Sometimes a living member of the Order played the part of the crucified Christ, bound to the Cross with ropes. But this, together with other such extreme manifestations of penance, was eventually prohibited by an order from the Pope.

The ceremonies, however, together with the all-night 'wakes' which follow them, still continue. The courts deal with cases of bloodshed which attend them, and flecks of blood may still be seen on the walls of the Penitente chapels. D. H. Lawrence, when he lived in Taos, was so horrified by their rites that he slept indoors with his windows closed, in order to shut himself off from the noise of the processions. But when they were over, he would himself walk reflectively up the road which led to 'Calvary.'

Realism was the quality inherent in the figures which now

surrounded us, realism to the point sometimes of crudity, but always compelling. Here was an effigy of Christ lying in the bier in which the Penitentes carried Him. A human being in evident agony, with a spear wound in the right side, another wound in the left cheek, inflicted by the mockers, and blood dripping from beneath the Crown of Thorns, the figure was so jointed as to move arms, legs and head, its jaw being so manipulated as to appear to utter the seven last words on the Cross. Here was another, mournful and dignified in a Spanish beard and a long red robe provided by the women of the village. He had eyes of mica, with realistic tears, and human hair, designed to emphasize his human aspect. The impact of his figure was essentially dramatic, helping to bring home the story of the Passion to these unlettered people in vivid, realistic terms. Sometimes human finger-nails were used, relics perhaps of a more pagan fetishist past, while the robes would be held to have magic properties of their own.

Most moving of all was the Christ Child lost in the temple. Childlike still, yet already with a solemn remote look, as though aware of his future destiny, the lost boy Christ is a favourite figure in New Mexican iconography. Often, prophetically, the wounds of the Crucifixion are portrayed on the feet, while here he held up a right hand which may have held a T-square, or a carpenter's tool, representing the Cross in shape or in shadow. The figure of Christ, and that of the Virgin, were often elongated out of respect to their place in the hierarchy, almost to the point of distortion, and their eyes were disproportionately enlarged as in some portrait by an expressionist painter. The Virgin Mary, Spanish features and dress, sometimes stood upon a half moon as in the paintings of Murillo. Many of the effigies resembled portraits of contemporary Spaniards, men and women both dressed in the bright, elegant costumes familiar in Spanish painting. Often, despite their primitive workmanship, they recalled, in their dignity and grace, Minoan, or Etruscan, or Tanagra figures, or the eighteenth-century glass figures of Verre de Nevers.

Here was St. Isidore, a Spanish gentleman in a smart Cordova hat; St. Michael, sword in hand, triumphing over a realistic dragon; St. Jerome with his lion; St. Barbara with her tower; Job, his body covered with sores like the broad arrows of a convict. But the most macabre figure of all was that of Death, with which the Spanish-American cult was much obsessed. Here he was a skeleton, armed with destructive bow and arrow and seated in a cart, with fixed wheels, which was drawn, loaded with rocks, through the streets on Good Friday. The penitents were harnessed to it with rawhide thongs and chains, cutting into their flesh.

Here was genuine folk art, European in inspiration but with a flavour of its own—art on a different plane from the Indian arts-and-crafts around us.

∽ 15 ∽

NEXT day we took the bus on to Denver. The 'Mile High City' (from the sea, not the ground), it is the 'capital' of the Rockies—the terminus, a century ago, of the Colorado Gold Rush. In those pioneer days it was a rough shack settlement, where it was usual enough to see a man being hanged in the public square, after a trial by the citizens, for murdering his mate with an axe. One of its more notorious characters was 'Old Phil the Cannibal,' who used to boast that, during the long trek westwards across the water-less plains, he had in an emergency eaten two Indians and a Frenchman. Upon being asked about the taste of human flesh, he answered that the head, hands, and feet, when thoroughly cooked, tasted not unlike pork. But the other parts of the body he disliked: they were gristly and tough.

Today it is a clean and thriving city, where a prosperous nineteenth-century past blends, architecturally, with as pros-perous a skyscraping present. Looking back to the great age of silver and gold, it looks forward perhaps to an age of uranium, its shops selling Geiger counters, as an alternative to fishing rods, for a weekend in the mountains. It is a city moreover whose wealthy inhabitants, descendants of pioneers, living in villas designed in an extravaganza of Edwardian styles, have a strong civic sense, and take a pride in being patrons of the arts.

Here John welcomed us expansively. With him was Ken, a reserved young man with a quiet wit, sensitive perceptions and a promising talent, who sought to follow in his footsteps as a writer for the musical stage. In the morning they drove us up into the mountains to Central City, where *The Ballad of Baby Doe* was in rehearsal. The sun was hot but the air was invigorating and cool, and we drove with the hood down, talking and laughing with exuberance as we wound up through a canyon, between steep slopes of spruce forest and crags speckled with juniper, by the banks of a clear running stream. Presently notices appeared beside it. 'Pan for Gold. See Gold Recovered.' 'Operate an Ore Crusher,' read an invitation on the cliff face. 'Visit the Bobtail Tunnel, with its 37 miles of Underground Workings.' Thus we turned into Central City, a 'ghost town' from the boom days, now rescued from dereliction, as a curiosity of the period, for the benefit of tourists.

Here, for a few shillings, they may buy nuggets of gold ore, together with such treasures as rose quartz, pitchblende, pyrites and uranium ore, and even a ticket in a raffle for a disused gold mine, while the gas station offers a nugget free to the motorist ready to buy its gas. 'Tour Mining Area. Visit Ghost Towns. Scan Breath-taking Vistas,' invites a line of red jeeps, driven by top-hatted, top-booted, frock-coated youths in 'Prospector' ties, like bootlaces.

The saloons where the pioneers caroused—the Grubstake Inn, the Glory Hole—have reopened their doors to the tourists, revealing interiors refurbished with Victorian mirrors and gasoliers and mahogany and marble bars. One is disguised as a mine, complete with pit-props and sacking. In another, behind 'the only original swinging doors in the county,' tinkles an ancient mechanical piano. The Glory Hole is dedicated to Diamond Lil, with candles in bottles on the tables and a Can-Can dancer, 'bottoms up,' on the ceiling. The shops on Eureka Street abound with the Victoriana of the West—kerosene lamps, old pharmaceutical bottles, reproductions of old-fashioned trivets. The visitor may be photographed astride a stuffed bucking bronco or, on a Victorian tin-type, in 'the authentic costume of the Gold Rush era—a token of Bygone Days.'

The Chain o' Mines Hotel, its chimneypiece fashioned not merely from silver and gold but from all Colorado's minerals; the Teller House, whose pavement was once paved with bricks for the visit of President Grant, do a roaring trade once more. The Teller, all plush and lace curtains, boasts a mirror backed with diamond dust, and in its bar-room the famous 'Face on the Floor,' painted there by a stranger crossed in love, and recorded by the author of *The Shooting of Dan McGrew*:

'Another drink, and with chalk in hand, the vagabond began
To sketch a face that might well buy the soul of any man;

Then, as he placed another lock upon the shapely head,
With a fearful shriek he leaped and fell across the picture—
dead.'

In the window of a neighbouring café was a notice, 'She ate
her burghers here.' It referred to Baby Doe, the heroine of the
opera we had come to see. For the focus of Central City is its
Opera House, a small theatre of character, with Victorian décor.
It was built in the 'seventies and restored by the rich families of
Denver in the nineteen-thirties. In a laudable effort to keep alive
the cultural traditions of the West, they devoted it to annual
festivals of opera and drama. The opening performance was of
Dumas' *Camille*, featuring Lillian Gish. Since then its productions
had ranged from *Diamond Lil*, featuring Mae West, to Mozart,
Verdi, Beethoven and Gilbert and Sullivan. Now in celebration
of the festival's twenty-fifth anniversary, *The Ballad of Baby Doe*,
for which John had written the words and Douglas Moore, a
distinguished New England composer, the music, was to have its
world première here in Central City, following a performance of
La Tosca.

'It's sure to go,' said John (whom a confused lady had addressed
as John La Tosca). 'It's about love and it's about money, and
there's no combination an American audience like more.'

Baby Doe was a young Irish belle, 'a blue-eyed darling,' from
Oshkosh, Wisconsin, who came, as the wife of a miner, first to
Central City and thence, after divorcing him, to Leadville, a
neighbouring 'boom town.' (Here Oscar Wilde had once lectured
to an audience of miners on 'Aesthetic Theory of Exterior and
Interior Decoration, with Observations on Dress and Personal
Adornment,' and, despite his flamboyant manner, long hair to
his shoulders, and black velvet costume with a cluster of diamonds
on his snow-white shirt-front, was voted by the miners a 'Prince
of good fellows,' with 'no piousness in his nature'). Here, in a
saloon opposite the Opera House, she met Horace Tabor, who
had built it—'the finest theatre west of the Mississippi . . . under
the full flood of gaslight, the cosiest place for lovers of the legiti-
mate drama to throw off the cares of life and yield to the fascina-
tions of music and imagery.' One of the early pioneers of the
region, he had, after twenty years of ill-luck in his prospection for
gold, suddenly struck a rich vein of silver, and had become over-
night one of the richest men in America. He fell in love at first
sight with Baby Doe, abandoned his stern middle-aged New

England wife, Augusta, causing considerable scandal, and married the young colleen in a lavish ceremony in Washington, where he had established a legend for himself as the 'Wild Western Senator'. The President himself, Chester Arthur, attended the ceremony.

Contemptuous of the scandal, Tabor took his bride back to live with him in Denver, where she reigned in splendour in Augusta's place. A man with a taste for display, he had kept, in Leadville, a private army of Highland Guards, wearing Royal Stuart kilts with goats'-hair sporrans. Now he bought and embellished a large Italianate villa, its gardens decked with Greek statuary and en-livened with a hundred strutting peacocks, while Baby Doe drove through the city in a carriage enamelled in black and pale blue and upholstered in azure satin, with two negroes in scarlet liveries on the box. Discomfiting the gossips, she proved a good wife to him, and bore him two girls, known respectively as Golden Eagle and Silver Dollar.

Then ruin fell upon Tabor, largely owing to the devaluation of silver and the establishment of the gold standard. With Baby Doe still staunch at his side, for she had fallen in love with him, he died a year or so afterwards in a small back room in the hotel which he had built and owned, rescued from penury only by a job as a postmaster which his friends had found for him. Baby Doe lived on for another forty years, dying shortly before the second World War, a penniless old crone, in an old cabin by the shaft of the disused Matchless Mine which had made and lost her husband's fortune.

John was right. The story made a spirited ballad opera, witty and tuneful, varying in the range of its drama from the romantic to the tragic, and in that of its music from operette to grand opera. Moreover, its period settings reflected the lush Gay 'Eighties in a fresh and spectacular style. Here, for the first time, was the folk-lore of the American West, enshrined in a medium more elevated than the screen and the music-hall—in its composition a harmoni-ous marriage of Western American drama with Eastern European-ized culture. It seemed sure of success. As the rehearsals proceeded, John's spirits were rising—and infecting us all.

Finally the day of the first performance came. All-day festivities preceded it. Post-horses raced across the mountains in a 'Pony Express,' the victor being rewarded with a gold cupful of silver dollars by Miss Kim Novak, wide-eyed and white-headed, look-ing a trifle scared as she rewarded both rider and horse with a 'real big Hollywood kiss'. Television cameras recorded the incident, the announcer, in a morning-coat and a *Daily Mail* hat, refreshing himself from a bottle of Coca Cola, as a kilted clown disported himself in the gutter and ladies in bustles and feather boas walked the pavement. Next, boys and girls danced down the street into the livery stables, there tripping, amid covered waggons and ploughs, into the steps of a square dance, reminiscent at once of English lancers and Scottish reel, performed to the music of a fiddle and a voice at a microphone.

As dusk fell there appeared, floodlit at the head of a rocky slope, a flight of hand-picked débutantes, graceful in crinolines with posies of rosebuds and lace, who floated serenely downward, one by one, to be welcomed on a lawn by frock-coated, top-booted ushers, and conveyed, arm-in-arm, to the door of the theatre. Here presently, as the television cameras whirred, a waggonette drew up, from which the Governor of Colorado descended to open the door of the Opera House with a massive golden key.

After a series of orations the audience, ladies and gentlemen from Denver and critics from New York, were admitted to their seats and the cameras turned on them from the stage, portraying a profusion of orchids and white fox, silks and diamonds, sharkskin and gold. Throughout the performance, fanning themselves with golden programmes, they laughed and cried and applauded and cheered, some murmuring with eager reminiscence of the days when their grandmothers had cut Baby Doe in Mr. Tabor's own Windsor Hotel. To mark the triumphant close, a rain of carnations fell on the stage. Afterwards we proceeded to a lavish reception, then slunk to the candlelit shadows of the Glory Hole, its proprietress fresh from the opera in diamonds and lace, like Diamond Lil in person.

The critics were full of praise for *The Ballad of Baby Doe*. An impresario from Broadway bought an option on it. John became the darling of Denver, responding eagerly to the limelight which the composer, more modestly, shunned. With irresistible energy he drew us along in his tide from party to party, back for a drink or two at the house where he was staying, and then out again. He would talk with exhilaration, thump at the piano, sing songs loudly and out of tune, invent games and make us play them, dispute furiously and drink recklessly, until, one after the other we dropped out exhausted—first Ken, then myself, and lastly Harry, leaving him to return home protesting, after the night clubs had closed and they had wandered through the streets talking still, for an hour or so more. After a few lean years on Broadway, his life was becoming full again. He was recapturing the sweet smell of admiration and success—and he was enjoying it without inhibition.

We shared his enjoyment. I remember an evening at an Amusement Park, a place dating from the Gay 'Nineties and still preserving a period flavour in the baroque design of its merry-go-rounds and sideshows, with John careering over the tops of the trees and down in among them on a roller-coaster of scarifying slopes and bends. I remember an afternoon party in the grounds of a house built in the style of a French château, with John as the central figure, and the hostess, in a brassière and a pair of tight Hawaiian pants embossed with lover's knots in velvet, serving her guests with cold curried prawns by a warmed-up swimming pool, and showing them photograph albums entitled respectively, 'Ellie gives a Party, Ellie gives another Party, Ellie's last Party,' and 'Look up at the Birdie.'

I remember an evening in the Brown Palace Hotel, trying in vain to console Margarett MacKean, who had flown out from New England for the première. An old friend of John, possessed with much of his surging energy and devouring need for people, she was a woman of passionate enthusiasms and downright ideas, with a rare sense of quality and fastidious critical values. It was her first visit to the West, and she was hating it—partly, no doubt, because John had not yet found time to see her, partly because her patrician New England reserve put her out of temper with the free and easy, all too welcoming manners of the Western people. Lying, with black smouldering looks, prone on the settee in her room, she growled miserably: 'They ask you how you *are*, all the time. They say good-morning to you in the streets—perfect strangers. The waiter talks to me as though we'd been in bed together the night before.'

Margarett was a close friend also of Alice, of whom the three of us spoke with affection. She had seen her only a few days before, harassed as ever by the torrid heat and the conflicting demands of New York, where her mother's illness still kept her.

*   *   *

One day Harry and I took John's car up into the mountains, for a picnic. We stopped on the way, to visit Denver's open-air theatre, an amphitheatre carved, like that of Delphi but on an even larger scale, from the flank of a mountain, with giant slabs of red rock, as smooth in texture as a waterfall, pouring down on either side of it to form a natural proscenium, then breaking and swirling away down to a rolling gold-dusted landscape. The programme alas! was no Greek drama but Liberace at the piano.

From here we proceeded up the mountain to the grave of Buffalo Bill, a shrine for pilgrims, like the Shrine of the Sun to Will Rogers farther south, with a museum containing his cowboy possessions and innumerable portraits, designed in a rustic Wild West style. The tomb had inspired a visiting poet to the lines:

> 'I've stood at the grave of Buffalo Bill
> On a mountain crest and I've felt the thrill
> Which he must have felt, as I saw below
> The prairies wide of his long ago.'

Retiring to a more secluded point of vantage, eating our sandwiches and drinking our Californian wine amid the clean scent of the spruce trees, we looked down over the prairies, then up over the mountains to the snow-capped peaks of the Great Continental Divide. Images of the other world beyond it tempted us. So a day or so later, after a rousing farewell evening with John and Ken, and many promises for other such evenings back in New York in the fall, we took the bus up to the top of the range and away to the west beyond it.

At the head of the pass, the snow lay over the flanks of the mountains in weird ribbed shapes, like cavalcades of White Horses on the Wiltshire Downs. Here was the watershed. The Atlantic lay behind us, the Pacific ahead. At once the landscape, caressed by the western breezes, grew softer in colour, more luxuriant in texture. We ran down into a deep canyon to the hot springs of Glenwood, then out in a local bus into a broad fertile valley, where a mountain peak soared ahead of us, cleanly grey between spurs of pink. Scattered over a plain at the foot of it lay the small town of Aspen, and the trees which ran up its slopes quivering a fresh diaphanous green between ranks of opaque dark spruces, were aspen trees, no less.

Aspen is, like Central City, a 'ghost' mining town of the 'seventy-niners, killed by the devaluation of silver and now revived as a tourist centre. Its Tyrolean-type holiday châlet contrast curiously with the Victorian urban buildings and sub urban villas as of some English Midland town. My friends at Yale had given me an introduction to Courtie and Treenie Barnes, who lived in the East but spent their summers here in the West, above Aspen. We stayed as their guests in a smart châlet hotel in the town, but visited them often in their welcoming ranch house, greeted by two schoolboy sons eager to show off to us the beauties around them. Built by a clear rushing trout-stream, among aspens and spruces, its windows gazed up a narrowing valley between the flanks of glowing, rose-red mountains. In a paddock before them a Welsh pony grazed, while a pair of Palomino horses tossed their heads and cavorted as in some Hellenistic frieze.

Here, as we were to find, was only one among a group of highly civilized American families who had built houses for themselves in this delectable landscape and lived vigorous, varied lives, enjoying the outdoor pursuits of riding and shooting and fishing, but combining them with the pleasures of music and intellectual discussion. For Aspen, throughout each summer, provided a festival of music, and a school of humanistic studies, as Central City provided a festival of opera and drama. Culture had indeed come to the Rockies. Here was America at its all-round best.

We awoke to the smell of the clean mountain air. For Aspen stands eight thousand feet up, and in the winter is a popular ski-ing resort. After breakfast we took the chair-lift another three thousand feet up to the summit of Aspen Mountain, swaying in the air over the tops of the aspens glittering silver, and of the cone-clustered spruces glinting blue, until we came into Alpine meadows bright with larkspur and columbine, delphinium and cranesbill and a richness of wild herbaceous flowers. Here was a silence broken only by the smart little chipmunks, nibbling and scurrying through the grass, and by the woodchucks burrowing more secretively beneath it. For there were strangely few birds to be heard or seen.

At the top was an octagonal sun-deck, run as a café by a family of Swiss. They told us that the mountain shepherds were, for the most part, Swiss and Basques and Austrians, the native Americans not caring for so lonely a life. Sunning ourselves, we looked out over a panorama of peaks, immense in scale but never forbidding, thanks to the lightness of the bone-grey and rose-pink rocks and of the sea-green aspens, transparent around and beneath them. There was no sign here of human life—no huts, no châlets, no patches of cultivation wrung from the rocks by peasant tenacity. For there was no peasantry, no indigenous population but for a handful of wandering Indians. These mountain ranges, unlike those of Europe, have never been inhabited and were never likely to be so, except by an occasional mining community. They were virgin territory still.

Next day the Barneses lent us a car, and we drove up into the heart of this mountain landscape. Havoc reigned along the banks of the stream at our side, for the beavers had dammed it industriously, making pools for themselves but thus diverting it to flood long strips of forest, the trunks of its trees lying uprooted and derelict in a wilderness of water and mud and rotting vegetation. The spectacle gave a new meaning to the words beaver brook. Presently we emerged from the forest to see a deep blue lake spread before us and, at the head of it, naked and corrugated with diagonal slats of snow, the triple-rose-coloured pyramid of the Maroon Peaks, towering skywards. We bathed and ate our luncheon, tanning ourselves in the hot mountain sunshine, while around us families fished for the leaping trout. Leaving Harry to sketch, I walked on up a shaded sandy path, aromatic with brushwood, to the crater lake above. Here the pink pyramidal slabs of the mountain closed in, skidding down into still waters coloured a deep bottle-green against banks of fresh green turf.

In the evening there was a concert to go to, in the mammoth tent designed by Saarinen, the illustrious architect, in the form of an amphitheatre, its scarlet flaps rolled up to release the melodies of a Mozart concerto or a Haydn symphony, and to reveal views of the mountainside, steaming a little in the cool of the dusk. All day long, in the town, ragged strains of arpeggios and arias had been ringing out over the swimming pools as zealous aspirants practised, and now, over drinks in the Victorian pub where cowboys and students dressed as cowboys hobnobbed to the the sound of the juke-box, the barman whistled, without shame, the Emperor Concerto. There was, in these English-style bars and continental-style restaurants an agreeable blend of pastiche and the genuine West, flavoured also, in the cosmopolitan accents round us, with a taste of Central Europe.

Genuine enough, in the Western sense, was the Rodeo, held one Saturday afternoon—though this again, in its informality and in the participation, as would-be cowboys, of some adventurous schoolboys, had the light-hearted atmosphere of some country gymkhana in England. Cowboys however there were, in good number, from all parts of Colorado and the neighbouring States, with names like Pete and Chuck and Wayne and Clyde, narrow-hipped and lean-limbed in their belted jeans and Texan boots, with a casual swagger in their stance and a rakish tilt to their wide-brimmed hats.

'Give them a hand,' urged the voice over the microphone. 'These cowboys like to hear a lot of applause.' And to the tune of Camptown Races we gave it them, round after round, as the events succeeded one another, each swifter in movement than the last. Mastering their mounts with one hand and coiling a rope with the other, they pursued scurrying calves, riding them down on to the ground and getting them trussed by the legs in a few seconds. Two by two they tackled the sturdier, warier steers, skilfully rounding them up, and with a flying lasso catching them by a single twitching leg. Digging spurred heels into the necks of bucking, plunging broncos, they fought, with prodigies of dexterity, to remain on their backs, as though cavorting in an acrobatic ballet of centaurs. A race by wild horses was to follow, but now the rain came down, prolonged and relentless, and after a fruitless pause the show was abandoned.

Splashing back to the town we were offered a lift by a Texan, driving a scarlet-and-white convertible. The afternoon, he re-marked, was 'as cold as a well-digger's ass in Idaho'. As for the town, it was as 'busy as a one-legged man at an ass-kicking'.

Harry and I, anxious not to trespass too far on the hospitality of the Barneses, had moved from our smart châlet to a humbler Alpine Lodge, on the outskirts of the town. Here we were in Europe, for the couple who ran it were an Austrian ski-instructor and guide named Toni, from Garmisch, and his German wife, Ilse, from Stuttgart. They had created around them a warm peasant atmosphere, with a log fire, and clean checked table-cloths, and homely possessions. Here Harry drew and I wrote. After a morning's work we took out a picnic each day to the banks of the river, the Roaring Fork, running dark and clear through a bed of stepped red stones. In solitude we bathed and ate and slept, while cattle grazed in the meadows around us.

A plan began to grow between us—that he should return to England with me, in the autumn. Alice, I had a feeling, might help him to get there. But meanwhile he had promised to drive John's car back to New York—for John himself was hurrying back by air, to discuss the production of *Baby Doe* on Broadway. Harry dreaded returning, to the heat and the inertia and the lone-ness and the material insecurities of New York in the summer.

But one morning a call came from John that he would soon be ready to go, and he left on the bus for Denver that afternoon.

I had decided to stay on at the Lodge for another few days, to finish some articles, before continuing my journey westwards. Two days later I was awoken by a call from Harry, still in Denver. 'Something tragic has happened,' he said. 'Alice has died. John has had a call from New York. She had a heart attack yesterday.'

∽ 16 ∽

Mesa Verde Plateau · In Trouble with the Rangers · The Grand
Canyon · 'The Hottest Place on Earth' · A Landscape of Temples ·
Factories of Money

MY mind still ran on Alice, a few days later, as I drove away westwards, out of the Aspen Valley. She had been a victim, I felt, of New York, with its disordered, high-strung rhythm. It was a rhythm which seemed to suit John, as though there were a dynamo inside him which generated energy for ever, on a cumulative scale. It did not suit Harry, whom it had all but destroyed when he was living John's life, and it was the kinder tempo of Europe that had helped to restore him. Nor had it suited Alice, for ever yearning as she was for that Europe which soothed her with its intimacy, and enabled her faculties to expand in peace.

I thought of Alice as we drove southwards, turning the range so that I now saw its familiar skyline, more faded in colour, from the obverse side. Here the country opened out into a plain flooded in the evening with ochre-and-amethyst lights, where eroded foothills deployed in depth towards the now-distant snow-covered peaks. Spending the night in Montrose, one of those Western towns which seem to exist for the car alone, I drove on over a prairie of beet and stubble towards a new and more undisciplined mountain skyline—an extravaganza of ridges and spurs shooting off in all directions, without thought of symmetrical form. But as I drew closer they began to assume an architectural shape—that of a series of castles with towers and battlements and high-pitched roofs, anarchic creations of fantasy each unrelated to the other.

We drove up into this range, by the gravel bed of a stream rushing with milk-yellow water, to a high amphitheatre of cliffs which enfolded the village of Ouray. A notice by the roadside read, THE SWITZERLAND OF AMERICA. This was a grotesque under-statement—like another notice which I was to see later in Upper New York State, describing a grand chain of lakes as THE COMO OF AMERICA. No mountain scenery I had seen in Europe could emulate this cauldron of rich flowing rock, so alive in its sculpted, stratified movement and in the glow of its crimsons and madders and golds and maroons.

I thought how much Alice, with her sense of natural beauty, would have enjoyed this place, as she had enjoyed the more lightly operatic mountain ranges of Austria. I thought also how strange it was that those only two friends whom Harry and I had found in common, Peter and Alice, had now suddenly gone, within six weeks of each other. I remembered how Alice had spoken of Peter's death, that last evening up on the Hudson. Though I am not, as a rule, prone to superstition, an uneasy sense of foreboding began to grow in my mind. I reflected that there is a pattern of fate by which tragedies happen often in threes. I became anxious for Harry lest, driving alone those two thousand miles back to New York, he might grow impatient and drive recklessly, or fall asleep at the wheel. That night I wrote to him, 'Drive carefully and write me the moment you get back to New York.'

*   *   *

Now we passed into a darker mountain landscape, as into a new movement in music, and came down into the ghost mining village of Silverton. It seemed to have about it a certain air of unreality, and soon I saw why. Much of it was two-dimensional, built in the style of its period as a Hollywood 'set' for Western films, with the façades of church, saloon, store, stables and Court-house. Behind it a plain spread away towards Durango, where I left the bus and, in a station wagon, drove up into another dimension. A natural tableland rose before us, fifteen hundred feet high: an Acropolis broader and vaster than the space of Europe allows, standing squarely in an undulating basin of cultivation and pasture. The ripe wheat licked at its cliffs, purple in the evening light, like tongues of yellow sand. This was the Mesa Verde plateau, for centuries a home of Indian tribes and today a National Park.

Here I found a holiday camp, with some hundreds of family huts, electrically lit amid the spruce trees, and outside each one, dwarfing it, a sleek family car. The station wagon would be back to collect passengers at eleven o'clock next morning, so I arose early and, after awaiting my turn for breakfast under the orders of a lady with the severity of a governess, enrolled in a squad of tourists which, under the command of a ranger, marched off to inspect some Indian cliff-dwellings. Though much restored, they were curious enough, huddling, stone-built, beneath an over-hanging bluff, and burrowing into it to form deep caves. But as the ranger discoursed learnedly on their origins—Basket Maker Period, Modified Basket Maker Period, Development Pueblo Period and such—I grew restless, hankering for the wider spaces below. Presently, unobserved by the rest, I stole away down the canyon.

Climbing over a rough wooden barrier, I entered a solitary world of oak and pine and scented brushwood. The path, winding downwards, showed no trace of the footprints of man, but only of the occasional hoof-marks of horses. The silence was broken only by bush-tits, flitting through the sage-brush, by the scream of a jay and the croak of a raven in apparent dispute with an eagle. A white-rumped deer scampered casually across the path, saw me and stopped short on a rock, pricking its ears in surprise. The path led down into a broader, flatter canyon, one of the many which carve their way through the tableland. I turned up it, between two escarpments of lion-coloured rock, eroded into forms like those of ruins. Here, in the throbbing dry heat, was a stillness complete but for the scurrying of lizards across the hot splintered stone.

Planning to be back by eleven o'clock, when the station wagon was due, and consulting my map, I had expected to find a path leading to the right and thus returning in a circle to the area of the camp. But I had walked for two hours, and there was still no sign of it. Then I realized that I had underestimated the scale of the map, and had long ago left this path behind. So I turned back, reaching the camp by the way I had come. It was now after one o'clock, and I had walked for four hours. The lady at the desk greeted me severely. Where had I been, she enquired? The car, she said, had waited for me for more than two hours, and had left only ten minutes ago. I had walked off without permission of the rangers, who had hence been alerted, and had been searching for me all over the roads. Had I not read the notice: 'Most trail trips require strenuous exertion, and because of the danger of getting lost, hikers must obtain maps and a *permit* before leaving the headquarters area.'?

I had not. I was sorry. But luckily no harm had come of it. The exertion had not been too strenuous. It was not easy to get lost on a trail. She gave me a look like that of a Brahmin confronting a sweeper, and asked me when I proposed to leave the camp.

'When the car returns in the evening,' I replied, and went hungrily off to have luncheon. But the lady guarding the door of the dining-room barred my way. No luncheons, she said sharply, were served after 1.30. It was now 1.35. I went to the bar, where I drank several cans of beer and ate several hot dogs. The bell-boy joined me.

'I've not eaten for two days,' he said.

'Why?' I asked.

'Guess I just forgot. I'll get me a Hamburger.' He ordered a glass of milk with it and talked of his car. It was a 1950 Buick, for which he had paid five hundred dollars—the eighteenth car he had owned. He was thinking of changing it for a Triumph. Another youth, with his two sisters, joined us. They were motoring to Phoenix, Arizona, via Durango. I dropped hints that I was anxious to get to Durango myself. But there was no response, and they drove off, one of the sisters lounging alone in the back.

I wandered across to the museum, which was stocked with Indian arts and crafts. It contained also a section devoted to the physical remains of the cliff-dwellers, illustrating especially the ailments from which they had suffered—fractured limbs, a cystoid abscess, decaying molars, a set of teeth ground to pulp. The milk-fed tourists looked at these with awestruck fascination. Tired after my walk, but without a bed, since I had given up my hut, I lay down under a spruce tree and fell asleep. When I awoke I had a bath and felt better. The station wagon returned with the evening passengers, and drove me—now the only one—back to Durango. Here, in a Mexican restaurant, with oil lamps on the tables to save electricity, I ate a meal for fifty cents—the cheapest and best I had yet tasted in America. The hotels were full but I finally found a room, without outside windows or skylight, for two-and-a-half dollars. By leaving the door open, I was able to get some sleep. Early next morning I left by the bus for Arizona.

*   *   *

The desert spread away in front of us, unending and comforting. It was pinker than other deserts I had known, peppered with a yellowish sage and throwing up deep red rocks. One of them, the Shiprock, stood high up in solitude, two thousand feet, like a vast Gothic cathedral, pointing the way to the West. The bus was late in leaving Gallup, where I changed, and it was dusk when we drove through the Painted Desert. But its many colours glowed brightly in the aftermath of the sunset. I spent the night in Flagstaff, taking a room in a suburban house, since the hotels were full, and next morning set off for the Grand Canyon. The bus drove up before the Bright Angel Lodge, decorated in the rustic style with varnished beams, knots and all, and furnished with stalls selling bric-à-brac. Beyond them was a sun-terrace, crowded with tourists. Over the edge of it the earth opened abruptly—and there, at my feet, spread a grandiose chasm, laying bare, as far below and almost as far across as the eye could see, a landscape more dramatic in scale, more fantastic in form and more vivid in colour than any I had yet seen on its surface. This was the Canyon.

Impatient to get down into the heart of this world, yet zealous, after my experience at Mesa Verde, to abide by the rules, I called upon a ranger and enquired of him the best way of walking down to the foot of the Canyon. He turned on me the deadpan Brahmin gaze and, looking me slowly up and down, replied: 'There is *no* good way of walking down into the Canyon.' I should, he recommended, join the daily mule train, complete with guide, at a cost of thirty-two dollars, which included a night at the Phantom Ranch. I did not care, I pointed out, to go by mule or in company; I preferred to walk, and alone. Shrugging his shoulders at such lunatic persistence, he pushed across to me a sheet of information and instructions for hikers, and turned in silence back to the work on his desk.

These hikers, it seemed, were a species of helot status, subordinated not merely to man but to beast. 'Hikers,' I read, 'must give way to mules on the Canyon trails. When approaching the animal train, stand quietly on the outside of the trail, preferably off the trail, until the train has passed.' Contradictorily, 'Stay on the trail,' I read further. 'Do not take short cuts . . . . When in doubt do not try to cross a stream.' Solemnly I was warned that there are neither garbage cans nor toilets in the wilderness ('Bring your trash back with you to civilization . . . Do not *ever* ever throw refuse of any sort over the Canyon to hide it.') More encouragingly, 'You need have no fear of wild animals—the noises, so apparent at night, are not made for your benefit and fear, but only from their own ways of existence.' Lest they had be dragged out of the Canyon in a state of exhaustion, hikers were instructed to carry not merely a canteen of water but a packet of salt tablets to counteract the effects of drinking too much of it. Supplying myself with the water but not with the salt, taking care to sign the Hikers' Register, I set off with some sandwiches to walk down into what appeared to be the centre of the earth—or was it perhaps the bottom of the sea?

In a sense it was. For the Colorado River, part of whose valley this is, had once sprawled seawards here through a flat, watered plain. Then the crust of the earth began gradually to rise, forcing it to narrow its path and to deepen its bed, until it found itself running, as now, between two high plateaus, each some five thousand feet above it. Meanwhile, thus imprisoned on either side, it had cut its channel downwards, not outwards, exposing its rock walls to the elements, to the disintegrating forces of rains and frosts which gnawed away at them, for ever widening them and carving tributary canyons around them, sculpting them moreover, on a mammoth scale, into weird but consistent shapes. It is a process still continuing, so that the Canyon, for all its static, suspended air, is undergoing, invisibly, a continuous process of change.

For the moment, zigzagging down the steep golden face of a rain-made amphitheatre, modulating into a world of pink precipices, then into a world of red, I was still far from fitting into a rational focus the fantastic shapes ahead of me. I was, after all, reversing the ordinary process of nature by walking, as it were, down a mountain, before having walked up it, and it would be only on reaching the foot of it that I should be able to gain any coherent impression of its form. Meanwhile I was happily alone in the silence and in the heat of the sun, for I was, it seemed, the only hiker, and the daily mule-train had gone down in the morning.

Then from above me I heard a whistling and a shuffling and a kicking of stones, and a snub-nosed schoolboy caught up with me, ejaculating a cheerful 'Hiya!' He was sixteen years old, his name was Bill, and he had hitch-hiked two thousand miles, at a cost of two dollars, from Grand Rapids, Michigan, to take a look at the Canyon. We walked on together. His town shoes looked worn. Was he used to walking, I asked? Well, yes, in town, to school and to the movies and home again. But he was good at all sports; this was nothing to him. At which he scampered ahead of me at some speed down the trail.

Two hours down, we stopped on a stretch of plateau in the shade of the Indian Gardens, where we drew some water from a well and ate some sandwiches. Beside us a pair of antelope ate from a garbage can. The path plunged on downwards into a winding, rock-walled canyon, black like a coal-face and narrow like a street, and after a further two hours we reached the banks of the Colorado River. Here we rested, sunning ourselves on a smooth white beach, but unable to bathe in the narrow river, so malignant did it look with its livid yellow waters and relentless, swirling current.

The Phantom Ranch was still two hours' walk ahead of us, the path winding along cliffs of a grey elephantine granite. The boy began to falter and to lag behind, his feet starting to blister, his bravado to wane. I walked ahead of him and he straggled into the ranch some ten minutes after me. It stood in a deep red gully, amid poplars and tamarisks, and had a swimming-pool of muddy red water. But in response to my request for a room the proprietor, a lean pale man dressed as a chef, gave me the Brahmin look, from head to foot, and replied:

'No, *sir*. I've been told nothing about you. Nobody phoned. How did you get here?'

'On foot,' I replied. He gave me a contemptuous glance, followed by a stern interrogation; then grudgingly showed me to a room, demanding ten dollars payment in advance. Presently the boy was shown in after me. We were allowed a meal but, as befitted tramps, in the kitchen, since the dining-room was occupied by the riders of mules. Afterwards the boy went to bed exhausted, and I sat around outside in the hot, windless night. A group of cow-punchers—or mule-drivers—with deadpan faces and ten-gallon hats, surveyed me with silent disapproval. The proprietor joined us. I would, he presumed, be riding up with the mule-train in the morning. The cost of a mule would be eighteen dollars. I thanked him politely. But I preferred, I said, to walk. At this he grew impatient. I must realize, he said, that it was a five hours' climb, by the shortest route (we had come down by the longest), and that this was the hottest place on earth.

Boasting a little, I remarked, 'Not so hot as some other places I've been in. The Dead Sea, for instance. Have you ever been to Sodom—or to Gomorrah?' He was silent.

The boy next morning had recovered his spirits. After some ten hours' sleep he was full of energy and bounce. He found a scorpion in the bedroom, climbing out of the tap. He claimed also to have seen a rattlesnake.

We were allowed into the dining-room for breakfast. We let

before the mule-train, and, when it passed, remembering the rules, drew reverently, unobtrusively aside. The boy, disobeying all rules, rolled rocks exuberantly down the mountainside—one so large that he almost rolled down with it himself. He teased lizards by the way. He announced casually that, after paying the bill at the ranch, he had only one dollar left. He would have to phone his mother in Michigan—reversing the charges—for more money. His mother in any case liked him to phone every few days. Usually he put through a Person-to-Person call, giving her a prearranged false name. She would answer, and deny the name, so neither would have to pay for the call; but she would know he was safe, and where he was.

Now, however, his shoes were in shreds and he started to linger behind once more, taking long rests and deep draughts of water. At first I would wait for him to catch up with me. Panting and blowing, he would explain: 'I just stopped to rest for a minute, two or three blocks back.'

But finally I grew impatient, for he was walking only a few hundred yards between rests and, leaving him with a full bottle of water, went ahead. I awaited him at the top, where eventually he flung himself down in exhaustion beside me. But he perked up in a few minutes at the approach of a car, and ran out to stop it. It was going north into Wyoming, where he wanted to go, and he scrambled into the back, forgetting to wave me goodbye.

The climb meanwhile had been hot, the early light and shade fusing, as the sun rose higher, into a uniform heat haze. But it had been rewarding. Looking from below up the north face of the Canyon, I began to grasp not merely in detail but as a whole the form of the landscape, resembling rather a cityscape, which rose in majestic stages to the flat surface of the earth far above me. It rested upon foundations of granite, the piled molten rocks of the gorge through which the river was carving its way. Above them nature began to give place, as it were, to architecture. This took vertical form in a continuous precipice of a dull gold stone, throwing out buttresses and battlements like the encircling walls of a colossal fortified city. Towering above them in a broken sequence of high-stepped terraces, jutting out into undulating drifts of shale, so smooth in their aspect as to suggest a rose-red—and sometimes a stone-green—downland, there arose in irregular echelon, like a city's soaring towers and rooftops, a huge assembly of structures, fantastic in conception, bold and curiously regular in style.

Structures indeed they were, rather than organic phenomena of nature. Pyramids of alternate steps and slopes, sweeping upwards to pinnacles or flat-topped roofs, the masonry of their deep-red walls topped by stratified bands in differing widths of pink and purple and rust and grey, they had been built by a consistent process of erosion and fracture, their design varying in detail but conforming to a general canon, as in that of some school of temple architecture. Temples indeed they seemed, built on Elysian rose-red fields; and as temples they are named on the map, from an eclectic series of oriental cults—the Temples of Shiva, Osiris, Confucius, Zoroaster, Cheops Pyramid, the Tower of Ra; while the crescents, spreading protective walls around them, are the Hindu or the Ottoman Amphitheatre, and the highest wall supports the Valhalla Plateau. Here, indeed, I reflected, as I paused time after time to absorb this perspective of fabulous forms and colours, is a landscape, above any other, where nature has emulated art on a truly Olympian scale.

*   *   *

As nature, to no great practical purpose, harnessed the Colorado River within its black granite walls, so did man, for his own purposes, harness it lower in its course, creating the other great phenomenon of this rockbound valley, the Boulder—or Hoover —Dam. A bus from Williams dropped me at Kingman, whence another conveyed me to the dam—a shade regretfully, since, had I continued on my journey, I should have passed successively, at intervals of a few miles only, through the towns of Baghdad, Siberia and Ludlow. (They might, however, have proved little more rewarding than some of the places I had seen, with names as evocative—notably Intercourse, Truth or Consequences and Surprise.)

The Dam ('the world's highest') controlling the waters of the lower river and thus irrigating a million acres of Nevada, Arizona, California and Mexico, was dramatic enough to see. An amphitheatrical cliff of smooth pink concrete, stretched as tight as a curtain between rough pink crags, it rose seven hundred feet above me with a simple assurance, containing beyond its parapet a man-made lake ('the world's largest, capable of covering New York State'). The interior of the damn contained a number of amenities, notably elevators, the equivalent of forty-four storeys high, and in one of these I descended with a party of tourists, inspecting mysterious chambers filled with turbines and other such machinery, circulating in air-cooled corridors, like those of a tube-station, and indeed with the sound as of trains coming from either hand, from the roaring invisible water. There was also a grandiloquent inscription, declaring it 'fitting that the flag of our country should fly here in honour of those men who, inspired by a vision of lonely lands made fruitful, conceived this great work, and of those others whose genius and labour made that vision a reality.'

But one amenity was missing. There was no café or restaurant, above or below water. Thus, rather than wait three hungry hours for the next bus to Las Vegas, I decided to walk two hours to Boulder City and await it there. I set off along the road in the pitiless midday sunshine, while cars at the rate of some six a minute overtook me, driving me not indeed into the ditch (for American roadsides have no ditches) but on to the gravelly verge. The well-groomed ladies or gentlemen at their wheels regarded me with indifferent disdain, their well-shaven children, bouncing about in the back among the family clothes-hangers, with shocked surprise. I was too proud to flag a lift, and they to offer one. But after I had walked for three miles a truck drew up, and its driver offered me a ride—not merely to Boulder City but to Las Vegas itself. No tourist, but a game warden under the Nevada State Government, he was poor, he said, but enjoyed his life. The countryside itself was poor, as indeed I could see from the arid lands around me, and survived largely on the proceeds of a major industry—legalized gambling.

Las Vegas had a busy air about it. From all the buildings on its main street came the sound of machines at work. They throbbed like the generators of the Boulder Dam, but were worked by hand, long lines of men and women pounding away at their levers with intent concentration, while at intervals a bell rang. They were the gambling machines, and the bell announced that a gambler had won a jackpot, the amount of his Stakhanovite bonus being flashed on a board. These factories of money—the Golden Nugget, the Westerner, the Frontier, the Apache—were gay, garish saloons, with a Victorian décor of plush and gilt mirrors and baroque electroliers.

Out on 'The Strip,' a long boulevard by the edge of the desert, the industry flourished at a more opulent level, moreover with a more silent intentness, the green-baize tables attracting the seekers of fortune more than the jackpot machines. Here, like a series of Hollywood sets, were the Desert Inn, the Dunes, the New

Frontier, the Sands, with the names in bright lights of Judy
Garland, Mickey Rooney, Sophie Tucker, vying one with the
other for custom.

At one of these, done up largely in purple with shaded white
lights, I spent the night, in an enormous bedroom overlooking
a blue-tiled swimming-pool. I lost little time in putting a call
through to Los Angeles, where Ivan Moffat awaited me. Eagerly
I responded to the voice of a friend, the first since I had parted
from Harry—so eagerly, indeed, that I agreed to take the plane,
instead of the bus, to Los Angeles next morning, and accepted an
invitation to a Sunday luncheon in Hollywood.

I went downstairs to dinner but, after my walk, lacked the
energy to work at the tables; Judy Garland was not singing until
two o'clock in the morning; so, alone I have no doubt among the
visitors to Las Vegas, I went to bed early. When I left in the
morning to catch my plane, they were still pulling at their levers
and staking their counters, for ever insulated, as it were, in a
shroud of purple plush, from the welcoming daylight of the desert
without.

∘ 17 ∘

*Muscle Men in Mourning · An Evening in
Mexico · The Third Victim*

IVAN met me at the airport, dressed as for the beach, and we drove
through interminable suburbs, enveloped in the local brand of
smog, to his house on the Santa Monica Canyon. Here, and in a
flat in the house of a friend, in Hollywood itself, I looked forward
to a spell of relaxation. That Sunday, however, there were
parties to go to: a fashionable luncheon in the élite park of Bel
Air, at which my neighbour, Miss Claudette Colbert, sought my
views, with some concern, about the situation in Suez; a fashionable barbecue given by Greeks in a garden, with Bourbon flowing
and meat revolving on spits; a fashionable cocktail party in a villa
built high on the Beverly Hills, with a view as from Settignano,
at which Miss Greer Garson was especially sorry to have missed
me since she had heard I was a famous naturalist, and at which
Miss Zsa Zsa Gabor was at pains to explain to me that the Gabors
are an older family than the Monroes or the Dorses. There were
some lady columnists present. The *Grandes Dames*, as I was to
discover, of Hollywood, decked out in fabulous feather-hats and

gowns encrusted with pearls, they give fashionable parties in a setting of silver-framed signed photographs of the monarchs of screen and throne.

But that was enough of film stars for the moment. My life, during the next weeks, became beach life. I spent long quiet days in Ivan's large modern room, looking out over the fresh Mediterranean vegetation of the Canyon, and with a glimpse of one of the beaches nearby. My favourite among these was the most popular, but not the most fashionable—Muscle Beach, where a mile of clean sand (periodically renewed, I was told, from a convoy of trucks) stretched away between the ocean and a beach promenade. This, with its bars and fish-and-chips stalls, was more English than continental in character; but here at one corner was a sign in the sand, No. o Pacific Terrace, and there beyond it was the Appian Way. In a pen, with a ring in the centre of it, the muscle men—boxers, wrestlers, weight-lifters—assembled to train each day, watched by awestruck groups of bathers. Slowly and solemnly they mortified the flesh, lifting weights like the bogies of trucks, standing on their heads and on their hands and on the shoulders of their friends, flexing muscles by force of habit to raise even the occasional cigarette to their lips. Now and again a Hercules would emerge from the pen and stroll, with heavy assurance, towards the ocean. He would stop to pose unconcernedly, plunge into the breakers for a few swift overarm strokes, then stroll back again as slowly, preening himself before the crowds as before.

One day tragedy befell a friend of the muscle men, as I read on a scribbled obituary attached to the notice-board:

'Last night Gipsy Gene was killed, the victim of a cowardly attack by a sick man. I remember well our last meeting. Love had come to Gipsy Gene, and with it had come a change. He was the same happy forever smiling Gipsy as before, but now there was contentment in his eyes, the look a man wears who feels wanted . . . He is gone. But to me the streets still show the image of a little man dressed only in a red bandana, shorts and sandals, pedeling his bicycle. I remember how the cars and people would slow down and how the mixture of mirth and envy that Gipsy Gene always provoked would appear on their faces . . . With this little eulogy I am saying goodbye to my friend Gipsy Gene, and I can hear him acknowledge my farewell with a hearty, "So long, taxpayer."

Jim Baker.'

The favourite resort of the muscle men was a fish-and-chips shop, selling also Muscle Burgers, Mile-long Hot Dogs and Over-stuffed Bikini Burgers, plastered with muscular photographs and run cheerily by an English couple called Vi and Jack, from south-east London. Here, where, as nowhere else, the fish was fried when ordered and not before, to sizzle fresh and inviting on its plate, I lunched each day between a bathe in the morning and a walk along the front in the afternoon. The Pacific, heaving its waves on to the beach, was seldom blue but rather an opaque muddy grey. But the sun, released from the smog of Los Angeles, was hot, and its rays gave me a renewal of energy.

On arrival I had found a letter from Harry, written just before his departure from Denver:

'Denver has been as you remember it: filled with John who, in turn, has been filled with liquor, people and indirections. Sunday we went to that Scott Fitzgerald château where Ellie had one of her parties, for some English Duke and Duchess. I spoke for a long time with a very British gentleman whom I assumed to be the Duke, but he turned out to be a neighbour of his in Kenya. He made one wonderful remark about the suppression of the Mau Mau. He said: "We knew they were in the jungle, but we couldn't burn it down because there were too many wonderful wild beasts in there with them, you know." John, of course, got drunk, and started to tell Ellie that she must "explode inside . . . there's not much time left, etc." and other revelations from the gospel according to St. John. He leaves for New York tomorrow morning by plane and I by car. When I get there I will write at once, and let you know my plans.'

But the days went by, no letter came, and I grew worried. Harry, I calculated, should have been back in New York at least ten days ago and the air mail to Los Angeles took only two or three days. My superstitious fears, following the deaths of Peter and Alice, returned. He could very easily have had an accident en route. Anxiously, each morning, I emptied the letter-box by the road outside Ivan's house. On Saturday there was still no letter: I could now hope for none until Monday.

By way of distraction Ivan, who sensed my disquiet, drove me down into Mexico for the weekend. The Corniche road, fringing sunlit bays and beaches, was thronged with cars longer and slinkier and gaudier, it seemed, than elsewhere. We lunched, without stirring from ours, in a drive-in café, giving our order over a telephone plugged into a post, eating our meal off a tray clipped to the side of the car. Before San Diego a roadside notice, advertising a local newspaper, reminded us that 'It's smart to be informed.' We crossed the frontier into Mexico, where all was at once haphazard, with a laxer rhythm and softer, more irregular sounds.

Tijuana, a garish, flyblown town without laws or restrictions, catering solely, it seemed, for the whims of visiting Americans, flaunted gambling saloons, and divorce lawyers' offices, and donkeys painted with stripes to resemble zebras, and ranks of bright yellow taxicabs, with nowhere to go. The driver of one of them offered to drive us around the block to call on two ladies he knew, both used, he said, to the society of 'broad-minded gentlemen.' He advised us to pay our call before seven o'clock, since a new police chief had just taken office, and was expected to raid all such premises after that hour.

Rejecting his invitation, we drove on southwards, striking the sea again by beaches long and white and deserted, then taking a rough un-American road over brown mountains, refreshing in their emptiness and austerity, to Ensinada. Here, avoiding the few American restaurants, we found a clean Mexican *bistro*, with a charcoal oven and bare scrubbed tables, where we drank dark Mexican beer and ate a freshly made *pasta*, served with minced meat and spiced with *chilis*. It was a momentary holiday from America—clouded a little though it was by my irrational fears.

On Monday there was no news from Harry. Ivan laughed off my anxieties, and sure enough on Tuesday a letter came. He had forgotten to stamp it for air mail, and it had been sent by the slow overland route. He wrote:

'I arrived in New York Sunday morning at 6.00 after a nineteen-hour drive straight through from Indianapolis. The trip was hazardous: two flat tyres on the plains of Kansas and Illinois: and a huge crap game in St. Joseph, Mo., that completely wiped out all my resources and necessitated a frantic phone call to John to wire me more money due to a large and unexpected outlay for car repairs (a large and unexpected lie!) by then I was lonely and dejected, so I decided to get back here jack-rabbit quick, enjoying the Dali-esque New Jersey landscape and metropolitan skyline plastered up against the dawn. Last night I saw John, chez lui, filled with alcohol and dire prophecies about my soul, his soul, the World soul. I was sober and shaken. Tomorrow we leave for Vermont. I will paint there, and his house is appealing. Nature more so, and John's voice, like his patron saint's, will be lost in the wilderness.'

So my superstitions had been groundless. There was to be no third victim.

The following Sunday I went with Ivan to a party in a beach-house, given by Shelley Winters, beyond Santa Monica. Some film people were there, and as I sun-bathed, I caught fragments of their casual gossip:

'Did you see about John Latouche?' said one.

'No. What's he been up to?'

'It was in the New York papers. He died a day or two ago, up at his place in Vermont. Thrombosis.'

Harry's letter came a few days later:

'John died here on Tuesday. I was alone with him. We had been out to dinner with some neighbours. At 3.30 in the morning he woke me, complaining of a terrific chest pain. The house is without phone, alone on a hilltop, so it was impossible to get help. At 4.30 he was dead, although at the time I didn't realize it, thinking rather he was sleeping. When I awoke in the morning I found him in the same position, and knew then what had happened. His body was shipped down to New York for funeral services, and then taken back up here for burial. I can say so little more now. I have never known a time like this when I feel so numb and unable to communicate. Today there are only four of us still here at the house: Ruth, Ken, Gerrit and myself. Effie, John's mother, her son Louis and his wife, have finally left for New York. Ken and Gerrit fly back today and Ruth and myself drive back tomorrow. There is so much I will tell you—but not now.'

So John it was that died—at the age of only thirty-eight. He had never been ill in his life: he might have lived if he had. His own energy had consumed him. The dynamo in which, in his lust for life, he had always trusted implicitly, had proved unable to carry the load. Destroying abruptly and without warning, his seemed to me a characteristically American death—a New York death—as Alice's had been.

John had never been to Europe. He loved all things European and especially English. He knew and loved and tried to sing, as he thumped at the piano, all the songs of the English music-hall and the less familiar songs of the English pub. He could recite Burns by heart, and often spoke to me of his dream to write an opera around his life. His mind was imbued with a classical culture, acquired eagerly and voraciously through self-education. He was always planning to visit Europe but, perhaps for some sub-conscious reason, drew back from so momentous a step. Possibly, ambitious as he was, moreover needing always to be loved and admired and to be the centre of the stage, he preferred to await the moment at which he might burst upon Britain as an acknow-ledged success—had he lived, who knows, with a London pro-duction of *Baby Doe*?

I had often wondered how John's high-powered organism would have reacted to the reduced voltage of European life. It might, evoking some chord of his French Huguenot ancestry, have led him to moderation in some things, and a completeness in civilized terms. As it was, rejoicing in the stresses and extremes of America, he had chosen to live recklessly, developing to the full the best American qualities of zest and warmth and unchecked enthusiasm. Tempting the Gods, he had chosen a life too exacting, perhaps, for the human species; and now Nemesis had destroyed him.

 ∽ **18** ∽

*Keeping Down with the Joneses · 'You feel you're at
the movies' · Pedestrians will be Prosecuted*

LOS ANGELES, straggling over a large area of plain below its circle of hills, has been described as nineteen suburbs in search of a city. At no time did it acquire an identity for me. Downtown, as far in time from my flat in Hollywood by bus as Brighton from London by train, a city of a kind did exist, complete with sky-scrapers and jangling streets. But it seemed to play little part in the life of the place, which was lived in a series of loosely con-nected suburbs, from Beverly Hills on the one hand to Pasadena on the other. The interminable boulevards, each one like the other, radiated in from the ocean: at first smugly domestic, then shoddily commercial or industrial, then petering out into waste-lands scattered with shacks, then alternately domestic and com-mercial and industrial once more, but never arriving at a centre, never acquiring a personality, for ever nondescript, scrappy, un-fulfilled. When, as in Sunset Boulevard, a certain character did emerge, it was as artificial as some neo-Regency cardboard set, two-dimensional, ephemeral, insubstantial. One afternoon indeed, driving down the avenues of Culver City after a tour of the various street-sets of Metro-Goldwyn Mayer—where, lunching in the canteen, I had missed Marlon Brando by only a day—I found myself wondering whether I was still in the studio or out of it, so indistinguishable seemed the real from the false.

Once the screen portrayed castles in the air, the cities and houses of a world of escape. Now in Los Angeles dreams had come true in a smog of prosperity. Aircraft factories bigger than film studios, oil derricks encroaching on country clubs (oil, indeed, whose deposits made it impossible to build basements in some residential areas), were enabling all to follow the stars in their courses. In this industrial paradise the once humble and meek might now enjoy a life once deemed fabulous, relishing the leisure and the luxury, the loves and the limousines once reserved for a fairy-tale few. Gracious Living, Glamour, Romance, were avail-able to all.

Around me the outside world had caught up with the dream-world. Here, scattered across the plains and up the hills of Los Angeles, advertised in fat supplements to the newspapers, were the architectural fantasies of a boom in real estate. Tens of thousands of Quality Houses, Executive Houses, Enchanted Homes were arising, built, like those sets of MGM, 'of genuine lathe and plaster,' gracing such romantic modern dreamlands as Parkwood Royale and Peter Pan Village, Sherwood Forest and Highland Glen, Cinderella Estates, Merryville ('Designed for a Queen, Picked for her Lady') and Paradise Square.

Here, reproduced in multiplicate, was the Forever House with the Dream Kitchen of Tomorrow. This, offered to millions, con-tained such starry amenities as Lawn with Sprinkler, Garbage Disposal, Oversized Two-Car Garage, Coloured Marble Pullman Lavatories, Bathrooms 'right out of *House Beautiful*.' Soon, to every man his swimming-pool, his 'beautiful den with bricked-up barbecue,' his 'large well-landscaped backyard.' As 'Better Living for You' grew Better Still, you could soon move up, among the stars, into a wooded estate, 'nestled behind large trees . . . wagon-wheeled fixtures and knotty-pine panelling . . . four hundred square feet of meandering roofed-over patio,' or a 'huge sprawling pumice block rancho home,' equipped with 'lots of glass both front and rear.' And, as is usual in America, the advertisements reflected the reality.

Modern America is a land, as Mr. Russell Lynes remarks in *A Surfeit of Honey*, where 'everybody's name becomes Jones'—and Los Angeles is the quintessence of Jonesism. As a man moves up, keeping up with the Joneses, the stars move down to them, to make him feel at home. One day I went on a bus tour, around the starry homes of Beverly Hills. Here was little lavish display; rather suburban discretion. True, each star displayed his own architectural fancy—Rosalind Russell for the French style, Hedy Lamarr for Queen Anne, Jimmy Durante for Spanish, James Stewart for Jacobean, Tab Hunter for Contemporary. But they were essentially the houses of Joneses, the palace giving place to the bungalow and cottage. A King might now look at a cat. Joan Crawford was selling up a mansionful of sumptuous furniture. The palmy days of Pickfair were over.

In such modest surroundings, Glenn Ford 'exults in a peaceful domestic environment, puttering in his garden, helping his wife Ellie prepare her TV Sunday School program'; Russ Tamblyn indulges his taste for bottled ketchup, pouring it over the eggs as he scrambles them in the frying-pan, and attends faithfully to the household duties assigned to him, namely emptying the ash-cans and keeping his room neat; while Rock Hudson, living in a 'den with a house round it,' aspires (do-it-yourself) to convert his garage into a rumpus room. So at least the movie magazines declared, and the stars of today read them assiduously, living down to the myth which they create for them. Conscientiously, in this spirit, they make frequent appearances in slacks, buying groceries at the Thriftimart or eating, perched on stools, at Schwab's Drug Store, cheek by jowl with all the other Joneses. 'If we're lucky, folks,' said the bus guide, 'we'll see Clark Gable doing his shopping.' We were unlucky, but 'Look. Here's a movie-star right here, coming out of the drug store. What's his name now—you remember him—the blond-headed kid who played with Dean in *East of Eden*?'

Industrious as any Joneses, in this most industrious of all cities, in bed by eleven and up by seven, the stars spent long, earnest hours on the business of income-tax deductions, the formation of themselves into companies to absorb capital gains, the manipulation of their investments in real estate. ('That apartment building was given to Norma Talmadge by her husband as a birthday present . . . That big block is owned by Red Skelton . . .')

They were, it seemed to me, growing to look like Joneses too. Two by two, up the red carpet strewn with the petals of flowers beneath a blaze of electricity turning night into day, I watched them sweep into the Gala Invitational World Première on the Hollywood Boulevard, pausing for a moment on a dais to face compère and cameras, pausing for another to say a few homely words down the barrels of the microphones of ABC, CBC, NBC —even BBC—lost finally amid a galaxy of 'socialites and civic chiefs,' factory kings and oil queens glittering hardly less brightly than themselves.

The film presented as a mirror to the audience was *High Society*, in which ladies and gentlemen danced, drank highballs, changed husbands, and jumped clothed into swimming-pools, in a style to which the least among them might now aspire. The crowd outside, in its grandstands built out over the pavement, glittered as brightly, stenographers and secretaries and salesgirls Cinderellas no longer but Princesses Charming, transfigured by the Beautician's art. For even the Hollywood face has now become so adapted as to fall within the reach of all. The nose, for example, has all but vanished. There are Garbos no longer but Kims and Virginias, their little heads all a-cluster with silvery curls, their little faces kittenish masks; there are Garys no longer but Gregorys and Rocks, their ruggedness within reach of the mere salesman and enabling him to look, if not like a cowboy, at least like a golfer.

It was a strange experience—after a morning spent on a Wild West set, where I was photographed gazing up into the eyes of the giant Clint Walker, till lately a policeman in Las Vegas—to lunch one day in the Warner Brothers canteen, amid a galaxy of these soft little mask-like creatures, and to compare their faces with that of the Duke of Albuquerque, a Spanish nobleman of ancient lineage, who was one of my fellow guests. With the proud Velazquez bone structure of his pointed head, aquiline nose and long, jutting chin, he resembled, by comparison, an extinct human species.

Life, throughout America today, is as good as a film. 'It's wonderful: you feel you're at the movies,' a lady had remarked to me, fresh from a horseback holiday in the wide open spaces of Wyoming. Men in bars, as I had observed in New York, talk in a language of wisecracks, derived from the gangsters of the screen. Cowboys and would-be cowboys, as I had observed in Colorado, dress and behave to the Western manner born. High Fidelity, as I saw here in Hollywood, turns parties into musicals, guests high-kicking together in chorus. On the roads and in the suburbs, in the cafés and on the beaches, life around me was imitating art.

Where, then, was the world of escape? I sought it one day in Disneyland, brought to my notice as 'a world of magic and fantasy, history and knowledge,' and offering a wide choice of inner worlds within worlds. Here were Fantasyland, featuring Dwarfs and such amid winds in willows, within the walls of a French baronial castle; Frontierland, featuring sheriffs and cowboys, with rides in mining-trains and covered wagons; Adventureland, where stuffed wild beasts wagged realistic tails in tropical jungles; Tomorrowland, with a TWA trip to Mars, and a ride for the kids driving a car on a highway as real and as earnest as that of their parents. But here was no fantasy. All the lands were as realistic as a series of film sets.

The last resort, it seemed, was death and a glamorous burial in the Forest Lawn Cemetery. 'Well,' said the bus driver, as the tourists piled in, 'we don't have room in here for one more soul, do we?'—at which there was general laughter. Beneath the well-mown, well-sprinkled lawns, Loved and Unloved Ones alike lay in Graceland, Vesperland, Lullabyland, Slumberland, reposing to the strains of music which ranged from sacred through grand operatic to 'The End of a Perfect Day,' and of disembodied voices, intoning and preaching through microphones; watched over by sculptural masterpieces which I had thought to be elsewhere—Donatello's David, Michelangelo's Moses—and shrines ranging eclectically from the Wee Kirk o' the Heather (without heather but with relics of Annie Laurie and Harry Lauder) to a temple of Apollo and Daphne or a pagan Wishing Chair. Here both Joneses and stars rested side by side, to all Eternity.

* * *

I led a quiet life in Los Angeles—as indeed Ivan did too, preferring, after a long day at the studios, not to become too much involved in the social round of the film world. He had a few close friends, mostly with a European background, and with those we would sometimes dine, in one of Hollywood's good restaurants or at some place on the beach. In this way I grew to know and like Gottfried Reinhardt and his wife, Shelley Winters, Speed Lamkin, Christopher Isherwood.

Throughout my visit the taxicabs were on strike. Thus during the day, since I had no car and moreover insufficient funds left to hire one, I was obliged to travel by bus, taking sometimes as much as three hours to reach Ivan's house at Santa Monica from Hollywood or Beverly Hills. The buses (advertising Funerals on Credit for Two Dollars Fifty a week) ran infrequently, and a twenty-minute wait at a bus stop was usual. The drivers treated their few passengers—some negroes, children, elderly widows and myself—with the monosyllabic scorn due to the underprivileged. A request for information of any kind produced merely a stare of astonished contempt.

One evening, when Ivan was busy, I decided to return to Hollywood instead of sleeping at Santa Monica. I walked for half an hour to a bus stop, waited for a bus for twenty minutes, travelled in it for half an hour, waited for a connecting bus for half an hour, and started to walk the last half-hour home along the shaded, flowered Santa Monica Boulevard, the Park Lane, as it were, which fringes the starry homes of Beverly Hills.

Suddenly a police car drew up beside me. A policeman signalled to me to stop. He demanded my papers, scrutinized them closely, interrogated me in detail as to my origins, my address, my business, my movements throughout the evening. What had I in that bag, he enquired. I opened it, to reveal my bathing trunks, my towel, a copy of *Time* magazine. What had I in my wallet? I opened it. He looked disappointed. There happened to be more than the minimum of fifteen dollars which, as I learnt later, can mean a prosecution for vagrancy in Beverly Hills.

'You still have some money,' he said.

'Some.'

'Why then are you walking?'

'The taxis are on strike. The last bus seems to have gone. It is a fine night.'

'It is most unusual,' he continued, 'to be walking alone, at this hour of the night.'

'At 11.30 p.m.? On a main thoroughfare? Not where I come from.'

Reluctant and unconvinced, he wrote at length in his notebook then let me go.

'We shall be seeing you again,' were his parting, menacing words.

When I told the story to an American friend he remarked, 'Yes, the authorities here like people to have cars.'

Walking, I had at last come to the regretful conclusion, is an un-American activity.

San Francisco · The Liking of Ike · Peace in our
Time · Figures from the Past

IT was on wheels that I left Los Angeles for San Francisco, driving
up the coast road with the Duquettes, a friendly pair of interior
decorators, in whose flat I had stayed in Hollywood. The Pacific
gleamed to the left of us, a sheet of dull silver cloaking its horizon
with a thin veil of fog. To the right of us glowed the soft forms
of hills, scattered with live-oaks and dried by the sun to a deep
tawny yellow. Then the coastline became grander, the rugged
grey-gold cliffs of the Santa Lucia range careering steeply into the
sea and flinging out rocks and islands to embrace chains of clean
white beaches. It was like a landscape of Southern Italy, but on a
more grandiose scale, moreover scantily inhabited by man.

Presently a notice by the roadside read 'Wild Animals. Unsafe
for Pedestrians.' This was St. Simeon, the lavish ranch of the
Hearsts, boasting its own harbour and village roofed with tiles
and designed in the Spanish manner. But we could see nothing
wilder than a herd of zebras. Then the air grew more moist and
the earth more luxuriant, cherished by the breezes and the cur-
rents of the North Californian 'Gulf Stream.' There were lush
flowers now in the gardens, giant begonias and fuchsias and suc-
culent cacti: and mammoth conifers in the forests, marching
grandly up the sides of the canyons. The sea, beyond links of rich
green turf, became slashed, as though spread with jam, by weeds
of crimson. At Cypress Point, by the edge of it, gnarled old
cypresses posed, brandishing arms weirdly contorted and thickly
encrusted with a brilliant scarlet fungus. On the rocks offshore a
school of seals performed, striking attitudes and slithering in and
out of the water before a crowded audience of cormorants.

We spent the night in Monterey, in a seventeenth-century
Spanish house, and drove next evening into San Francisco, a
blanket of white sea mist unfurling swiftly over its hillsides as in
some romantic Celtic twilight scene.

I had been thinking of Harry with constant concern, and now
at my hotel I found a letter, the first since he had written me the
news of John's death:

'I sat down to do battle with this erratic typewriter with the promise not to express any negative thoughts (bolstered by my own instinctive belief in this plus an ultra-esoteric book on the teaching of Gurdjieff and Ouspensky, which John happened to be reading when he died). I have been rummaging through some old letters of John, and although this may sound macabre, they are still vital and warm testimonies of his like qualities. The bulk of them were written to me when we first met while I was still in college, that tenuous and formative period when he was filled with desires that I find myself and discover my centers of creativity, reach fuller awareness, etc. What I subsequently did discover was due so much to him, and what I find subsequently from now on will still be largely due to him, but it shall not be bogged down because of his absence. (I almost said, "and this is the way he would have wanted it," but I shy from that insistent cliché because it implies a kind of forethought of death that John never had.)

Of course I am still lonely and finding it hard to re-adjust to everyday life without him (that is not a negative statement and cannot be counted as a breach of my original promise!) The Gurdjieff-Ouspensky clan say we cannot talk of a collected I, there are too many isolated I's, one of mine being very confused and without direction. But the real me (like those people at Hollywood parties who always desperately exclaim: "You don't know the real me") is singing for life and filled with expectancy. I await your return.'

The resilience of youth, and of America—one of John's own best qualities—would soon, I felt, do its work.

*   *   *

San Francisco I found to be a city which marries in perfect harmony the contrasting elements of land and water. In this it resembles Istanbul, but on a more open and expansive scale. Its streets are as steep, if not steeper, a series of switchbacks scarifying to a motorist unsure of his brakes; its houses crane one above the other for a view which, on all hands, encompasses the sea. But the Bay is broader than the Bosporus, and an Ocean laps the city, the feel and the smell of its mists and soft westerly breezes pervading the streets and relaxing the rhythm of life. The Golden Gate spans the water like a graceful bowstring, with a backward view across its silvery expanse to the San Francisco skyline, its skyscrapers rising in a diffused blue light like the towers of some city dreamed up by El Greco. Life here is lived on the sea, i innumerable suburbs and ports clustering around its inlets, and on the wharves of the city where fish restaurants thrive, serving sweet abalone from luminous shells, swordfish steaks, live crabs and small fresh soles. With its mixture of races—American, Chinese, Japanese, Negro, Italian, French—it is a city cosmopolitan in the purest sense, neither American nor European in its atmosphere, but simply and uniquely San Franciscan.

Its period is Edwardian; a crumbling roman rotunda proves to be the abandoned site of an early twentieth-century international fair. The Opera is still the centre of social life. The hotels, gathering around Nob Hill, where the nobs used to live, are all a-glitter with an Edwardian splendour of marble and ormolu and gold, in luxuriant palm courts muted with rich Turkey carpets. South along the bay, beyond humbler suburbs— huddles of white cubes with a curiously North African look, piling up over the bare tawny hillsides—is the elegant suburb (or rather city) of Burlingame, where hostesses entertain still in a lavish Edwardian style. Here in Italianate villas is the taste of *foie-gras* and the odour of tuberoses, diamonds and champagne sparkling, bibelots gleaming, ladies and gentlemen conversing on immaculate lawns beneath the shade of immaculate trees. And now at the Burlingame Country Club, till a year or so ago the stately home of an old San Francisco family, there were balls several nights a week.

For this was no ordinary season. All day at intervals the sirens were screaming and the fire-engines were roaring through San Francisco—not indeed for a fire, such as had once destroyed it (nobody likes to call it an earthquake) but for the Republican Convention, described by the Press as 'The Greatest Show on Earth.' The city had become the stage, as it were, for a musicale, 'The Liking of Ike,' whose theme was PROSPERITY and (in smaller letters) Peace.

Ikery shone everywhere in the form of buttons and brooches, earrings and ties, hats made into elephants, handbags made into elephants, Ike balloons, Mamie balloons, Ike girls in Ike dresses with Ike parasols held up against the misty skies, and a helicopter hovering up in them with 'I like Ike' painted all over it. 'Ike likes You. . . . Let's Win, Keep Ike in. . . . Abe and Ike, In deed alike. . . .' Sideshows included a bandwagon drawn by Clydesdale horses, followed by jeeps containing girls dressed as drummajorettes, and vintage cars containing actors dressed as former Presidents; a procession of belles, liking Ike in bikinis with a

faint quiver of gooseflesh in the wind from the Bay, led by saxo-
phonists in tartan jackets; lavish issues of free cigars, free beer,
free chewing-gum, free Alka Seltzer, free fruit juice, free Coke
('Ike likes Coke'). Hardly a disliker of Ike was to be seen: only
a schoolboy, demanding Go for Pogo, an old man demanding
Dump Everybody, a defiant young man, long-haired and egg-
headed, posing in front of a bookshop with an outsize Adlai
rosette.

The Governor of California gave a ball, treating eleven
thousand Republicans to three thousand magnums of Californian
champagne, two tons of crab, orchids for all, and a ten-foot
elephant, composed of Malmaisons, revolving on a gilded dais.
A real elephant named Dollie, a 'Young Republican' led by a
lady in Turkish trousers, lazily pawed at the guests with her
trunk, disarranging an occasional corsage. (Ominously, she was
killed in a road accident on her way home from the Convention.)
A Beautician gave another ball, with French champagne but
no elephants, to which four hundred Republicans were invited
and six hundred came. Lesser entertainments, crowding the
days, included caucus breakfasts, briefing brunches, round-ups,
barbecues, rallies, coffee conferences, gang dinners and suppers
for the cream of Republican Buffet Society.

Meanwhile one evening, before the St. Francis Hotel, a kilted
bagpipe band had paraded, dispersing when the sirens shrieked,
the motor bicycles roared, a shower of waste paper poured down
from the windows, and Ike himself arrived, standing, all tanned
and boyish, hands up in surrender to the crowd, in a Cadillac
with a special Plexiglass sunshine roof. Preceding him was a car
of the Special Accident Investigation Bureau; accompanying him
Mamie, smothered in roses; following him a second car, containing his doctor.

In a golden room, with a golden vaulted ceiling, the Press
assembled with a clattering of typewriters, a whirring of television cameras, a blazing of arc lamps, men crawling on all fours
amid a tangle of rubberized cables. 'Gimme a mike, gimme a
mike,' cried one in a frenzy, and somebody threw him a rope.
Others, as they waited, killed time taking flashlight pictures of
each other. Others, mouth pieces in hand and earphones on head,
killed it telephoning, it seemed, to themselves.

Ike, liking as well as liked, presently beamed down upon them
telling his story. Everybody liked Everybody, there was Peace
to say nothing of Prosperity—not only in the world but in th

Republican Party. And how was Ike himself? 'Well, when I try to hit some balls, after a little while I seem to be dragging the club, which I don't like.' But what of that?

With all this liking, the spectre of the dragged club hidden firmly off stage, the show presented little in the way of a plot. But a Hollywood director made up for this. The Cow Palace, where the lowing of oxen ceded to the rumbling of Republicans, was ablaze and aspangle with stars and stripes and spotlights, with golden emblems of a century—but particularly four years—of Peace and Prosperity.

Dressed in their best, seated in the best of their cars and wreathed in the best of smiles, the delegates drove up as though for a race-meeting at which the winners are known in advance. Police, white-hatted and dressed as cowboys, controlled the traffic. A red-bearded negro declaimed from a Bible, in an un-heard chant of warning. Men waved flags at each other across the arena, in some Republican tictac code. Smartly tailored young ladies carried, strapped to their sides, not race-glasses but tele-phones with elegant little aerials. Usherettes, arrayed in tight blue coatees and loose red slacks, showed the thousands to their seats. The ladies of Kansas burgeoned with sunflower hats; the gentle-men of Idaho with russet potatoes; Oklahoma proclaimed 'Oke for Ike.' Hundreds addressed perambulating microphones, posed for the flashlight, talked unwittingly into eavesdropping tape-recorders. For the millions preferring the image to the reality, a TV platform towered high above the rostrum, portraying it all.

The organ broke into strains reminiscent of the oxen. A dance band, interrupting it, struck up 'Blue Skies,' and a Broadway singer sang it. The show had begun. A roll of drums and a flourish of trumpets prefaced a parade of young Republicans, waving star-spangled banners. Then the compère took over. 'Is every-body happy?' he demanded. There was an affirmative roar, as of those who believe in fairies. 'Who likes Ike?' The roar was repeated, followed by a roar of Allegiance. Then the four-day flow of panegyric began, relieved by frequent musical numbers.

Loud applause followed a marching song, 'Vote for Ike'; a tribute to Mamie to the tune of Lindy ('You're the one we like in the White House; We're in love, all in love with you'), and two special lyrics sung to familiar tunes by Miss Ethel Merman, who transformed 'Alexander's Ragtime Band' into the 'Eisen-hower Parade.' A notable film star intoned a prayer composed by Ike. Thanks to the Hollywood director there was never a dull moment, often even a touch of surprise. 'Never,' declaimed the compère, 'in the history of the entertainment business has a man performed greater service to his fellow men.' And there stepped to the microphones, not the Honourable Mr. Dewey, as the programme promised, but Mr. Irving Berlin, singing 'Ike for Four More Years,' with a choir to accompany him.

The orators, Honourables and well-trained Republicans all, billed to fill the gaps in this musical programme, knew their lines and stuck close to their theme. It was Peace and Prosperity. Prosperity without War. 'Everything is booming but the guns. . . . The prayer of every American has been answered; not a single American boy is fighting today any place in the world.' Already, in the newspapers, the Suez headlines were shrinking.

Finally, in a fever of expectancy, with a series of state roars proclaiming a unanimous vote, the winner was announced: none other than Ike. The fever broke out into a delirium; a riot of banners, State-names, Ike signs, mops, balloons, confetti and streamers; a hubbub of roars, yells, whoops, cheers, yoo-hoos and halloas; a pandemonium of organ, dance-band, choir, drums, trumpets, megaphones, microphones, dinner-bells. After some ten unbroken moments of frenzy, a covey of doves was released, doves of peace as white as Picasso's, homing pigeons winging off with rude messages to Libertyville, the home-town of the war-mongering Democrat Stevenson. Terror-struck, they flew hither and thither among the banners, then found some way out—all but one which dropped ominously dead at the foot of a spectator, unheeded as the spectral, dragging golf club. Prosperity was vindicated. Peace was assured.

*   *   *

I wrote to Harry:

'The Convention is over, thank goodness! All that "Peace in our Time" stuff gave me quite a nasty turn. Now I am able to breathe and to look around me for other distractions than mass democracy. I went and saw a revival of John's *Golden Apple*, miles away somewhere in a Theatre in the Round like a boxing ring. An amateurish company of boys and girls, but his lyrics got across, gay and original. The music not nearly as good as *Baby Doe*, I thought.

This is an eclectic city. Last night, on Market Street, I hesitated between a movie house and a Burlesk theatre, side by side, one billing *The Body is a Shell* (your Ouspensky friends?

and the other *The Body Beautiful*. Across the street at another movie house there was a double bill—a nudist film and *The Well of Loneliness* by Colette [*sic*]. Naturally I couldn't resist this, and sat impatiently through the nudes (ingeniously and decently photographed) until the big film came on. It proved to be—what? *Olivia*, that Bloomsbury story about a girl at school, featuring Edwige Feuillère, whose name wasn't even on the bill.

Afterwards I went to talk to an eccentric character, who has a newspaper pitch on Market Street. He is called Gavin Arthur, grandson of that American President who attended Baby Doe's wedding, and is writing an autobiography at the moment called *The President, Petronius and the Poet*—he being the poet, of course, and Petronius his father, who seems to have been a sort of Edwardian dandy. He has his pitch very well organized, farming it out to a team of serfs whenever he goes out to dinner. You might try this, when you get tired of your taxi. He called up one of them, and took me off to supper—toasted cheese cooked in beer—in his cold-water flat "the wrong side of the tracks." Every inch of the wall-space was covered with a collage of photographs—family-album stuff of the President, Edwardian, Tallulah characters in cloche hats, nudes, muscle men, things out of *Life*, personal snapshots, all pasted up together regardless, and sloshed in among them a number of horoscopes. He is an astrologer, and does them for people at ten dollars a time. He says he has got through all his money and anyway is tired of the rich and prefers living this way. He hadn't heard of Alice's and John's deaths, though he was a friend of them both, and was distressed when I told him. Clearly he doesn't read his own newspapers.

I met him on Saturday at a nice lunch out in the country, right up in the treetops in a forest of redwoods—sequoias they are, hundreds of feet high like great fluted columns, dating from 1066 and All That, and impressive. The lunch was given by an amiable English painter called Onslow Ford and his American wife, and there were two Chinese poets there, both charming and polite. There were two friends of Alice's and John's there too, and as we were talking sadly about them the telephone rang and someone came back with the news that Dr. Kinsey had just died. He seemed to have been a friend of all, and there was great consternation.

Then there is an old pal of mine here from the 'twenties, a

Greek painter called Varda, who lives on a ferry-boat which he
has converted into a studio with plenty of atmosphere. He has
a new saucer-eyed wife from Athens, whom he seems very fond
of, and gave me lovely Greek food—but alas, not Retsina.

I met an old Oxford friend with him, Hilary Belloc, now a
greybeard, who gave me a delicious meal, specially ordered,
in an Italian restaurant, with two bottles of vintage Californian
wine—Château Beaulieu, I think—which he had brought with
him. He has spent most of his life bumming happily around in
boats, but now seems to be settling down with a good wife—
an American one—and children. His only worry is that his
wife has come into some money, and he is afraid this will be
bad for the children. I suppose that's one of the snags you must
put up with if you go marrying American wives.

I leave in a few days for Nevada, then the Middle West,
and back to New York before too long. Go on cultivating the
I that lives, and write me your news.'

'Thank you for your report from planet Earth [he replied].
Life here in my personal cosmos is much less entertaining and
there are few bulletins to pass along that will not sound like
excerpts from Plotinus. I am aching to get back to terrestrial
reality, but finding it difficult. Every time I attempt "practical"
thinking and formulating "realistic" schemes I get bogged
down in dead ends. I keep thinking of that role in life that will
be spiritually and financially rewarding while my rapidly
dwindling fortune will probably have me taxi-ing again in a
few days. So back I go to philosophic musings about the end
of being, and ideal man.

New York has been hot and disagreeable, August refusing to
leave without a good dose of its notorious weather. My only
consistent activity has been tennis with Ken. I see Ellsworth,
who despite all the reasons for contentment seems to be yearning for that Dostoievskian torment that suits him so well.
Howard and Gerrit ask for you often, and are always filled with
sweetness and light, respectively. But little happens, except in
the untidy confines of my psyche, which I promised not to
report on.'

THE road back into Nevada led me up eastwards over the Sierra Nevada, through spectacular mountain and lakeland scenery. It did not attract my neighbour in the bus, a truck-driver returning thankfully to his home in Michigan.

'California stinks,' he said. 'Even the women stink. The coffee tastes of soapsuds. Nothing ain't no good there.'

Turning to the local newspaper, my eye was caught by a cryptic notice: 'Deer found wearing necklaces and earrings in Elko County should be reported promptly.' I read also, with some fellow-feeling, that two young men had been fined twenty-five dollars for climbing a mountain—Mount Rainier, in the nearby State of Washington—without permission. Such, I reflected, were the rewards bestowed on the pioneer spirit today.

At Reno, Lucius Beebe and his friend Chuck Clegg met me at the bus station in their sleek Rolls Royce (was it the first time, I wondered, that a Rolls had met a Greyhound bus?) and took me off to dine at a restaurant where we ate a well-grilled steak and drank vintage claret, for my host was a gourmet. On the way he explained to me that he had had trouble over the Rolls—the latest model (1956) to join his 'stable' of these vehicles, old and new—with the manufacturers at Derby. He had insisted that it be painted in two colours—colours, moreover, which he had defined as Vanderbilt Maroon and Taft Cream. The manufacturers protested with conservative asperity. Anyway, they said, they could trace no such colour as Taft Cream. But Lucius was insistent, conceding that Caramel Cream would do. Greatly saddened, they had shrugged their shoulders, painted the elegant creature and shipped her quickly away. She was now the prize pet of the Nevadan highways.

Lucius Beebe belongs to a Bostonian banking family, of English Northcountry origin. He was for many years a famed columnist and theatre critic on a daily newspaper in New York. Now he had retired to Nevada, where he had bought and ran, with the aid of Chuck, his literary partner, a local newspaper, *The Territorial Enterprise*. As 'squire' of Virginia City, a revived

'ghost town' which he had taken under his wing, he was a flamboyant figure, with the panache of the dandy and the wit of the
man of the world. For some years he and Chuck had lived in a
private railroad car designed in the Victorian manner—and containing a marble mantelpiece—nearby in Carson City, hitching
it, when they began to feel restless, to any train they fancied. But
the speed of the modern trains threatened to rattle it to pieces.
Now they had a steel-built car, designed in a more opulent
Edwardian style, which was kept in Reno. It cost five thousand
dollars to get it going on the railroad. So they used it less often,
living instead in a Victorian-Edwardian villa in Virginia City, to
which we drove after dinner. Its amenities included a number of
jackpot-machines in Lucius' dressing-room, and a Turkish bath
adjoining it, where he sensibly sweated out the poisons of the
evening before retiring to bed.

Next morning I explored Virginia City, set high among its
arid, rolling mountains. Here was the familiar Western set: the
Silver Dollar Hotel, where I stayed; the street of saloons—the
Sawdust, the Brass Rail, the Crystal (famed for its chandeliers),
the Bucket of Blood (with a macabre 'Dead Wagon' outside it);
the Presbyterian, Episcopalian and Catholic churches; Piper's
Opera House, sacred to such names as Buffalo Bill and Lily
Langtry, but now a dance-hall; the Castle, a villa in the 'gingerbread' style, built by a silver-digging miner in the 'sixties, with
silver door-knobs and stair-rails, doors and balusters from Germany, lace curtains from Brussels, marble fireplaces from Italy,
crystal chandeliers from Bohemia, clocks and statuary from France
and some furniture from England, all specially shipped round the
Horn. Finally, on sale at the street corner, there was *The Territorial Enterprise* itself, 'Mark Twain's Newspaper,' conserving the
typography of the period and shedding a glow of Western
nostalgia over all its news.

Lucius came to call for me in the Rolls around midday, and
took me on a tour of the surrounding countryside. He wore a
Stetson hat, with a spotted bandana round it, a white-brocade tie
and a bright-patterned shirt. We drove through the Comstock
Lode, the source, between the 'sixties and the 'eighties, of the
wealth of the Nevada gold rush. But every sign of it had vanished:
the wilderness had reclaimed its mines and buildings and railroads
more completely than the desert sands bury any Roman city, and
the archaeologists were unlikely ever to be tempted to excavate
it. Nevada, as I had already learnt, was now poor, dependent on

gambling and divorce, and now on atomic experiment, for a living. But it had compensations. It was empty, containing only one person for each square mile. It had no income tax. Moreover murder was easy: the State could afford few police, juries were expensive, and the lawyers were preoccupied with divorce.

Lucius saw his West in humorous but Romantic terms, and had written several books on its folklore. He considered the Wild West film to be the only indigenous American art form, and talked of starting an annual film festival in Reno, showing Westerns of different periods, from the silent days onwards.

In the evening we had a picnic dinner, with a barbecue, in the haphazard garden of two hospitable ladies who worked on *The Territorial Enterprise*. Afterwards Chuck drove me into Reno, not in the Rolls but in a Jaguar. ('Chuck prefers Jaguars,' Lucius explained.) We spent an hour or so in a gambling palace as large as a department store. It had a different casino, catering for a different income group, on every floor, and providing every conceivable game of chance. At the bar on the top floor, muffled and discreet and expensive, we got into conversation with a businessman from California. He asked me how I was travelling. I replied, by bus.

'Fourth-class travel,' he exclaimed contemptuously, and turned away to Chuck. I left them together and went to bed.

Early in the morning I took the bus to Salt Lake City. On the eastern frontier of Nevada there stood, twenty feet high, the Largest Mechanical Cowboy in the World. We piled out of the bus and into the station where, for a last twenty minutes of feverish industry, we pulled silently away at the levers of the gambling machines. With my last dime I won a miniature jackpot. Then we drove into the more straitlaced State of Utah.

This, it seemed, was Asia. A high flat prairie stretched ahead of us, its white sands sprinkled with a yellowish sage. Clouds played with their shadows over a rim of bare eroded mountains, and a salt lake gleamed silver like a frozen sea, towards the horizon. At sunset the sky turned to a luminous green and the clouds to pink, settling now on the tops of the mountains, to which the light gave a bold silhouette. I might have been on the Anatolian plateau.

Moreover Salt Lake City, standing like Damascus in an oasis of trees beneath its wide semicircle of mountains, is a sacred city, a place of pilgrimage like the cities of Asia. 'This is the place,' exclaimed Brigham Young, the leader of the Mormons fleeing from persecution in the East, as the pilgrim band emerged from the pass and saw the well-watered plain beneath them. It was their Promised Land, and here a century ago they built the tabernacle and temple which dominate the city.

They were good builders. The Tabernacle, where the Mormon choir performs and the organ plays daily, is a great oval rotunda, its dome containing no steel but only a lattice of timbers, no nails, but only pins of wood. The Temple, to which only priests and initiates are admitted, is a stone building of original style, Gothic in feeling but less so in detail, shooting six great spires up into the sky. They stand in precincts shaded by trees, with an elegant column surmounted by a pair of seagulls in bronze. For when the pioneers had planted their acres of grain there came an invasion of locusts to devour it, threatening to convert sown land into desert once more. They fought against the hordes in vain, then prayed for divine intervention. In due course they heard the sound of another invasion, on wings, from the West. Hordes of seagulls flew in and began to devour, not the grain but the locusts. Their prayers were answered: the crop was saved.

At the opulent headquarters of the Mormons, well-furnished with inlaid woods and marbles, I was received by their President or 'Pope,' David McKay, an aged but virile Scottish giant, a minor prophet with a mane of white hair, a deep resonant voice, and the clear blue eyes of the believer. He spoke of the pioneer days and of the building of the temple which, under Young's direction, had taken the Faithful twenty years to complete. He himself had had an uncle, no Mormon at first, who refused to pray or to preach or to attend meetings, but nevertheless worked for six months as a builder on the site—and was finally converted. The President had lived for a time in Stirling, in Scotland, where his beliefs had incurred some suspicion from the local inhabitants. 'Ye're no gonna take *oor* lassies,' they enjoined him.

Polygamy, in fact, which no longer prevails among the Mormons, was never, he assured me, practised by more than a small percentage, and then only at a high social level. It derived, by revelation, from the Old Testament custom by which the patriarchs took more than one wife. But there was no harem in the oriental sense: each wife and her family occupied a separate house or separate quarters, and was treated alike—as indeed the Koran lays down that Moslem wives should be. Marriage and family life are sacred institutions in the Mormon theology, and the marital state is held to continue after death. Thus God the Mother plays as significant a part in the heavenly hierarchy as

God the Father. A verse of a hymn which I heard sung in the
Tabernacle ran:

> When I leave this frail existence,
> When I lay this mortal by,
> Father, Mother, may I meet you
> In your royal courts on high?
> Then at length, when I've completed
> All you sent me forth to do,
> With your mutual approbation
> Let me come and dwell with you.

The Mormons are a prosperous community, wise investors and
administrators of real estate and industry. They were wise town-
planners too. Though Salt Lake City was laid out a century ago,
its streets were made, as though by the gift of prophecy, wide
enough for modern traffic, and there is little sense of disproportion
about its skyscrapers today. On the roof of the chief bank is a
tall pylon which indicates the approaching weather by coloured
lights: still blue for sunshine, flashing blue for cloud, still yellow
for rain and flashing yellow for a storm.

The acquaintance who showed me around the city was a banker,
but not a Mormon, and in the evening I dined with the wife
of his partner. She lived in a house outside the city, where we
sat, relaxing after the heat of the day, on a cool verandah, looking
out on to an all-white garden, with a fountain at the end of it
and a mountain beyond it, glowing softly pink, while the scent
of petunias drifted around us in the transparent twilight. I was
interrupted by a call to the telephone from a local newspaper
reporter, to whom I expatiated on the beauties of the landscape.
He seemed gratified by this, remarking that most visitors to Salt
Lake City were interested only in Mormons, and the next day
published my remarks with a headline, 'Briton Lauds Utah
Scenes.'

The drawing-room was done up in soft dove-greys and pinks,
picked out with gold. Its Edwardian family portraits blended with
neo-French furniture and with an occasional ornament of the
period, which might have come from a Third Avenue antique
shop. The table was laid with cut glass, and we had wine for
dinner—a welcome amenity, since we were afterwards to go to
a Mormon party, at which no drink or stimulants, not even
coffee or tea, would be served. The conversation was of the opening of the Opera in Vienna, which my hostess had attended, and

the lady next to me said later, with simplicity and feeling, 'How I love to go to Europe! I find that it makes me live better.'

This was no snobbish affectation, but a remark of obvious sincerity. It warmed my heart to the wide open spaces of America.

MIDDLE WEST

21

Saddle and Sirloin

WHEN first I arrived in the States a shrewd American said to me: 'A European, coming to America for the first time, should skip New York and fly direct to Kansas City. Start from the Middle. The East will only mislead you.' Disregarding his advice, I was only now, towards the end of my journey, approaching the centre of America, having first explored East, South and West. Each had been in its way tinged with the past, and with an imported culture: the East with Georgian England and the Puritan tradition; the South with colonial Africa and the nostalgia of reaction; the West at first with a hybrid Spain, then with something wholly American but nostalgic too in its reversion to Frontier romanticism, then on the Coast with Europe again —but a Mediterranean Europe. But now, from that evening in Salt Lake City onwards, the picture began to form in my mind of an authentically American America, foreign only in so far as it deliberately chose to draw from European culture, moreover forgetting the past to live self-confidently and optimistically in the present and future. Here indeed was a new and distinct civilization. I began to perceive what my shrewd American friend had meant.

Already I had sensed something of this spirit on a flying visit from New York to Chicago, during the first month of my journey. Here, in the 'capital' of the Middle West, all that jarred in the East seemed to fall into place. Brash as the city was, it had an integrity of its own, it made sense. In its raw, alive, restless vulgarity there was no clash, as in New York, with an earlier immigrant culture. Chicago had been initially, and was still, defiantly American.

The skyscrapers, not huddled one in front of the other but overlooking the wide open spaces of the Michigan Boulevard and the Park and the lake beyond, were in scale—and I felt at ease with them. The population, hybrid as it might be with its hundreds of thousands of Poles and Czechs, seemed to have cut its ties with Europe: the Atlantic, after all, was a long way away. In this new atmosphere, the perpetual motion of the elevated railroads like roller-coasters roaring along above the streets, of bridges leaping in all directions, carrying roads over railroads, railroads over railroads, roads over roads, railroads and roads over river and canals, stimulated more than it tired. There was a gaiety in the whirligig of freeways, like speedways, encircling and spiralling around the city, even in the immensity of the parking lots, horizontal or vertical, and in the gaudiness of the sleek, shining cars within them. There was a fantasy in the design of the buildings themselves, with here an aquamarine dome, there black polished walls and gilded windows, here a Venetian façade, there a castellated roof, and everywhere the iron fire-escapes, zig-zagging nakedly up the sides of the man-built canyons. Here was the vitality of an unabashed materialism, independent of tradition and creating its own, rejoicing positively in the ambitions and the rewards and the pleasures of a mechanical civilization. Withal it was a city close enough to the earth, with no ocean around it like Manhattan Island, but planted right in the heart of America's deep-soiled lands.

With my old friend Jerome Colloredo-Mansfeld, a Central European who had settled in Canada, and who had flown down from Montreal to spend a few days with me, I visited the stock-yards, looking no longer on tens of thousands of cars but on tens of thousands of cattle and sheep and hogs. Brought hundreds of miles by hundreds of trains from the Western prairies and the Middle Western grain belt, policed now by picturesque cowboys on horses, they queued and processed to the slaughter like human beings to the subway. Then, stunned by sledge-hammers, strung up ungainly by the legs, throats slashed, heads cut, corpses skinned as adroitly as a child is undressed for bed, they disappeared in a welter of blood to become, on various floors, chilled carcasses, joints and hams, sausages, canned meats, but above all steaks, for this is essentially a beef-eating race.

Man-size steaks awaited us a few steps away, in the Stockyard Inn, 'where the steak is born.' Built in the style of Shakespeare's house at Stratford on Avon, with a post-chaise anchored outside the door, the inn, embodying also the Saddle and Sirloin Club, had its stools and its banquettes upholstered in cowhide, and a Matador Bar tastefully frescoed with the prehistoric herds of the Altamira caves. In a windowless luncheon-room, fluorescent with amber, the man-size eater studied a menu bound in a cowhide design. Then he proceeded to a throne, decked with steaks.

'Choose and brand your own steak,' his menu instructed him. 'Then we'll whisk it out for broiling.' He might choose a Sirloin

Room Special for the equivalent of £2 ('16 ounces of luscious eating. Specially selected and aged for tenderness and finish. Real he-man size—and wonderful'), a double one for £4 ('double the delight, doubly wonderful'), or a Saddle and Sirloin Very Special for £2 10s. ('World-famous. A single steak extra aged, specially cut and trimmed.') Alternatively he might try Roast Prime Ribs of Beef ('real corn-fed, with that "just-right" marbling that ensures mighty tender eating') or Lamb Chops ('tender young spring lamb . . . all dressed up in the latest style of french "panties" ').

So man devoured beast, noting, as he did so, 'Two out-of-the-ordinary touches. The hot platter on which your steak reposes in all its glory is the one from which you are expected to eat. This helps keep the steak hot long as possible and all juices are retained. Secondly, your salad is placed at the right of your plate for modern American convenience . . . not at the left, in passé European style.'

After a drink here, we preferred to lunch more modestly at a restaurant, billed as frequented by senators ('Yes, Sir, *Senators*!'), whose wines nevertheless came 'from the cellars of the purveyors to His Holiness Pope Pius XII.'

The university quarter was an enclave of European culture, which served merely to give point to the Americanism of the rest of the city. We stayed here, Jerome as the guest of his friend, P. H. von Blankenhagen, who was a member of the Faculty, myself at a cheap hotel nearby. Unaware that it did not serve meals, I made the mistake of ordering my breakfast in bed in the morning. It came—with the coffee in a cardboard cup, the butter in a cardboard saucer, the jam in a piece of paper, a slice of bread in the bell-boy's hand; and without a plate, a spoon to stir the coffee, or a knife to spread the butter and the jam. (It was just such a breakfast as had once been brought to me in the wilds of Anatolia, where, as here, guests breakfasted out). With the professor, we talked of many things—of the American Constitution. to which he referred as a constitutional—or did he say unconstitutional?—monarchy, and of the American character. He was thinking, he said, of writing a book of essays, entitled 'Nobody Loves Me: Studies in American Psychology.' One of a number of Germans who give Chicago University an especial European character, he had collected around him, in European fashion, a group of intelligent students who dropped in and out of his rooms, as often at Oxford and Cambridge but seldom at Harvard or Yale, and with them too we drank and talked and joked, often far into the night.

During the day we rejoiced in the Chicago Art Gallery, and in various private collections—born, not of mere snobbery but of a genuine enthusiasm for the arts. For Chicago is a city of serious collectors. The Professor had a friend, a millionaire of recent origin, who one day, with time on his hands between air flights in London, visited one or two art galleries and bought one or two pictures—a Picasso, a Monet, a Braque. The purchases stimulated in him an interest in painting, of which he knew nothing; and now, one of the city's wealthiest citizens, he was humbly attending a university course in the history of art. Here was a culture not traditional, as on the Eastern seaboard, but one which, as the generations went by, would surely develop, selecting at will from the European heritage, until it achieved the force of a tradition of its own.

∽ 22 ∽

The American Press · Blow-fish and
Spice · The Childish Hubby

NOW, on my journey back from West to East, I did not return to Chicago, but passed to the south of it across the centre of the continent, feeling at home in the Middle West as in the Middle East, with its vast flowing expanses of earth and sky. In two days from Salt Lake City via Cheyenne, Wyoming, to Omaha, Nebraska, I travelled nearly a thousand miles. This no longer seemed too long a journey, so used was I to the soporific comfort of the bus, and to the stops, at two-hour intervals, for a cup of coffee or a snack at some Greyhound station or roadside café. I had grown familiar with these places, each one so like the other, with its warm smell, compounded of hamburger and hot milk and cardboard and central heating; its armoury of intimidating machines, steaming for coffee or freezing for ice-cream; the bright but timeworn plastic 'leather' of its bar stools and booths its slot machines, supplying so many needs (the oxygen machine for example, and the 'mechanical valet,' dispensing shave cream toothbrush, nail clippers and styptic pencil); its counters stacked with candy and souvenirs and ten-cent cigars, and its racks with such enticing magazines as *Uncensored Confessions* and *Darin*

Romances; and, to accompany all, the monotonous muted psalmody of the juke-box, canned and unchanging from coast to coast.

There was one commodity they did not supply—and that was alcohol. Seldom was I able to get beer even with my luncheon or before it. In the evenings, needing whisky, I carried a flask, ordered simply ice-water with my meal, poured the whisky into the water under cover of the table, then hid the glass behind the various bottles of condiments and sauces with which it was furnished. There was always one high, rectangular container especially suited to this form of concealment. One day I looked at it closely and saw that it contained paper tissues, for which, being a user of the conservative handkerchief, I had never before found an appropriate use. Now I took one of these and wrapped it carefully around my glass, thus effectively concealing not only the liquor but, I hoped, my appearance of guilt. In these places—as indeed in most American restaurants—I found it always a problem to know what to do with the litter of screwed-up paper wrappings for sugar and crackers (biscuits to me, just as American biscuits are scones) and other eatables, together with the cardboard cups and cardboard saucers that lay strewn all over the table as a meal progressed. Why not, I thought, a little trash-can, in a Contemporary design, before each place?

Sometimes I ran out of reading-matter, for the supply of readable paper-backs—though it included works by such writers as Aldous Huxley, Henry Miller, Truman Capote, Carson McCullers, and J. D. Salinger—was limited. But I never tired of the provincial newspapers—so numerous that there was often a new one to buy at each stop. I had been surprised, in New York, by the respectability of the American Press. Here was nothing so frivolous as the London *Daily Express* or so sensational as the London *Daily Mirror*, but a series of tabloids which, beneath their sky-scraping headlines, were by comparison models of decorum and gravity. The social columnists, it is true, retailed some scandal—which was often, moreover, inexact. Once at luncheon I met a columnist, Leonard Lyons, who talked throughout the meal without pausing to ask me a question. A week or so later he mentioned my name in a paragraph, spelling it wrongly and attaching it to an inaccurate story, of which I could have given him the correct version. He had evidently no idea that we had met.

Otherwise it was only in the correspondence columns of the *Daily News*—the Voice, not of the Editor, but of the People—

that an element of astringency sometimes raised its head: 'Does anyone know the I.Q. of Harry Truman? . . . I am heartily in favour of giving Eisenhower another term as President—of Columbia University. . . . Something should be done about the pigeon problem in New York City. Twice within the last year I have had my hair shampooed and my jacket cleaned due to the thoughtless habits of these birds. . . . If anybody can do it, Grace Kelly will make pregnancy popular.'

The average reader, for ever in search of useful information, doubtless preferred the brief laconic items of it used to fill up a column in the *New York Times*: 'Easter Island is fourteen miles long and seven miles wide. . . . An estimated 27,000 Americans went blind in 1955. . . . Small clams steamed in garlic and wine are a popular dish for tourists in Southern Spain. . . . More than half of all United States farms have trucks and three-fourths of them have automobiles . . .'

But for pure entertainment many Americans turned from the news to the comics. It was a familiar sight in the Subway to see a middle-aged gentleman solemnly engrossed in one of those bright-coloured supplements, while in San Francisco and other such cities of pleasure they were promoted to Page 1, Section 1, of the mammoth Sunday editions.

The provincial Press, with which I grew so familiar, was less serious in its content than the Press of New York. It contained, for example, little foreign news. A friend of mine, Michael Padev, a European journalist who was now foreign editor of a group of newspapers in Arizona and Indiana, had told me, when I saw him in San Francisco, that only twenty per cent of the foreign agency news from the East got beyond Dallas, Texas; and here it was drastically cut before onward transmission. (Such a dearth of information explained, no doubt, the views of a Texan who, at the time of the visit of Kruschev and Bulganin to London, expressed to me the conviction that the goddam British were on the point of signing a treaty of alliance with Russia, directed against the United States. He offered to bet with me on the subject and, since he was a millionaire, I have never ceased to regret my refusal to do so.) Yet the West is not indifferent to the affairs of the world. Michael, organizing independent sources of information and relying on his own European political background, had now introduced into his papers a regular column of foreign comment, which was attracting widespread interest—not to say surprise at the unfamiliar truths it revealed.

As I travelled I liked to delve into the women's pages. Is not America, after all, a woman's country? Here I was struck by an old-fashioned primness of language. Young ladies were not merely engaged but 'betrothed' or 'affianced.' I read not simply of marriages taking place but of 'vows exchanged' and 'nuptials repeated.' Acting once as best man at a New York wedding, I remember the slight shock which ran round the table at a preliminary party for ushers and bridesmaids, when the bridegroom, an Englishman, declared his intention of having the English as opposed to the American marriage service. This included, as he explained, the endowment of his bride with all his worldly goods (certainly an un-American conception) and the worshipping of her with his body. There was an embarrassed pause at this; and then one of the bridesmaids remarked, 'A bit ranchy, that.' Later the ceremony, thus carried out with some misgiving by the parson, was voted to have been 'rather a sexy service.'

In American language, as in American manners, there is often this old-world flavour. Formal compliments are exchanged with a flowery politeness long since forgotten in Europe. A party is a 'gracious occasion,' with manners as grave and as decorous as in any Jane Austen novel. On the *Queen Mary*, meeting a lady from Philadelphia, I had asked her what kind of a city it was, expecting some such answer as 'Gee, but it's swell!' Instead she replied, 'I like it well,' using unconsciously the style and the grammar of her grandmother. Similarly, when I first called a lady on the telephone, I was surprised to receive the melodious, grammatical reply, 'This is she'—not 'It's her speaking,' or merely plain 'Speaking,' as in the more casual jargon of the British. My lawyer friend, Andrew Jackson, told me of a document he had received with the poetic title, 'The Brief of the Grieving Pilot.' On the other hand, words were used like 'slenderizing, tenderizing, climaxing, vacationing, socializing. . . .'

The ladies of the wide open spaces—or so it seemed from their newspapers—led vivid and manifold social lives. From headlines only a few points less large than those of the New York *Daily Mirror*, I quote at random: BRIDGE LUNCHEON IS GIVEN . . . MMES SKOUSEN, ELLIS AND HAMPTON ARE ISSUING INVITATIONS FOR COFFEE . . . MISS BAILEY ENTERTAINS MISS LANE. . . . MRS. BAKER CHOSEN TO ATTEND MEETING. More romantically MISS VIRTUE IS MARRIED; more eccentrically HANDKERCHIEF SHOWER HONORS MRS. BOGUS. ICE CREAM SOCIAL SLATED BY CHURCH diverted me by its hint of disreputability until I learnt that 'slated' meant, not 'denounced' but merely put on the slate.

The *Social Calendar*, in any week, promised a riot of breakfasts and brunches and lunches, receptions and lectures and meetings, dinners and socials and barbecues, coffee parties and cocktail supper parties and bridge parties, culminating perhaps in a 'twilight mixed golf event and chuck wagon dinner' at a fashionable country club. A faithful account of these events was given day after day by battalions of columnists (*The San Francisco Chronicle* has about seven). For example, in Denver I read:

> 'MONDAY: Bang-up partygiver this p.m. was Baroness V. Kuhn von Poushantal, who tossed her annual shindig at her Troutdale canyon home, Hacienda del Sol. Party candids: Anne and Herbert Mueller talking about plans for a future trip to the Orient . . . pretty Mrs. Kirk Howry talking about her European junket and the Dior showing where she sat next to the Duchess of Windsor . . . male fashion pace setter Bill Glass in a gray and brown charcoal blazer . . . new addition to the spectacular hillside house: a Swiss room overlooking the canyon . . . hanging lights of Hawaiian blow-fish and beautiful shell panels.'

And in Dallas:

> ' "We're going to put some spice in this game," a Dallas hostess announced at a dessert bridge party Monday night for a Dallas bride-elect. Prize for a grand slam, bid and made, was a can of spice wrapped up in pink and white. Anyone taking a trick with a deuce won the prize for a "hot game"—a pink and white can of black pepper.'

On another such occasion, in Pinocchio Drive, the buffet was planted with three-foot pretzel trees, with 'vari-sized' pretzels and clusters of balloons on their branches.

But all, alas! was not blow-fish and pretzels and spice. There was a dark side to the glitter of American social life. Side by side with the society chronicles were oracles of syndicated wisdom, where some lady of elevated standing supplied other lesser ladies with intricate advice—and myself with a valuable insight into the problems of American social and personal life. My favourite among these was Mrs. Molly Mayfield, whom I came upon syndicated in the *Rocky Mountain News*, a lady of tact and understanding smartly flavoured with wit. Here is an example of one of the social dilemmas with which she had, day after day, to contend:

'Dear Mrs. Mayfield,

I have a most perplexing problem, and it involves my husband. He is a quiet, intelligent professional man. He has a wide variety of interests, most of which he brings into the conversation when we have guests. This is all right except recently he has become interested in a system of fortune telling by reading the lines on people's feet. Now every time we have guests he insists on going around making them remove their shoes, so he can show off his new talent. This is most embarrassing to me. Recently our Minister, who happens to be an old friend of ours, visited us and my husband "read" his right foot. In all seriousness my husband told the minister that he had strong criminal tendencies. Just suppose the minister had not been our friend! He has done the same thing to several *important* guests of ours. . . . Other than this he is a wonderful guy and I hate to hurt his feelings. But people are starting to whisper.

Worried Wife.'

Mrs. Mayfield replied that she was drawn to the husband's sense of humour ('He must get a real bang out of life'). But of course, if people were starting to whisper, he might start to get his name into the society columns, and that indeed might become serious. So why not, on threat of exposure to the society editor, ration him to one pair of feet at any given party, and two on Saturdays, and hope that he would eventually lose interest in his hobby?

Another of these worldly-wise ladies was Miss Abigail ('Abby') von Buren, the oracle of the *Mirror*, whose pronouncements are syndicated far and wide throughout the open spaces. 'Dear Seventeen,' ran one of them, 'A girl should wear her clothes just tight enough to show she is a woman, and just loose enough to show she is a lady.' Counsels of patience were addressed to the Spouse who Objects to Hospitalization:

'Dear Abby,

I am a lady one year younger than Jack Benny. Lately I have had the feeling that my husband would like to trade me in for a newer model. He and a doctor friend of ours have engineered me into this hospital for a "check-up" and I have

lived here for five weeks without finding out what is wrong
with me. Every night my husband and my doctor (a bachelor)
tuck me into bed at 8 o'clock and THEY go out on the town.
I know I'm all right, but who will take my word against the
doctor's?'

The trials of life, in America, seemed to begin at an early age.
'College Boy Puzzles over Meaning of Life' was a harrowing cry
from the heart. So was that of 'Wanting Forgiveness': 'I went
too far when I was a teenager . . . became blissfully infatuated at
the age of 13½ with a young man . . . was indiscreet with him.'
Now she wanted to marry another. Should she tell? To which
Molly replied, 'Dear Wanting . . . I see no reason why.'
Then there was the 'Childish Hubby' (aged 21) who 'Strains
Wife's Nerves':

'. . . so childish you wouldn't believe it. He likes to play with
a yo-yo and water guns. I am a nervous wreck. In the middle
of the night he wakes me up to get him ice-water or make
popcorn. If he wants to go anywhere during the baby's nap
time, I have to get the baby up and take him along. . . .'

Sterner stuff, however, suggesting drastic remedies, filled the
column of The Man of Mystery in *Bronze Thrills*, a negro
magazine published in Fort Worth, which I found one day dis-
carded on a bus seat. Mrs. V. J., of Rockford, Illinois, wrote
to him:

'I really don't understand my husband. We've been separated almost a year. I caught him with another woman. He still
comes to my home and eats. I cook his supper at night. We
have eight children. . . . I really don't know what to do about
it unless I kill, and I can't see why that would do me any good.
He takes her and her children to church and leaves his. Enclosed
is $2.'

The Man of Mystery, clearly also a Man of Moderation,
replied: 'You are right. Murder wouldn't help the situation at
all. . . .'

23

*The Heart of America · Ideal Homes and
Chimpanzees · Back to the East*

AT Omaha my host, Louis Drew, met me at the bus-station in
his car—the first time, I am sure, that a guest of his had arrived
by such fourth-class means of transport. Fortunately the station
was downtown, and it was a Sunday evening, so there was nobody
to see us. I had learnt to avoid mutual embarrassment in various
cities, when asked how I had come and how I proposed to leave,
by replying, with a non-committal shrug of the shoulders, 'By
road.'

Louis ran an antique shop with his brother Jack, who had just
left, on an annual buying trip, for Europe. I had met the brothers
in London, where one or other of them came each year, combing
the markets and the junk-shops of the slums and the suburbs for
bargains in furniture to be sold to the ladies of Omaha for handsome prices, showing especial ingenuity over the transformation
of mundane objects into fashionable adornments for the home. A
Victorian night-commode, fitted with a top, became a coffee-
table; a washstand became a plant-stand, its basin and its soapdish
planted with flowers, while its jug was transformed into an
electric lamp; bedroom chests-of-drawers, at thirty shillings,
made of varnished pitch-pine, were stripped down and smartened
up to sell at seventy-five dollars; Georgian soup-ladles, with
handles bent back, became ashtrays handy for the arms of chairs.

'They make good conversation pieces,' Louis had said. 'Something to talk about at table. You can't just go downtown and get
one the same.'

Now for the first time I was to see the houses of Omaha, for
which these treasures had been destined. They proved for the
most part to be villas of an Edwardian character, with a tendency
to the Jacobean style unusual in other suburbs I had visited. They
showed a taste for neo-French furniture, vitrines full of knick-
nacks, ormolu ornaments, and satin-glass epergnes. Jack and his
wife, in their house in Omaha, discreetly dark behind lattice
windows, had converted silver presentation cups into lamps, and
on the walls had put silver Georgian dish-covers, cut in half to
make sconces, with a dish inside to hold flowers; while Louis and

his wife had resourcefully made a lamp out of an old-fashioned telephone. They had the advantage of living across the river in Council Bluffs, in the State of Iowa, where the drink laws were easier. Here one night we dined at a club, and I was able to add another to the list of States in which I could claim to have set foot—a list which, in the end, added up to thirty-four, or nearly three-quarters of the whole.

The pride of Omaha was its Boys' Town, an institution to which we drove next day, aimed against delinquency, and resembling rather, in its amenities, some university in the Eastern States. Around us spread an undulating park-like landscape, surprisingly green owing to the moderation of the season, but spread with fields of bright-gold maize and dark-gold popcorn. Clean white farmsteads with silos, in groups of trees, woods of oak and elm and a suggestion of downs beyond the blue horizon gave it the aspect rather of Central Europe than of the conventional Middle Western spaces.

Next day we drove to Lincoln, where from the roof of the Capitol a colossus in the guise of a sower flung symbolical seed over the prairies around. Beneath, Nebraska displayed the progeny of its deep prolific soil in a State Fair, a concourse of beasts fabulous in form and proportions. Here, shampooed and beribboned, were sheep as square and as broad as upholstered settees; mammoth cows, immaculately groomed and crimped and permed; ponies with cute little coiffures; pigs as fat and pot-bellied as armchaired clubmen, barely able to drag themselves to their feet. Here also were mighty marrows and melons and corn-cobs; such sideshows as a baby in a bottle, with two heads and one buttock, and a cathedral made from ten thousand match-sticks; and a clinic, broadcasting throughout the fair-ground: 'It could be worth your while to get your chest X-rayed right away . . . right away. Just go right down to the Agricultural Building . . . right down . . . right down . . .' At this passers-by listened nervously—and some of them turned in the indicated direction.

These Middle Western cities, far apart and separate as islands in an ocean of land, differ one from the other as distinctly and as proudly as Greek city states, showing their rivalry not merely in wealth and production but in manifestations of culture—in their art galleries, symphony orchestras, programmes of lectures. Omaha looked down on Kansas City, my next destination, and Kansas City, Missouri, as I found when I reached it, looked down not merely on Omaha but on Kansas City, Kansas, occupying, t

the confusion of postal sorters, the other bank—the wrong bank
—of the river. The city, describing itself proudly as the 'Heart of
America,' seemed like a miniature Chicago, its tempo quicker,
its atmosphere more prosperous, its spirit more thrusting than
that of Omaha. From the apartment of Bill Kemper, comfortably
furnished and hung with excellent pictures, I looked down
through a broad plate-glass window over a stately bend in the
Missouri, alive with silos and oil-drums and wharves and railway
sidings, containing a harbour, embracing an airport and crossed
by an imposing new toll-bridge. It had been opened that very
afternoon by a young lady of fourteen, breaking over it a champagne bottle, filled with Missouri water, while a band played
'Everything's up-to-date in Kansas City.'

Among the spectators, as I read in the *Kansas City Star*, printed
on pink newsprint, was a man who had worked on the bridge and
had helped to build four others, all spanning the Missouri. The
experience had inspired him to poetry, notably an ode, distinctly
anthropomorphic in spirit, on a derrick named 'Old Elmer':

Old Elmer had stood through wind and rain,
   He had lifted each load and withstood every strain,
Not a man on the job had the slightest of doubts,
   That old Elmer would finish and set the job out.
But once in a lifetime, be it derrick or man,
   There comes a sad thought—can we finish this span?
Old Elmer had travelled quite far from his base,
   Although his cables were tight he was winning the race.
But who could foresee when he took the big lunge
   That Old Elmer could not handle twenty-six tons.
He died as he lived when he crashed with a bang.
   He picked a good spot, killing none of his gang,
So let's hope that Elmer don't go down below
   But gets his just dues where good derricks go.

But the pride of Kansas City is its art gallery. Museums thrive
in America as perhaps nowhere in Europe. Sixty millions—one
third of the population—visit them annually. In terms of such
statistics it is possible to prove that art—and indeed classical music
is more popular than baseball. In New York, wandering in the
Metropolitan Museum or in the Museum of Modern Art, in
Washington in the National Gallery, I had always found myself
one among thousands earnestly examining the pictures, either
singly or in conducted groups, and indeed spending a great part

of the day there, for the museums of New York have inviting cafeterias and restaurants, and gardens in which it is agreeable to sit, while the Metropolitan gives a daily programme of film shows. In Boston and Philadelphia and Washington, I had found myself similarly one among hundreds. Many of them had yet to develop a true feeling for painting. But the curiosity was there, and that went half way towards it.

The cultural snobbery which prevails throughout the States may well, in another generation, become cultural understanding. Patronage of the arts is general, and is extended not merely through the big Foundations but through business firms, zealous to embellish their buildings as their more Philistine British counterparts seldom do. Ellsworth was now working on a large decoration for a building in Philadelphia; Harry found a market for his sketches in an advertising firm, which hung them on the walls of business offices and boardrooms. America may not provide an atmosphere in which it is sympathetic for an artist to live; but at least it provides him with a living, if he is not too proud to take advantage of it.

Moreover, taste in interior decoration, throughout the States, is in many ways superior to that of Britain. It may be standardized, negative, impersonal, in that it is the taste of the decorator, following a prevalent fashion rather than of the owner following his natural choice. But it seldom achieves that degree of pretension to which the British suburbanite aspires in his Ideal Home.

The Nelson Art Gallery in Kansas City gave me perhaps more satisfaction than any I saw in the States. It must indeed contain one of the best and most representative small collections of pictures in the world. It inherited, I was told, some thirty million dollars in cash, not in depreciated securities, at the lowest ebb of the great depression in the nineteen-twenties, and an enlightened director was able to buy all he wanted in Europe at the lowest prices.

St. Louis too, the 'Gateway to the West' and my next port of call on the continental 'ocean,' had a rewarding gallery, in which I spent a morning, enjoying not only pictures but Etruscan statues, Chinese bronzes, a medieval chapel, and a Pompeian Room designed for Mrs. Fitzherbert. St. Louis is a city much aware of its French origin, like New Orleans, farther down the Mississippi River. It is, in fact, French in the planning of its spacious parks and gardens and in the mansard roofs of its older streets, but with a strong flavour of Victorian England in its commercial buildings and wharves. Its Zoo houses a company of chimpanzees, of whom it is boasted that they have the highest I.Q. of any of their kind in the world. They give accomplished theatrical performances before applauding crowds, and throw fits of temperament backstage.

Along the Mississippi riverfront, more inviting than that of New Orleans, the Mid-American Jubilee Fair was in progress. Here such marvels were shown as a Super-Fortress comparable to that which dropped the atom bomb on Hiroshima; a model farm stocked with enormous beasts; exhibits of electrical and industrial gadgets ('Better Living Company. Electronics and You'); a German beer-garden, serving meals with *bratwurst* and *sauerbraten*. There was an exhibition of the activities of Pinkerton's, their detectives undetected in crowds (Contest: 'Find the Pinkerton Man') and as they work side by side with unsuspecting employees to check their reliability. There was a Parisian street, complete with bistro and Eiffel Tower ('*Soyez le bienvenu*. That means Hello there!'). A pageant of some length was enacted before the façade of the old cathedral, entitled 'Heartland U.S.A.' and recapitulating the history of St. Louis. A fashion display, beneath a geodesic dome, offered, to the sounds of an organ, hairstyles in real hair coloured pale sand, red pepper, blonde ash, steel smoke and tropical splendour.

I stayed at the Sheraton-Jefferson Hotel, finding a notice pushed under my door in the morning: 'You neglected to lock your door last night. Our Night Officer, rather than awaken you, took the liberty of doing this for you. We hope you enjoyed a good night's rest.' This zeal to please the customers of American hotels takes various forms. At the Lafayette in Portland, Maine, I was asked on departure to fill in a questionnaire: 'CLERK: courteous, haughty, helpful, discourteous, disinterested, gruff? BELL MAN: pleasant, impertinent, eager to serve, disinterested? ELEVATOR OPERATOR: obliging, polite, rude, efficient? MAID: polite, surly, talkative, quiet, noisy, impolite? TELEPHONE SERVICE: prompt, slow, pleasing, annoying?'

At Cheyenne, Wyoming, my towels were wrapped in Cellophane paper, hard to tear open, and were hence, I read, 'as clean and fresh as December snow in the Rockies'; at Chapel Hill, North Carolina, the lavatory seat (one of those church seats, probably, 'the best seat in the house') was sealed with a ring of paper marked 'Sanitized for your Protection.' Most hotels provided a notice to hang outside the door: 'Don't Disturb,' varied sometimes colloquially to 'Whoa Thar!' or 'Please Go 'Way and Let Me Sleep.' I was not easy to disturb, since I had learnt to plug my ears with anti-noise ear 'stopples,' against the throb of the traffic, and to mask my eyes with a slumber shade from the drug store, against the early sunlight streaming in through the venetian blinds on the normally curtainless—or in Americanese 'drapeless'—windows.

I never stayed, however, in the hotel in New York where it is possible for the visitor to plug in to sounds which will make him feel at home—bird sounds, for example, babies crying, oxen lowing, traffic throbbing or the sounds of the sea. Nor alas! did I stay—though I drove past it—in the Crazy Hotel at Mineral Wells, Texas, whose amenities I can only imagine.

* * *

Indianapolis too proved to have a certain French atmosphere—but in terms rather of some extravagant Paris exhibition of the early nineteen hundreds. Here were broad radiating boulevards; gardens designed like a travesty of the Tuileries, with elaborate monuments and fountains; sumptuous public buildings, with mansard roofs and imposing clocks; a circular 'Place Vendôme,' with a towering memorial in the centre of it to Indiana's 'silent victors' in four wars and a revolution. Mammoth in size and flamboyant in conception, it was a Statue of Victory, some three hundred feet high, surrounded by four of the world's largest fountains, and embodying a galaxy of swashbuckling goddesses. Here were guns firing, ships tossing, eagles spreading their wings symbolic ladies waving star-spangled banners and flaunting voluptuous limbs.

But now we were moving back into the orbit of the East once more. In the bus-station at Columbus, Ohio, I bought a *New York Times*—the first I had seen for some months. The Ohio landscape undulated cosily; the towns had squares, like market-places. At Cleveland, a city which, despite its industrial wealth, scorns a connection with the Middle West, Kay Halle, whom I had last seen in Washington, met me and drove me out to the home of her family, a Georgian country house looking down on a river and out over a countryside as gentle and civilized as any in Europe. Here I relaxed for a while before embarking on the last lap of my three months' journey, over the Ohio turnpike to Philadelphia and New York.

'I liked the Middle West [I wrote to Constance]. It isn't

beautiful—at least the cities aren't, though much of the landscape is. But to begin to understand America, I realize, you have to forget about beauty, stop being an old-fashioned European aesthete and look for other things instead. Vitality, for instance. There's plenty of that—the vitality of people who live in the moment and don't ask too many questions. And they've their own brand of democracy. It's a strong feeling of loyalty to the community—a civic sense, which I suppose is weakening in Europe. One sees it very clearly in the Middle West. A woman said to me, criticizing somebody, "He's no sense of service." What matters more than the person, or even the nation, is the city and the fraternity and the lodge and the shrine and the club and the committee, all blossoming into the convention; and, of course, there's the church—usually Low Church—which is one of the strongest (and incidentally richest) social influences of all. What they call "group adjustment" is more important than personal adjustment. All these groups are stronger, I think, than the family, which tends to get scattered once the babes are weaned. This is probably a Good Thing in its way, though I think it does mean that this civilization may develop on collectivist rather than individualist lines. But it won't be an inhuman sort of collectivism. There's too much warmth and enthusiasm and sound liberal principle behind it all. The raw material may still be raw, but it's good human material.'

NEW YORK

24

*Dark Accusations · Through New East Anglia · With Friends on
the Caspian · United States of Euphoria · Winter of Discontent ·
Good-bye to Babylon*

HARRY was drinking beer alone in the flat when I arrived back
in New York late in the evening. He had drawn a life-size post-
humous head of John, which brooded a little ominously over the
room. He looked nervous and worn and I soon learnt why. The
story he told was at first hard to believe.

John had had a brother named Louis, whom he saw seldom.
He himself had risen above his family's modest origins. But
Louis had stayed more or less where he was—a contractor of sorts,
in Virginia. He was said always to have been jealous of John.
There had been some awkwardness between John's friends and
Louis, when he had come up with his wife to the funeral in
Vermont. Since then, it seemed, John's death had been preying
on him. The cause of it had been given as thrombosis, to which,
so a doctor had told him, he himself had a tendency. Reluctant
perhaps to believe this, he had sought about for an alternative
cause of his brother's death; and suspicions began to develop in
his mind.

Harry's first inkling of this came a few days before my return.
He had paid a visit to John's mother, as he often did, since she had
kept house for John, and they had been friends. But on this
occasion her attitude was unexpectedly cold. She seemed to in-
sinuate that Harry was in some way to blame for her son's death;
if she, with a mother's love, had been there to look after him, he
would not have died.

Then, from Ken, Harry learnt what had happened. Louis had
convinced himself that the cause of death was not as the doctor
had certified. There had been a haemorrhage, and this did not
accord with thrombosis. Could it have been brought on by
violence? With the approval of his mother, Louis had asked the
Vermont authorities for an exhumation of the body that a full
autopsy might be held. In terms of the law of the State such a
request from a nearest relative would automatically be granted.
Harry's state of mind was easy to imagine. After some six weeks

the wounds created by his friend's death had begun slowly to heal. Now they were harshly and sordidly re-opened.

Louis had engaged an enquiry agent, a personal friend who had worked for the F.B.I., to investigate the case. Harry, sensibly, had refused to see him; he would talk to the police, if they required it, but to nobody else. But the man continued to call him up on the telephone, and had begun to use threats. He did so twice next day, giving a different name each time. I took the calls and said Harry was not available. Finally, hoping to stop this persecution and having nothing to hide, he consented to see him.

I left them together, but returned before the end of their interview. The enquiry agent was a little man with shifting eyes and a rat-like neurotic expression. Harry was recapitulating for him, patiently, the story of John's death. They had dined out quietly that night with some neighbours. They had gone to bed not long after midnight. At about 3.30 in the morning Harry had been awoken by John, who complained of a severe pain in the chest. It might, he thought, be acute indigestion. He asked Harry to fetch a medical dictionary, which they consulted together. John took some bicarbonate of soda. Since there was no telephone in the house, Harry suggested going for a doctor. But John did not want to be left alone; it would be best to wait a little; the pain might subside. He lay down on his bed and, after a while, turned on his side and appeared to go to sleep. Harry left him. Next morning he found him lying in the same position, and realized that he was dead. There was blood on the pillow and the sheets, presumably from a haemorrhage. Harry went for the doctor, who pronounced that the cause of death was thrombosis. That was all.

The little man asked him a number of questions. Had he been on good terms with Mr. Latouche? Certainly. They had had no quarrel that evening? Certainly not. After Mr. Latouche's death, had he instructed the servant to burn his mattress? Yes. Why had he done this? Because it was stained with his friend's blood, so was not a thing to keep. Was he aware that the Vermont State Police wanted to interview him? No. Did he not think it would be in his interest to go up to Vermont, to help them clear the matter up? No. If the Vermont Police wanted to see him they had only to say so. The little man hesitated. Possibly my presence in the background embarrassed him. Then he said to Harry, "Your story seems fairly clear. Will you come round with me now and tell it to Mrs. Latouche?" His tone was reasonably polite.

After a moment's thought, Harry shrugged his shoulders and agreed: 'I've told it to her before, several times. But if it's going to put an end to this nonsense, I don't mind telling her once more.'

They went round to Mrs. Latouche's flat. A little later Harry returned, angry and shaken. In Mrs. Latouche's presence, the enquiry agent's tone had changed abruptly. He turned on Harry and virtually accused him of killing John. Mrs. Latouche looked at him and said nothing. Harry refused to continue the conversation, and left.

The little man called up once or twice more. He was abusive. 'You little weasel,' he threatened Harry. 'We're gonna get you. We're gonna get you.'

Then the calls ceased. We heard that the exhumation had taken place. Harry might now expect to be left in peace until the result of the autopsy was known, in about ten days' time. He began to regain some of his spirits. But he needed to be alone. I was in the way. A friend of mine, who had just arrived from England, asked me to go with him for a few days to Montreal. Before leaving I saw Ruth, who promised to keep her eye on Harry.

'I always respected John,' she said. 'But I must say I do respect him twenty times more, now that I see just what he sprang from.'

*   *   *

From Montreal—a city still American in its atmosphere, where it was strange to drink good English tea, and see the Queen's head on the stamps, and hear French spoken in the streets, and drink wine with meals as a matter of course—I drove down through the forests of New Hampshire into Maine, where Ruth Moore, a woman novelist whom I had met in New York, had lent me her cottage for a week or two. Here I proposed to write and rest. The cottage stood close to the sea, at McKinley, a fishing village on Mount Desert Island, among woods whose leaves were beginning to flaunt the bright scarlets and golds of the fall. I took long walks, but always with a slight sense of frustration, since the woods made a thick belt between the road and the sea and, though this was a National Park, few paths ran through them or along the rough rocky beaches. It was a country not for walkers but for motorists and boatmen.

I was troubled about Harry. But I felt close to the soil and relaxed as I had not done since leaving the Rockies. There was a garden by the cottage, and here I dug up cabbages and carrots, and picked beans, staining my hands with the brown earth and the fresh-smelling greenness, cleansing and chopping the vegetables to make soups and stews. I became the peasant—and this was the tonic I needed.

Ruth Moore's family, who were fisherfolk, looked after me thoughtfully. Her niece and sister-in-law drove me up to Bar Harbour at the north end of the island. Until a year or so before this had been a fashionable resort, where millionaires had built villas in the earlier part of the century, looking out to sea and up the coast towards New Brunswick. But a forest fire had raged suddenly through it, consuming the villas and reducing a large tract of mountainous landscape to a charred and desolate waste. Her brother, a ruddy, shrewd fisherman, took me out in his boat one still October afternoon, to catch lobsters, hauling up the pots with a mechanical windlass, scrupulously measuring each lobster and throwing back those that were still too small for the New York lunch-tables, while the seagulls drifted around us like out-size snowflakes. He entertained me with stories of the coast—of the lonely lives of the lighthouse-keepers, marooned on the distant offshore islands; of the old woman, living in one of them, who, year in year out, kept a lamp lit in her window to guide the incoming fishermen. One night there was no lamp, and the next day her house was found burned to the ground, with her body charred amid the ruins.

I spoke to Harry on the telephone. He had had a polite note from the Vermont State Police, inviting him to call on them, or offering to send two officers down to New York to see him. He preferred this alternative. The interview had concluded satis-factorily, though in his depression he had stayed up drinking half the night before, and had thus felt at his worst during a long morning's interrogation. The autopsy had confirmed the cause of John's death as thrombosis, of which a haemorrhage was a known if unfamiliar feature. The record was closed. I suggested to Harry that he should join me for a few days in Maine; but he was reluctant to move. Moreover he had an idea for a story and wanted to work on it. A day or so later he wrote:

'You sounded well on the telephone on Friday. Your letter finally reached me, and your state of Thoreauean well-being was confirmed by the description of Maine. I have thought about making the trip up there, but decided against it. I think it's better for me to stay here. I feel positive and stronger, less aimless, and that's important to maintain. I've been writing writing, writing, and I'm feeling rooted to this place; the window, the brick walls and blue sky, the green blanket, that insulate me and my muse. Write when you expect to be back.'

Before returning I decided to pay a visit to Kay and Andrew Jackson, the friends of my first day in New York, at their small house up in Northern Vermont. Equipped with three fat lobsters, cooked by the fisherman's wife, I took the bus down the coast to Portland. From Bangor, a city of English aspect whose shops included the Puritan Clothing Stores and a draper named Coffin and Wimple, it proceeded appropriately to Belfast, where I ate a filling 'New England Boiled Dinner,' thence to Bath which stood on an estuary opposite Woolwich, and so to Yarmouth and Portland. (Here I found a post card of a sign in Maine, pointing in close succession to Norway, Parish, Denmark, Naples, Sweden, Poland, Mexico, Peru and China.) Along the road the glittering light of a still autumn day bejewelled a Nordic landscape of blue lakes and golden forests, decorated with white Georgian towns like those of East Anglia.

From Portland, a city adorned with a statue of Longfellow, the road climbed northwards into the steeper landscape of New Hampshire, its forest flaring and glowing in an extravaganza of hot colour above the blue lakes, cold as steel. Raging up the mountainsides were flames of scarlet and crimson and orange, maples and oaks, as it were, devouring the white trunks of the birches and the evergreen trees. Beneath them cinder-pink leaves smouldered over the earth like embers, seeming to kindle the undergrowth to an even fiercer blaze. It was a spectacle, showy and a trifle outrageous, characteristic of a continent with an indigenous trend to extremes.

Farther north, mounting into the State of Vermont, we came into a season of mistier, mellower fruitfulness. Here the tapestry of the forest had faded, orange dimming to yellow and crimson to pink, trees now bare of their leaves muting the pattern with lavenders and greys, while the pink of the leaves strewn over the earth had a rose-petal softness. Along the valleys and up the foot-hills this was a country of farms, their white clapboarded houses and high-pitched barns grouped as trimly as in a sampler or in a painting by Grandma Moses. In the mountains enfolding them was a profusion of stone, notably granite. Yet the farmers hardly used it as a material for domestic building. Despite their rigorous northern winters they preferred to build, for all its flimsiness, in the traditional clapboard, as though reluctant to commit themselves to too permanent a home. Subconsciously, perhaps, the nomadic instincts of the early settlers, the frontier itch to be up and moving, still prevailed.

For an hour or so I waited in the town of Barre, where I admired an unexpected and elegant statue of Robert Burns, in granite. Then a station wagon, carrying the mails, took me up a winding valley, reminiscent of Devon, to Greensboro' Bend. The driver flung out bundles of mail, without stopping, to left and to right of us, leaving the farmers to collect it from the roadside. Sometimes he stopped for a second to put the letters in a rough tin mail-box, once remarking of a full one: 'Terrible fellow that. No ambition. He don't collect his mail.' Steeples punctuated the villages, one of which was Calais. John's house was close by, and the driver had known of him, and spoke of his death. He lay buried in one of these cemeteries with the plain granite stones.

Andrew met me, and drove me to the house, near the edge of the Caspian Lake, which he and Kay had built for themselves, for summer holiday use, on her family's land. They had designed it with love and care, to be built one Winter, in the local architectural tradition, the sash-windows of the living-room facing a view of the lake and the wooded mountains beyond it. But when they arrived in the Spring they found, to their dismay, that the builder had turned the plan sideways, orientating the house away from the view that it might be protected against the prevailing winter snows. Unrepentant, he declared that to his knowledge no house had ever been built in these parts facing in any other direction. He consented, however, to put in a side window, facing the view, and the resulting room, with a log fire burning in the grate, had an atmosphere of ease and taste and comfort.

Next day we gardened, and walked over the hillsides—for here at last was a country to walk in. Russell Lynes and his wife Mildred arrived from their own summer house in the Berkshire Hills, and we spent an evening memorable for friendliness and amusing talk—also for the taste of the Maine lobsters, for once, as at no New York lunch-table, unfrozen thanks to two days on a bus, and thus of a fresh subtle flavour, brought out by a bottle or two of New York State white wine. Russell stimulated with his wit and his civilized understanding of American taste and behaviour, Mildred with her omnivorous interests and provocative views, Kay as a foil to them both, warm in sympathy and acute in perception, while Andrew beamed over all, preferring rather to listen than to talk as he filled and refilled our glasses. The night was cold, and was the last they would spend here until the following Spring.

On Sunday they drove me back as far as Rutland to catch the bus to Boston, winding across the Green Mountains behind convoys of trucks carrying loads of granite, destined to become tombstones in the New York cemeteries. Andrew, who was remaining behind for a few days to shut up the house while Kay returned to her publishing office in New York, waved us off with his lazy benevolent smile. It was the last time I was to see him. He died of a heart attack in New York, two months later.

I spent only a few days in New York, then went to Washington to cover the approaching Presidential election. I saw little of Harry, who had fallen into a mood of restless gaiety, staying up and drinking late each night, perhaps with a subconscious need to recapture the New York life he had enjoyed with John. I was usually out in the morning before he was up. He was worried about his flat. The block was to be demolished and, as a condition for this, each of the tenants had been offered and had accepted an agreed sum in compensation for notice to quit within two months. But the money had not yet been paid; moreover, the prospect of finding good alternative accommodation was small.

*   *   *

In Washington, trying to reflect the mood of the election, I wrote an article for *Punch*, entitled *Wake Up and Dream*, from which the following is an extract:

This America is a somewhat Victorian country. Millions of its people live in Victorian villas, and among the rest Victorian furniture is all the rage. It is a polite society, with stern social conventions and moral aspirations and romantic leanings, now caught up in a kind of wave of nineteenth-century prosperity which God is assumed to have had a good deal to do with. Watching over the elections, in the guise of a President, we have had, as it were, the dear Queen herself, in the evening of her days —with just an occasional whiff of the grand old Duke of Wellington. There, presiding over the Republic, is a kind of constitutional monarch reigning in the odour of sanctity, whom not even the damnedest of Radicals would dare openly to contradict or displease.

Thus it has been a velvet-gloved, not to say velvet-handed, election. For fear of displeasing the People, Mr. Stevenson has dared not to question peace, but only tentatively to propose another kind of it. For fear of displeasing Majesty he has been toning down his drafts: Mr. Eisenhower cannot lie, he is merely 'guilty of a gross misstatement of fact'; his 'fakery' boils down to no more than 'sinister, divisive talk'. For fear of displeasing the neighbours large numbers of his supporters have not dared to admit that they intended to vote for him.

A shocked silence greeted the suggestion of an adviser that a small boy with a pea-shooter be planted in a Republican audience, to cause the President's hand to fly to his heart at a crucial moment. That would Not be the Thing. It has been an election almost without jokes. There was one about Nixon racing Eisenhower to the top of the Capitol steps. But it was considered in Bad Taste and was not repeated.

The doves of Peace, released at the Republican Convention at San Francisco, seem to have found their way into the branches of the autumn-tinted trees of Washington, where they coo away happily day and night, lulling the people into Peaceful dreams and so helping to build up a brave new United States of Euphoria. . . .

Thus all America is Feeling Fine. The candidates have seldom stopped saying how Fine they Feel. Their doctors, for ever in attendance, confirm these feelings of theirs at medical press conferences: Mr. Eisenhower's thirteen (perhaps an ominous number); Mr. Stevenson's, announcing the fine results of a check-up on his patient 'from skull to toe,' and denying Mr. Nixon's ungentlemanly insinuation that he has only one kidney (he has two); Mr. Kefauver's, making announcements almost hourly: 'The Senator is suffering from respiratory trouble. That's a cold . . . The Senator took a throat spray. His respiratory trouble showed immediate signs of easing . . . The Senator has just been given a shot of penicillin—in the arm.'

And the People, of course, Feel Fine too. 'I haven't seen quite so much happiness in a long time,' said the dear Sovereign, 'and you don't know how good that makes me feel . . . I don't know of anything that's more worthwhile than just to see America having a good time.' The *New York Times* writes of America's 'peaceful, dreamy, faraway smile of pure contentment' in the

Presence: 'rather, some say, like the smile of the fourth Martini, rather, say others, like the smile of the sanctified.' Smiling it, they vote or don't vote, either way, secure in the feeling that, whatever happens or doesn't, this is the Age of a kind of Diamond Jubilee which can surely be prolonged for ever.

The truth may be that America is passing from one age to another—from the Benzedrine Age to the Equanil. Today the nation-wide slogan is RELAX. You see it written up in offices. You are lured to a movie which promises to be 'Exciting! Relaxing!' By your bedside in hotels you are invited to 'Relax on the long-distance telephone.' Relaxation, like Victorian decoration, is all the rage—'dynamic relaxation,' as a friend of mine, in Bad Taste, put it. Fulfilling the prophecies of Mr. Huxley and Mr. Orwell, it may be bought at the drugstore, the blessed tranquillizing pills of Milltown and Equanil, promising, in the words of *Life* magazine, Nirvana, 'calming down the raging personality or lifting up those who remain inordinately depressed'.

From the hurly-burly of the driving seat, this country is slowly but surely sinking into the deep, deep peace of the twin beds. 'Don't worry your pretty heads about political problems,' the politicians say. Are there not 35 million families with motor cars, 43 million with refrigerators, 39 million with electrical washing machines? Ike or Dick or Adlai or Elvis Presley or Billy Graham—what's the difference? What more can Europe want from us? Have we not sent them Marilyn Monroe? So Ole Man River goes rock'n and roll'n himself to sleep.

'Apathy sanctified by morality', a journalist has called it. There has only been one basic electoral issue. Is this great big slumberous beauty to start waking up now? Or is she to sleep on for another four years, in wait for Prince Charming 1960? On one thing only all are agreed. Peace, in the Equanil Age is secure.

Peace, it must be assumed, with Honour.

*   *   *

Having a few days to spare before Election Day, I paid my second visit to the Southern States, spending a night on the way back with a hospitable couple at Chapel Hill, a small university in North Carolina with a civilized atmosphere all its own. Back in Washington, I went with Kay on Election Night to a party given by a Democratic hostess. As the results of the voting came through on the television, and Eisenhower's return became certain, the guests grew morose, starting to talk of letting their houses and

going abroad for a year or two. I found myself laying down the
law on the subject of Suez to a polite gentleman who disagreed
with my arguments. Impatiently I asked him if he had ever been
to the Middle East. He replied as politely, Yes: he had until lately
been American Ambassador to Turkey.

Harry had written to me:

> 'The week has been exhausting. The days have been cluttered
> with people even beyond my extroverted consumption. Last
> night I went chez Howard for a party and enjoyed it very
> little, a commentary on my testiness with people, not the
> collection he had assembled. Others seemed to enjoy them-
> selves. I am cold. This is the winter of my discontent.'

In this mood, on my return to New York, I found him. An
added source of depression was the fact that he was now unlikely
to receive his money in compensation for the loss of the flat.
The company concerned had appealed to a higher court against
the obligation to pay; the case might take some time to come up,
and its outcome was uncertain. But meanwhile the demolition,
and the ejection of the tenants, was to proceed. I expressed
indignation. Was there nothing that he, on behalf of his poorer
neighbours, could do against such an injustice: write to the newspapers? get in touch with his Congressman?

He smiled at my English naïveté. 'Nothing.'

Clearly the time had come for me to return to England.
Reviving the idea which we had discussed in Colorado, I suggested to Harry that, faced as he now was with the problem of
homelessness, he should accompany me. But he shook his head.
He could not leave New York without a home to return to.
Besides, he was not ready for Europe. Too many wounds still
required to be healed. He must be alone for a while to work out
his inner problem here in New York, where John had belonged,
and where they had shared so much together. In the Spring,
when he was himself once more, perhaps he would come.

So I was to return home, soon to be wrapped in the cocoon
of low skies which enveloped the green English island, soothed by
the slow muted sounds of the London streets, warmed by a life
which stemmed from friends, from the affection of one human
being for another, in the intimate ease of familiar homes. As
time went on I was to find a new joy in Europe, seeing it for the
first time as one, London, Paris, Venice, Athens uniting as parts
of a single civilized whole, to which I belonged, whereas America,

so remote and so different, was another, to which I did not. I was to find, above all, a new joy in England, in that deep countryside which for centuries human beings had loved and lived in and nourished, fashioning out of it a supreme unconscious wholeness of nature and art and life.

Harry, healed of his wounds, was to follow me with Howard, and to share some of this joy throughout the long glowing miracle of a summer which followed. It was to inspire him to a new lease of creative activity. Ken was to come later, with Ruth, when Harry had returned to America to hold his first exhibition, leaving Howard settled for two years in a Bloomsbury flat. Ellsworth was to come too, for his second exhibition in Paris. All were to delight in the peace and the beauty and the humanity of the civilization around them, in the people as people, in the variety of the life, in the wit and the wisdom and the quickness, in the harmony of the values and the maturity of the ideas. And they were to bring to it their own American vitality, their directness and quick curiosity, their easy elasticity to temper the rigidities of European tradition and habit and class. They were the new world —the young world—come to redress and have its balance re- dressed by the old. For does not each of the two civilizations need the other?

But all this was still to come. Now I booked a passage on the *Franconia*, a slow Cunarder, looking forward to a leisurely nine- day trip. I flew down to spend a last weekend with Nin Ryan at Newport, Rhode Island, enjoying her easy hospitality and good- tempered company, and the curious survival around me of an Edwardian past, in lavish Frenchified châteaux and the sumptuous Italiante palazzo of the Vanderbilts.

The sky was high on the day of my departure, and there was a November nip in the sunlit air. With Harry and Howard and Ellsworth I had a long last luncheon, eating French food and drinking carafes of red wine in a Breton restaurant, used by the crews of the French boats, near the Docks. They came on board to see me off. An old friend, Helène Yourievitch, whom I had run into a few nights before, unexpectedly appeared with a pitcher of Burgundy, which we drank in my cabin. Howard had brought me a half-bottle of Scotch, and we drank this too. Ellsworth drew extravagant nudes with a piece of soap, all over the mirrors. Harry looked morose and drank whisky, which he seldom did. The bell rang for visitors to leave the ship. They filed away down the gangway, Howard turning to wave and smile back at me like a benevolent owl. I lay down for a while, then went on deck to see the last of New York.

Night had fallen. The ship hooted mournfully as we approached the Battery Point. The Babylonian skyscrapers of Wall Street, above Ellsworth's studio, were hard bright cages, black-barred and unblinking against a restless, purpling sky. The Statue of Liberty stood forward, floodlit white. In my mood of momentary dejection, she seemed to be wearing a jewelled Crown of Thorns. But I knew this was not so.

America had not given me nothing. Nor had it given me everything. Or perhaps, in an oblique sense, it had. It had given me new loves, new hopes, new memories, new ideas—and new eyes for the rest of the world.

London, 1958.